THE NORTHERN GARDENER

Perennials that Survive and Thrive

Habitat Gardening

Habitat Gardening

One of the biggest challenges in running a nursery can be giving customers enough information to be successful with the plants they purchase. This became a *Goldilocks and the Three Bears* kind of challenge for me. Too much information was overwhelming and forgotten by the time they were in the car, too little and I would be dealing with a complaint about a "defective" plant later in the season. The worst outcome would be someone who was put off gardening because it was "too difficult" or because "nothing will grow here."

This "Habitat" classification system grew out of that ongoing dialectic, and from discussions with gardening friends and students about this problem. Each habitat essentially represents a matrix of soil, moisture and light conditions. "Forest Floor" is, as you would expect, dry and shady. "Woodland" is semi-shady and more moist, with humus-rich soil from layers of decomposing leaf litter. "Prairie" is exposed, dry and sunny; "Meadow" is also sunny but sheltered and more moist. "Rain Garden" is an artificial construct, a depression in the ground built or enhanced to collect runoff and release it downwards into the underlying soil layers right away; "Bog Garden" is deep in mucky organic soil that holds water, being built on clay or with some kind of liner, but not holding standing water, the

A sleeping garden spirit, carved by Prince George artist Elmer Gunderson, is clothed with *Lysimachia nummularia*.

Photo Darwin Paton

Dedication

To all the gardeners everywhere who cope with short growing seasons, poor soil, untimely frosts, drought, windstorms, rainstorms, hailstorms, and arguments about political correctness in the garden—and yet still continue to experiment, try new varieties and methods, and share plants and information with each other. It's what we do.

Acknowledgements

I couldn't even begin to list all the people who have helped me over the years, sharing plants, sharing knowledge, and giving freely of encouragement. For fifteen years the customers and staff of Birch Creek Nursery contributed greatly to my ongoing and probably life-long project of compiling data on the huge variety of hardy plants for cold-climate gardens, and building a photographic record of those. I am grateful for the many photos in this book that were taken by the friends and staff of Birch Creek Nursery.

Three cohorts of Master Gardener students and I taught each other, and we were all richer for it. The general-interest gardening courses at the College of New Caledonia are proving to be both interesting and educational—I hope as much so for the students as for me. The most important thing that we all continue to learn is how much there is to learn—it never ends, and that's the joy of gardening.

Darwin Paton, wilderness photographer and owner of Wild & Free Outdoor Photography (wfphoto.com) in Prince George, BC, contributed many beautiful plant photographs taken especially for this book, and I am honoured to have his permission to include them.

The world-renowned German seed house of Jelitto Perennial Seeds generously permitted use of a number of their photos where time and weather had conspired against us here in Prince George. The Jelitto photos are used by permission and are copyright Georg Ubelhart, Jelitto Perennial Seeds (jelitto.com).

Diane Sales contributed the photo of her lovely Lucy (one of McDuff's favourite girlfriends) in her garden, as well as allowing access to her garden for photography. Willa Osis and several others of the Master Gardener group in Prince George were also kind enough to open their gardens to us.

The half dozen photos otherwise credited and marked with an asterisk are used with permission under the Wiki Creative Commons agreement found at http://en.wikipedia.org/wiki/CreativeCommons.

Many of the people I should thank are those I have never met, but whose books I have read. They shared their gardens and their knowledge, and through them I have travelled the world—and in some cases through time as well.

Closer to home, my thanks will always go to Jim Tingle (now retired from the BC Ministry of Agriculture), who encouraged me to write the first book back in 1999, and to Susan Hallum, friend and editor extraordinaire, who kept me sane through the writing of this book.

Last but not least, thanks are due to Harbour Publishing for decades of supporting BC writers and supplying BC readers with a wide variety of regionally relevant books.

Fritillaria meleagris.

CONTENTS

Introduction

There are no rose-coloured glasses in my garden—it is survival of the fittest. Plants die, others struggle, and some do far too well. This is gardening in the real world, replete with pets and pests, moose and mice, and a wide assortment of mostly mysterious bugs.

When I was running Birch Creek as a retail nursery in Prince George for a dozen or so years, there were staff to assist in the planting and maintenance of an acre of what was then a display garden. For the past five years, the same garden—now mainly a very large and well-landscaped dog run—has been pretty much on its own, with no watering, no fertilizer or deadheading or staking, and only occasional inadequate weeding. It is amazing how well the garden and many of the individual plants have survived this regime. It has been a lesson in what really happens in a "low-maintenance" zone-3 landscape.

Gardening can be about creating beauty, spending time in an activity you enjoy, increasing your property's value, sharing experiences with your children or grandchildren, or being the steward of a unique habitat and ecosystem in your own outdoor space. Your yard is a habitat to you as well as to your plants, so it needs to be functional and low-maintenance, as well as easy on the eye. Habitat means "home"—and this is your home as well.

Epilobium sp. in a natural rockery.

Photo Darwin Paton

Birch Creek Nursery, 2007.

When it comes to the plants, too, I have found myself speaking more and more of "habitat" type, to reference the interrelated web of soil, light and moisture conditions in which each plant species grows the best. Focusing on habitat enables gardeners to create a mental picture of the environment that a plant originated in and where it could then be grown without a great deal of fuss. A one- or two-word descriptor is easier to keep in mind than a list of seemingly unrelated conditions. Gardeners collectively have a tendency to purchase plants whose origins are in all kinds of different habitats all over the world—in varying types of soil, moisture and humidity regimes and distinctive plant and animal communities—then plunking them into gardens sorted by flower colour and height. The amazing thing is that this works as often as it does.

Once you get beyond the dozen or so most popular garden-centre varieties that have become ubiquitous in the trade simply because they will grow under almost any conditions, there are literally thousands of beautiful, interesting and garden-worthy plants to consider. Many are reputed to be "hard to grow" because they will not flourish just anywhere. Yet, as a friend points out, we don't "grow" plants, they grow themselves. We simply have to be smart enough to plant them in the right place so they *can* grow—and so we can enjoy them instead of fighting with them. Hence "right plant in the right place" is the mantra, and information becomes our best gardening tool.

I have grown, tested (and in many cases killed) virtually all the plants in this book. The following pages contain much of what I have learned over my lifetime, in the hopes that this will save you from wasting your time and money, losing plants, and perhaps even losing enthusiasm for playing in the garden.

Next page photo spread:
Dore River, BC.

Photo Darwin Paton

Barbara Rayment

Aconitum septentrionale weaves through an iris.

THE NORTHERN GARDENER

Perennials that Survive and Thrive

Barbara Rayment

Harbour Publishing

Harbour Publishing Co. Ltd.
P.O. Box 219, Madeira Park, BC, V0N 2H0
www.harbourpublishing.com

Edited by Carol Pope and Cliff Rowland
Additional editing support by Susan Hallum
Index by Joyce Wan
Cover design by Anna Comfort O'Keeffe
Text design by Roger Handling
Printed and bound in Canada

Additional image credits: Front cover, top — Frost-covered hardy geranium, Lida Perfetto photo. Front cover, bottom — Prince George garden, Darwin Paton photo. Back cover, left to right — Moose, Birch Creek Nursery photo; *Lupinus* x *polyphyllus* 'Russell Hybrids', Darwin Paton photo; *Bouteloua gracilis*, Darwin Paton photo. P. 1 — *Althaea cannabina*. Georg Ubelhart photo, Jelitto Perennial Seeds. Pp. 2–3 — Robson Valley and McBride, BC, Darwin Paton photo. P. 5 — *Bergenia crassifolia*, Darwin Paton photo. P. 6 — *Bouteloua gracilis*, Darwin Paton photo. Additional photographer information, see page 7.

 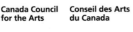 

Harbour Publishing acknowledges financial support from the Government of Canada through the Canada Book Fund and the Canada Council for the Arts, and from the Province of British Columbia through the BC Arts Council and the Book Publishing Tax Credit.

Library and Archives Canada Cataloguing in Publication
Rayment, Barbara, 1955-
    The northern gardener : perennials that survive and
thrive / Barbara Rayment ; with photographs by Darwin Paton.

Includes index.
ISBN 978-1-55017-578-3

    1. Gardening—Canada. 2. Perennials—Canada.
I. Paton, Darwin, 1963- II. Title.

SB453.3.C2R39 2012   635.0971   C2012-900572-X

preserve of "Water and Pond." "Rockery" is high, dry and exposed, the home of alpine plants and those others that require perfect drainage. "Herb Garden" is a bit of a hodge-podge, but most of the plants that fit in this category originated in a Mediterranean climate and on nutrient-poor, dry, and well-drained soils. Nine different habitat types are not really enough to explain the elegant complexity of the natural world, but they are a good starting point for a functional system that goes beyond just "sun" or "shade."

There are so many ways to classify plants: we sort by family, height, colour, season, hardiness, growth habit, use and any number of other qualities. I have come more and more to value habitat as a useful sorting feature. Plants originate in specific habitats, and perform best in our gardens if we can replicate that habitat to a certain extent. Prairies, bogs, meadows, alpine scree or woodlands each present basically the same plant environment wherever they are found around the world, although the specific plant communities will be different in China than they are in Chile or Canada.

In theory then, if we place plants that originated in meadow-type environments from all over the world together in a corner of our garden, they will all require similar growing conditions. Given these conditions, they will form a functioning community that works well and is aesthetically pleasing. Trying to grow a desert plant, an alpine, two bog and three meadow varieties all together in the same bed is bound to cause us grief, not to mention extra work and frustration.

I have arrived at an intuitive rather than scientific understanding of what constitutes a habitat, based on a lifetime of studying plants and their growing conditions. The requirements of most plants are not as rigid as some people believe, and they will survive a fairly broad range of conditions. Those plants that aren't that adaptable seldom show up in garden centres because retailers do not like the unhappy customers that result from dead and dying plants. The outcome is a very limited selection of generic plants, but that is a complaint for another day.

There are, of course, gardeners who are attracted to extremely difficult and tricky species, enjoying the challenge and the rarity. I am not one of them. A challenge is nice, but there is a limit to how much time and money I am willing to put into any one plant. I want to grow everything that will grow here on my zone-3 property, but not to fight with any of them.

Bog Habitat

In summary: A bog habitat has acidic, organically rich soil and is constantly moist, with a bit of standing water from time to time. Drainage underneath a bog is poor to non-existent, and the ecosystem relies on sedges (Carex) and other wetland plants to filter the water so the area does not become stagnant.

A bog is an area that is always wet, but not underwater, except for perhaps short periods in early spring or after heavy rains. It can be natural or constructed, very wet or just moist. The soil tends to be acidic and the plants that grow naturally in bogs prefer this. A man-made bog differs from a rain garden in that although rain gardens are also created to collect and manage water runoff, the latter are designed to filter water and dry out between storms, so plants in them must be drought tolerant as well. Bogs stay moist, and bog plants expect

Typha angustifolia in winter.

Photo Darwin Paton

to always have wet feet. That said there is some crossover between plants that can be grown in these two habitats.

Many plants that will grow in a moist bog are also perfectly happy in a garden bed that receives regular watering, but they are definitely not drought tolerant. Generally speaking, the more sun these plants get, the more water they need—*Astilbe* is a fine case in point here. *Astilbe* thrives in full sun in rich, consistently moist soil, but only given enough water. An astilbe that has dried out is a small and ragged thing, not worth growing.

In bogs, even more so than in other types of garden beds, the use of vertical accents seems to be important. Many of the plants adapted to living in fluctuating water conditions have vertical stems and grassy foliage (iris, rush, sedges, cattails) rather than large or horizontally attached leaves branching out from stems that may or may not be underwater at any given time. Vertical plants tend to look more at home in and around water, perhaps simply because nature has trained our eye to appreciate this combination.

Perennials for Wet Sunny Conditions

Butterfly weed – *Asclepias*
Cinnamon fern, royal fern – *Osmunda*
Dwarf cattail – *Typha minima*
Goat's beard – *Aruncus dioicus*
Golden Alexander – *Lysimachia punctata*
Iris (some but definitely not all) – *Iris*
Lady fern – *Athyrium filix-femina*
Pagoda primrose – *Primula vialii*
Ragged robin – *Lychnis flos-cuculi*
Sedge (some) – *Carex*
Water avens – *Geum rivale*

Perennials for Moist Sunny Conditions

Astilbe – *Astilbe*
Bee balm – *Monarda*
Bleeding heart (large species – formerly *Dicentra*) – *Lamprocapnos spectabilis*
Bugleweed – *Ajuga reptans*
Culver's root – *Veronicastrum*
Daylily – *Hemerocallis*
Elephant's ear, pig squeak – *Bergenia*
Foxglove – *Digitalis purpurea*
Globeflower – *Trollius*
Japanese painted fern – *Athyrium filix-femina* var. *nipponicum*
Joe-Pye weed, bone-set – *Eupatorium, Eutrochium*
Lady's mantle – *Alchemilla mollis*
Loosestrife – *Lysimachia*
Lungwort – *Pulmonaria*
Meadowrue – *Thalictrum*
Meadowsweet – *Filipendula*
Ostrich fern – *Matteuccia*
Plantain lily – *Hosta*
Primrose (some) – *Primula*
Ray flower – *Ligularia*
Snakeweed – *Polygonum*
Snakeroot – *Actaea*
Spiderwort – *Tradescantia*
Turtlehead – *Chelone*
Valerian – *Valeriana*
Vervain – *Verbena hastata*
Wood rush – *Luzula*

Plants for Moist Shady Conditions

Astilbe – *Astilbe*
Avens – *Geum*
Bleeding heart – *Dicentra*
Bugleweed – *Ajuga reptans*
Coral bells – *Heuchera*
Foamflower – *Tiarella*
Foamy Bells – *Heucherella*
Gentian – *Gentiana*
Goat's beard – *Aruncus*
Lungwort – *Pulmonaria*
Maidenhair fern – *Adiantum*
Male fern – *Dryopteris*
Monk's hood – *Aconitum*
Oak fern – *Gymnocarpium*
Phlox (some creeping varieties) – *Phlox*
Rodgersia – *Rodgersia*
Scotch moss, Irish moss – *Sagina*
Shooting star – *Dodecatheon*
Turtlehead – *Chelone*
Violet, pansy – *Viola*
Windflower (most species) – *Anemone*
Wood rush – *Luzula*

Forest Floor Habitat

In summary: The forest floor in a mature coniferous forest is a dry, calm place with little in the way of mid-height understory due to the lack of sunlight, moisture and nutrients. The forest floor itself is rich in small plants well adapted to those poor growing conditions.

A walk in the woods in most northern sub-boreal forests is very different from a walk in an eastern hardwood forest. Our spruce/pine/fir trees are conifers and evergreen, and the soil is thin, not built up and enriched by the annual leaf fall. The organic duff layer on the ground is shallow, and the forest floor is a fairly dry habitat, with less moisture, less variety, and less plant height than in "richer" woodland habitats. Nonetheless, there are a number of plants that can grow well in this environment, whether they originated in northern BC forests or the dry pine forests of northern China. These are the species we are looking for to plant in the dry shade under large trees, at the base of hedges, and in other relatively barren shady locations.

Gardening in dry shade areas is as much about management as it is about plant selection. Add a liberal but not excessive amount of finished compost or topsoil to the existing soil, but do not mix it in, as this will damage any shallow tree roots in the area. Adding too

An undisturbed forest floor habitat.

Photo Darwin Paton

much can smother the tree roots just beneath the surface—4 in. (10 cm) is generally sufficient. It is essential not to push soil or mulch up against existing tree trunks or shrub stems,
as this can cause them to rot. Hold the soil or mulch back a good hand-span of 4 in. (10 cm)
so that the bark can breathe. The arborists advise "think bagel, not volcano."

Mix the old and new soils together as planting holes are dug, placing the plants with
care for surrounding tree roots. Plant between tree roots, not on top of them, and avoid
damaging roots wherever possible. Plants selected should be shallow-rooted varieties and
small sizes so that the holes are as small as possible; an exception to the usual "dig a really
large hole" advice. After planting and watering, apply a layer of bark or aged wood-chip
mulch 3–4 in. (8–10 cm) thick on the surface around the plants. This replicates the natural
duff layer, keeps the moisture in and encourages vigorous root growth, ensuring healthier
and more drought-tolerant plants.

Tree roots will work their way to the top of the new soil and mulch over time of course,
but hopefully a stable plant community will have established itself by then. If the tree is a
poplar or cottonwood, you may not be able to win this battle—a clean mulched surface may
be as good as it gets; the more you enrich the soil the more the tree will send up suckers
from the roots. The more you damage the tree by cutting off the suckers, the more it will
respond by sending up new suckers. And if you cut the tree down it will really send up
suckers, all along the extensive spreading root system, unless you apply a systemic poison
to the trunk as soon as the tree is felled. These trees are programmed for survival in a harsh
world.

Some of the plants listed below (marked *) can be invasive under better growing conditions, but are perfect in short-season, cold-climate gardens in those tough areas under large
trees, or in the shady strips between the sidewalk and house.

A dozen low-growing species
share time and space in a square
foot of natural forest floor.

Plants for Dry Shade

Bugleweed – *Ajuga*	Periwinkle – *Vinca*
Cinquefoil – *Potentilla tridentata*	Stonecrop (some are amazingly shade tolerant, all are drought tolerant) – *Sedum*
Crane's bill – *Geranium nodosum*	
Goutweed, Bishop's weed – *Aegopodium**	Wild strawberry – *Fragaria vesca*
Jacob's ladder – *Polemoniun pulcherrimum*	Yellow archangel – *Lamiastrum**

Herb Garden Habitat

In summary: Maybe this should be called the Mediterranean habitat. Most herbs, having come from that part of the world, thrive in poor, hot, dry and well-drained soils. A herb gardener does what she can to replicate those conditions, trapping heat, creating barriers to wind, and making sure the soil is open and well drained, and not over-fertilized.

This habitat classification is for all those herbs that originated in the Mediterranean region and still long for the heat and sunshine. It is in many ways similar to Prairie Habitat, except that it needs shelter from winds, especially in winter, and the soils should be nutrient-poor, well-drained or even rocky. (Many prairie plants are quite tolerant of heavy clay soil; most herbs are not.) A herb garden could be perfect created as a walled garden, or enclosed by a low hedge—keeping in mind that it needs a lot of sun.

A herb garden in raised beds.

Most herbs that are hardy will grow quite happily without irrigation in a dry garden, walled or otherwise, although there are a few exceptions such as parsley and cilantro—the leafy green plants that prefer moister conditions. They could be given their own area to one side with a soaker hose or drip-irrigation system, perhaps. The mints, of course, not only need moist soil; they also need to be firmly corralled or they will try to take over the whole garden, dry or not.

Room could be left in the herb garden for the annual herbs, although some, most notably basil, will be happier in a container in a warm spot or in the greenhouse. Dill, fennel, summer savory, winter savory, the less-hardy thymes and oreganos can all be started from seed or purchased as bedding plants. They grow well enough to supply the kitchen during the growing season with some left over for drying for the winter. The tender perennials can be grown in containers and moved inside for the winter if there is a sunny, but not too hot, place to put them. It isn't impossible to have fresh herbs all winter.

Herbs have many uses. Apart from culinary and medicinal applications there is growing interest in the use of herbs in natural cosmetics, in place of bath salts, and in aromatherapy. Mint juleps, herbal teas and punch bowls with decorative edible flowers floating by themselves or encased in the ice cubes can count as a form of therapy too, of course. All of the ingredients for these could find a home in the Herb Garden—along with a bench or an arbour to remind us to sit and just breathe while watching the plants grow.

Meadow Habitat

In summary: Meadows have fairly rich soil relatively high in organic matter, good moisture retention and a diverse plant community. Natural meadows often have a creek running through them, or a spring. Plants are usually fairly tall and aggressive, thriving when provided with abundant nutrients and full or partial sunlight. I picture the average meadow as being surrounded by trees, so not totally exposed, and possibly with varying patches of shade throughout the day. Meadow plants tend to bloom in the spring and early summer, not trusting late-summer moisture levels to hold on.

Natural meadows are characterized by reasonably rich, moist soils fairly high in organic matter due to both the lush perennial growth of the mixed plant life and the leaf fall from surrounding deciduous trees. They are protected from the extremes of wind and weather by

A meadow in the garden.

those trees, yet still cope with bitter winter temperatures and a heavy snow load. Meadows are generally sunny, but may have periods of lower, filtered light throughout the day thanks to the surrounding trees.

In the urban setting, houses, fences and hedges play the part of the protecting woodland, but the microclimate is much the same. Small perimeter trees, or vines growing up fences, can help create the same sense of a protected glade far from the madding crowd.

Natural meadows often have creeks running through them or natural springs that provide moisture; created meadows may require irrigation in drier years. The lush, although not necessarily tropical, appearance of the meadow plant community can lend itself to making a well-designed man-made garden pond seem quite natural. This kind of pond would be in a low-lying area and in the way of being a discovery as one wandered a path, not an artificial focal point with accent lighting and a waterfall or two. A strategically located rustic bird bath, and a bench or two, would not be out of place.

Meadow plants are usually fairly tall and aggressive, thriving with abundant nutrients and full or partial sunlight, and competing for that sunlight. Small flowering shrubs are at home here. It is a diverse habitat, and a peaceful one. Meadow plants tend to bloom in the spring and early summer, attracting and feeding hummingbirds and butterflies, and then nourishing the songbirds later in the summer with their seeds.

Many plants native to meadow habitats adapt easily to garden conditions.

Water attracts wildlife.

Photo Darwin Paton

Pond & Water Habitat

In summary: It goes without saying that a pond has standing water. Garden ponds can be as small as a half-barrel or as large as a small lake. They can have liners or clay bottoms, but either way are designed to keep water in. If they have a liner, it is more difficult to create a rich and diverse pond habitat, as plants cannot root through the liner, and the pond edges around the outside of the liner are dry and the soil conditions not at all similar to those of a natural pond edge. It is difficult, although not impossible, to make this look natural.

It is important to know before you begin planting in and around a pond whether or not it is a natural clay-lined pond or if it has a liner in it. This makes a difference not only to which plants you can grow in the pond and how you manage them, but also to what can be grown around the outside edges.

A large lined pond generally has benches built into it, so that plants in containers can be placed at various water depths. Some plants need to barely have their feet in the water; others live with their crowns just at or under the water surface. These are collectively known as "marginals" because they live at the margins of the pond. (This has nothing to do with being marginally hardy, although you could have a marginal marginal.)

Edge-of-the-pond marginals include such reliable standbys as the water-loving irises, of which there are many, some very hardy. Marginal dwelling plants are a bit trickier to grow in lined ponds because their hardiness is partly a result of their being able to root deeply into the soil beneath the water surface. This isn't possible when they are in a pot or a shallow-lined trench at the pond edge. They naturalize easily at the rim of clay- or dirt-bottomed ponds.

An iris at pond edge.
Photo Darwin Paton

There are also "floaters." These plants have adapted to fill a water-borne niche, and drift with their roots in the water. These all tend to be tropical species and can be invasive outside their native territories without the pests and predators that kept them in check there. Again, this invasiveness is not thought to be so much of an issue in colder climates, however many of our Canadian rivers run from north to south, and weeds that escape into a waterway in Vanderhoof can end up causing a problem in Vancouver, which already has enough problems.

Waterlilies, both the native *Nuphar* and the exotic *Nymphaea*, are in a class of their own and grow beneath the water surface, rooted in pots or in the soil at the bottom of the pond, sending flowers and foliage up to the surface on long stems. To survive through a frozen northern winter, the exotic varieties have to be either sunk (below the freezing level) or lifted (and overwintered in tubs in the basement).

The native water plants buckbean (*Menyanthes*), cattail (*Typha*) and arum-leaf arrowroot (*Sagittaria cuneata*) are seldom if ever available at garden centres and not included in this book for reasons of space and because I had to draw the line somewhere. Northern water-garden enthusiasts warn that it is dangerous to bring plants from natural "wild" ponds into the home pond if you have fish, as you can also transplant pests or diseases.

While water-edge plants, in nature, are adapted to living in constantly moist soil, plants growing alongside a pond with a liner are actually living in near-desert conditions. This makes it necessary to find choices that have a look similar to naturally occurring pond-side inhabitants (rushes, water irises, reeds, etc.) but that are actually drought-tolerant Prairie Habitat plants.

Prairie Habitat

In summary: Prairie plants are adapted to the wide open spaces, to cold winters and hot dry summers, deep but not particularly rich soils, occasional droughts, and grazing by herds of large animals. Whether this is a pampas, a prairie or a steppe, it is going to be a mix of similar-height (tall grass prairie, short grass prairie) tough plants that rebound after mowing or burning, surviving by developing deep and/or fibrous root systems. The shorter prairie plants tend to bloom early in the spring before the competition gets going; the majority of prairie plants put their energy into growth for the first half of the season and then into flowering and seeds from midsummer on. They tend to be productive in terms of creating biomass and building up the soil.

A prairie in the garden.

Many, but not all, of the plants that are lumped together here as belonging in a Prairie Habitat originated on North American prairies (or Russian steppes or the South American pampas, which are similar ecosystems). What the plants have in common is a hardiness of soul that allows them to tolerate many types of soil and a wide range of moisture regimes. In their native habitats they are used to being wet in the spring and dry in the summer. In the northern hemisphere they are also used to harsh winters and a lot of snow. They all do best in full sun, and many actually grow to be their finest in rather poor soil, getting too tall and floppy if coddled with rich soil.

Monarda didyma.

A number of our attractive North American native plants have been borrowed by European plant breeders, notably in Holland and Germany, and are now coming back to us in new improved forms, usually with more and bigger flowers, and in a wider range of colours than nature intended. In many cases this is an improvement, especially when it results in more compact forms, or ones with brighter colours or a longer bloom period. The "improvement" can sometimes result in a loss of hardiness or backbone, but for the most part we are the winners in these transactions.

The many new forms of bee balm (*Monarda*), for instance, are spectacular, and far more mildew resistant than their ancestors. The compact form of Canada goldenrod (*Solidago*), which goes by the German 'Goldkind' or the English 'Baby Gold,' is two-thirds the size of the wild form and not so likely to flop over towards the end of the summer. Blanket flowers (*Gaillardia*) are now available in a wider array of colours, as are coneflowers (*Echinacea*), although the non-purple varieties (in shades of yellow, orange and other sunset colours) aren't proving to be very hardy in zone 3.

Many of the prairie plants are tall, late-blooming and have a tendency to self-seed, as indeed they should, for survival of the genes is the name of the game in the plant world as it is in the animal world. With a whole prairie to expand on, being able to take over territory is a good thing. They can be overwhelming in a small or formal garden, but splendid when given room to express themselves.

A rain garden created to manage runoff.

Rain Garden Habitat

In summary: Rain gardens are a relatively new concept, designed to manage rainwater and make best use of it on the property rather than simply channel it into storm sewers and the nearest river as quickly as possible. A rain garden is, at its simplest, a depression in the ground that collects surface water and allows it to percolate down into the soil at a natural rate. Plants in this habitat must be able to tolerate occasional wet feet as well as periods of drought. At their most complex, rain gardens can consist of acres of channels and canals, swales and berms, and a series of depressions, each acting to direct, slow down and filter the runoff from summer storms as well as spring snow. In the home garden, a small depression at a strategic point may be sufficient.

The observant reader will note that the plants listed below are mostly prairie natives which evolved in a climate where abundant spring moisture gives way to summer drought. Any plants adapted to similar conditions are probably going to do well in the rain garden.

Rain gardens are functional man-made areas, designed to trap excess rainwater and prevent it from running into storm sewers or flooding other areas. Essentially, a rain garden is a depression large enough to hold the runoff from the surrounding area in the worst of storms. This means that after the heaviest rainfall of the year the rain garden is, very temporarily, a pond. Unless the soil is totally impermeable (in which case it really is a pond garden), the water will then percolate down into the soil, being filtered by the plants and organisms that live there. This contributes to a recharged aquifer instead of an accumulated massive runoff into storm sewers and creeks that can cause erosion and flooding downstream.

Rain gardens are generally designed with gently sloped or benched sides that can be planted with an assortment of water-tolerant species. Those at the bottom will be sitting in moist soil much of the time, those near the top of the slope will be wet only occasionally throughout the year. In an ideally designed rain garden, a heavy rain or spring runoff will completely fill it, but it will not overflow. Any deeper than this is a waste of space and resources. Rain gardens, obviously, are not lined with plastic or anything else that impedes drainage, and are planted with vigorous plant species whose strong roots will aid in keeping the soil porous.

Although a well-designed rain garden doesn't need additional irrigation, a sort of "hybrid" rain garden/bog can be created, and this is the route I have taken. If the area can be kept permanently moist by artificial means during periods when it doesn't rain, it can be planted with a mixture of the tough plants listed below and other moisture-loving species such as *Astilboides, Ligularia* and *Rheum tanguticum*. My rain garden serves an essential purpose in diverting and controlling runoff that previously flooded the shop, but I couldn't resist taking advantage of the opportunity to plant a few water-hungry plants that I couldn't grow elsewhere. The hollow (15 by 20 ft./4.5 by 6 m) gets watered during dry spells, with the need for watering determined by physically checking under the mulch layer. (Watering almost always ensures that it rains the next day, of course.)

Veronicastrum virginicum 'Fascination.'
Photo Darwin Paton

Perennials for Sunny Rain Gardens

Aster (most native asters, heath aster) — *Aster*
Bergamot, bee balm — *Monarda didyma*
Black-eyed Susan — *Rudbeckia*
Blazing star — *Liatris*
Columbine — *Aquilegia*
Culver's root — *Veronicastrum*
False sunflower — *Heliopsis*
Golden Alexanders — *Zizia*
Goldenrod — *Solidago*
Iris — *Iris* (species and varieties for wet areas)

Ironweed — *Vernonia*
Joe-Pye weed, bone-set — *Eupatorium, Eutrochium*
Meadowrue — *Thalictrum*
Meadowsweet — *Filipendula*
Milkweed — *Asclepias*
Prairie coneflower — *Ratibida*
Purple coneflower — *Echinacea purpurea*
Sedge — *Carex*
Sneezeweed — *Helenium*
Vervain — *Verbena*

Rockery Habitat

In summary: This is the alpine, with rocky soil, very little organic matter and excellent drainage. It is exposed and usually, but not always, sunny (in nature, some small alpine plants will adjust quite well to the shady microclimate created on the north side of a boulder). Alpine/rockery plants tend to prefer alkaline soil, although there are exceptions. Alpine plants tend to bloom early in the spring, taking advantage of snow melt for moisture and rushing to flower and set seed during what may be a short season.

Rockeries are the garden equivalent of alpine settings, with the important factor being very good drainage down through the soil as well as downhill on the soil surface. Unlike most of our other garden plants, alpine varieties do not appreciate a lot of organic matter in

Natural and man-made elements blend in a well-designed rockery.

the soil, and will probably not overwinter if planted into that lovely humus-rich and moist but well-drained soil we keep dreaming about.

Alpine and rockery soils in the garden should be composed mostly of gravel, sand and loam (finer than sand but not as fine as silt). Alpine soils are coarse textured and do not hold moisture well, so their native plants are usually drought tolerant in one of two ways. They tend to have either very long wiry root systems that will wind way down into the substrate to anchor the plant and find moisture there, or fat tuberous roots that store moisture.

Many alpine and rockery plants also prefer soil on the alkaline (high) end of the scale; this is convenient because at least one of the more common sources of rock around Prince George is a limestone quarry, which leaches enough of that lime to raise the pH. Retaining walls built out of concrete, including all the interlocking block systems, also leach lime from the concrete, for the same effect. This and the lack of acidifying humus to buffer the pH in the soil generally provide a suitable pH for all but the fussiest alpine (and there are some very fussy ones, and gardeners who collect them, of course).

Campanula rotundifolia.

Although we tend to think of rockeries as being sunny and exposed, almost every one has a shadier side and shady microclimates behind small shrubs or large rocks. These can be taken advantage of for those small plants that need some protection from the elements.

Rockery Plants

Bellflower – *Campanula*
Bitterroot – *Lewisia*
Candytuft – *Iberis*
Cinquefoil – *Potentilla*
Columbine – *Aquilegia*
Creeping phlox – *Phlox subulata*
Hen and chicks – *Sempervivum*
Ornamental onions – *Allium*

Pin cushion flower – *Scabiosa*
Pussy-toes – *Antennaria*
Sea holly – *Eryngium*
Stonecrop – *Sedum*
Speedwell – *Veronica*
Spurge – *Euphorbia*
Tickseed – *Coreopsis*

Woodland Habitat

In summary: Woodlands are deciduous forests, and greatly influenced by the annual leaf drop and accumulated organic matter. They tend to be a bit sunnier in the spring, before the trees leaf out, so are often the home of spring ephemerals. The mix of sun and shade and the rich moisture-retentive soil can create a fertile habitat where it is great fun to play with the many textures of plant foliage.

Woodland Habitats are protected areas, with both shade and shelter provided by deciduous trees. In nature, trees provide the windbreak, in urban gardens, buildings and fences can do that job. Woodland soil is undisturbed for the most part, and its upper layers tend to be high in organic matter due to the annual addition of a layer of fallen leaves. The high percentage of decayed and decaying organic matter in the soil plays an important role in the ecology of the place. This is where undisturbed woodland tends to differ from a *backyard* woodland—no one is raking up the raw gold of those leaves and hauling them away.

Lush textures help to recreate the feeling of a woodland setting.

Photo Darwin Paton

A peaceful retreat in the middle of the city.

Photo Darwin Paton

The natural mulch that the top duff layer creates holds moisture like a sponge, and is also home to millions of little living things. Some of the inhabitants are familiar creatures such as worms and centipedes, but most are microscopic. All of them fill specialized roles in processing the varying types of leaf litter and debris, breaking raw organic matter down into useable nutrients. For every size and shape and stage of decaying matter to be found on a woodland forest floor there is a dedicated organism—or a thousand—breaking it down into smaller pieces.

The trees, the wildlife they attract, the plants—all the by-products of life and death in the woodland—eventually end up decaying gently into the ground and becoming part of the soil. The soil feeds the next generation. No trees, no life. This is why some of our ancestors worshipped trees.

As for the flowering and foliage plants—the colour and texture that gardeners are so fond of in shade gardens—there are a thousand choices once the shade and the soil are established. This is the home for ferns and hostas, primroses and coral bells, and dozens of lesser-known genera. Start with the list that follows, but don't take it as gospel. A great many shade plants will grow in northern climates, and many plants that references and plant tags say need full sun will actually adapt quite nicely to the shade, even if they may not flower as much there.

Native and non-native plants both flourish together in the right soil and light conditions.

Preserving the integrity of the top layer of natural mulch is a good reason not to till or dig soil any more than is necessary. Each of the organisms that live in the soil and the mulch layer is adapted to live at a specific depth in the soil, a balancing act governed by the amount of moisture and sunlight available in that layer at that time of year. If you mix all those layers together it does not "improve" the soil—it kills all of those organisms.

In our man-made woodland gardens, no matter how large or small, we can replicate the duff layer with mulch. Mulch can be imported bark mulch (coloured to match your siding, if you must) or locally sourced aged wood chips (common in many parts of the north, found at old sawmill sites), finished compost or chopped leaves and assorted garden debris. For debris of every size there is some living thing that will use it as food and habitat; however, if you are developing your garden from bare earth, those organisms will not be there at first, maybe not for several years.

The populations of decomposers will eventually appear and build up to maximum capacity to match the food source, but this doesn't happen overnight. When I started leaving my leaves on the Siberian irises, the immediate result was a messy garden and some doubts on my part. (It was time, stress and a bad back that motivated the change, as much as any personal philosophy.) Now, five years later, the system has reached some kind of equilibrium, and the iris leaves break down in the garden as they do in the wild. The previous year's foliage falls outward as the fibrous material begins to break down, suppressing weeds in a ring around the growing centre of the plant. The soil builds up as the foliage disintegrates down, and the plants grow larger every year, expanding into this improved soil.

Nature adds mulch ingredients in small increments rather than by the truckload. If you add 12 in. (30 cm) of mixed coarse dead plant material to the top of the soil, it is going to take several years for the organisms in your garden to build up a large enough population to process it. (In fact, this is not a bad strategy around large trees, as long as the mulch isn't pushed up around the trunk. It keeps the grass and weeds—and herbicides and string trimmer—away from the base of the tree until it grows large enough to shade out that competition and take care of itself.)

In northern sub-boreal forests, the summers are short and cool, and organic material breaks down more slowly than it would in more moist, warmer coastal rainforests. In mixed pine/spruce/fir coniferous forests, which hold more biomass in the living trees and shed needles only gradually over a longer period of time, the composition of the duff layer is obviously quite different, and there is less variety and less biomass in the understory as a result. If you live in a dry continental coniferous forest and want the same kind of rich lush understory growth that is commonly found in the coastal rainforest or eastern deciduous woodlands, the simplest solution lies in building up the organic matter layer with scavenged leaves. Fortunately there will always be people who rake their lawns and put bags of those leaves out at the curb. Making prior arrangements with one or two of these tidy people should ensure an annual supply of clean herbicide-free rakings.

The closer you get to the particular natural ecosystem that exists wherever you live (and this shifts with region and climate, even from one side of town to another, as soils and

A quiet woodland garden in a city yard.

Photo Darwin Paton

altitude and exposure vary), the healthier and lower maintenance your garden is going to be. You can create a small-scale lush cedar/fern/rhododendron ecosystem on the high and dry central plateau around Prince George; it just requires a fair amount of initial work (including an irrigation system) and ongoing maintenance.

It has to be said that there is nothing wrong with a high-maintenance garden if that brings you pleasure. If you are young and/or rich and/or have a strong back, and love gardening and have lots of time to devote to your garden, I can't imagine any better way to spend it. For the rest of us, the trick is to get maximum results with minimum effort, while being kind to this earth (and perhaps having as many different plants as we have room for). As much as I hate to admit it, sometimes compromises are necessary.

People differ from each other in a wonderful variety of ways, including their ability to visualize and imagine. For some, one small rhododendron bush that barely blooms every year can bring back a flood of happy childhood memories. For others, that same plant will never be anything more than a taunting reminder that in Prince George we cannot replicate the famous Rhododendron Walk at VanDusen Botanical Garden. You are part of your garden habitat, and your perception of that habitat is going to play a huge role in shaping it. As Hugh Johnson said, the hardest thing to control in any garden is the gardener.

Despite common complaints about the difficulty of growing plants in the shade, there are actually a wide variety of hardy plants that can be grown there if the soil is not hard-packed and dead (or after it is rehabilitated from that state). There are at least half a dozen readily available plant genera and dozens of less common ones that are shade tolerant. A blend of native and introduced plants of different shapes, sizes, textures and foliage colours can create a living tapestry, making woodland gardening one of the more rewarding themes to indulge in.

Woodland Plants

Anemone, windflower – *Anemone*
Arnica – *Arnica*
Astilbe – *Astilbe*
Astrantia, masterwort – *Astrantia*
Barrenwort – *Epimedium*
Bleeding heart – *Dicentra*
Bugloss, Siberian bugloss – *Brunnera*
Columbine – *Aquilegia*
Coral bells – *Heuchera*
Cortusa – *Cortusa*
Dead nettle – *Lamium*
Elephant's ear – *Bergenia*
Ferns – *most*
Foamflower – *Tiarella*
Fringecup – *Tellima*
Geranium, crane's bill – *Geranium*

Ground ivy – *Glechoma*
Hellebore, Christmas rose – *Helleborus*
Hosta – *Hosta*
Lady's mantle – *Alchemilla*
Leopard's bane – *Doronicum*
Periwinkle – *Vinca*
Phlox – *Phlox*
Primrose – *Primula*
Pulmonaria – *Pulmonaria*
Saxifrage – *Saxifraga*
Solomon's seal – *Polygonatum*
Strawberry, wild – *Fragaria*
Violet, pansy – *Viola*
Wild Solomon's seal – *Maianthemum*
Wood rush – *Luzula*
Yellow archangel – *Lamiastrum*

From Habitat to Garden

Gardening, like much of the rest of life, is not a linear process, so any attempt to beat information on it into a straight line is bound to be somewhat artificial. Everything is connected to everything else.

As you dig into this book, you will find sections that deal with the specific problems and issues northern gardeners have to contend with—from moose to snow load to clay soil. Other sections offer solutions—as in perennials to attract beneficial insects (under B for Beneficial-insect Attractors) or perennials that deer generally avoid (under D for Deer-resistant). All of the sections that follow are organized alphabetically, with plants and other gardening topics interspersed. Plant listings within each genus are ordered by botanical name, which are not written in stone but are at least easier to track on the Internet than the many regionally variable—and often multiple—common names. The many lists included here (Salt-tolerant Perennials, Groundcovers, Foliage Favourites, etc.) are organized by common name. Those lists are short enough for anyone who enjoys working with botanical names to scan them quickly, while still keeping the information accessible for others who just want to play in the garden, not learn a second language.

The plants described here are those that not only survive but also thrive in zone-3 gardens—and it turns out that there are a lot of different plants that will. These are not always common species or varieties that are easy to find. I would encourage you to search out and support small nurseries, local growers and obscure seed sources. The University of British Columbia has introduced a number of plants that are registered with the Canadian Ornamental Plant Foundation (COPF), which collects royalties from commercial growers and distributes them back to the registered breeders. It is a self-reported payment that, in the case of UBC, supports their Botanical Garden. Be aware that anyone propagating and selling licensed or patented plants without paying this royalty is cheating the Botanical Garden as well as the future of plant breeding.

Refuse to settle for generic lowest-common-denominator offerings wherever you buy plants. Why buy a generic red peony when you can have 'Barrington Belle,' "a lush semi-double Japanese type with gently ruffled rich maroon-red cupped flowers, each accented by a tuft of lemon-yellow stamens," or 'Early Scout,' "a former American Peony Society Gold Medal winner, with large satiny deep-red flowers and a prominent cluster of dark-gold stamens; early blooming and gently fragrant."

Diversity is not just beautiful and satisfying for the soul, it is also environmentally healthy. We have all heard the dire warnings about mono-crop agriculture and the dangers that come with species extinction. These things are true on the micro as well as macro scale.

Nature is not linear or simple, and everything is connected to everything else in a myriad of ways we are only beginning to understand. One of the things I love about gardening is that it is so complex and ultimately uncontrollable; any one simple alteration can affect two or ten elements, and the whole garden can change in ways we haven't expected. It's always a mystery—and a joy—if we let it be.

Arabis self seeds through a limestone rockery.

Photo Darwin Paton

A to Z of
Perennial
Gardening in
the North

Achillea millefolium 'Colorado.'

Achillea ptarmica 'Ballerina.'

Achillea – Yarrow

Prairie | *Compositae*

Yarrow comprises a large, easily grown genus of sun-loving, drought-tolerant plants, many with a tendency to spread. The longer-stemmed varieties make good cut flowers, and all are useful for attracting beneficial insects. They tend to be mid-sized summer-blooming plants, often used as part of natural gardens or in the middle of sunny borders. A few are smaller, and suitable for sunny rockeries or at the front of borders. They thrive in poor soil and are clay tolerant, but may become leggy and floppy in rich soils where they can grow too fast.

VARIETIES

Achillea ageratum. Not quite as tough as the other yellow species (*A. filipendulina*) but a very pretty soft yellow. 'Moonwalker' ('Moonshine') grows to 32 in. (80 cm).

A. filipendulina. Usually available as the mustard-yellow 'Parker's Variety,' a.k.a. 'Cloth of Gold,' up to 48 in. (120 cm). Zone 3.

A. millefolium. The finely cut foliage gives this popular species its species epithet, *millefolium,* which translates as "thousand leaves." There are numerous cultivars and seed strains with flowers ranging from pale pastels to deep reds; the native form is white. Some of the darker colours fade as the flowers age; 'Paprika' holds its colour well. 'Summer Pastels' is a pale mix that blends nicely with other pastel flowers, but appears faded next to strong colours. I have seen it looking stunning planted with the pale 'Sea Lavender' (*Limonium tataricum*). The hybrid 'Terracotta' is excellent, with silvery blue-green foliage; it tends to get too leggy in rich soil. All are mid-sized, usually around 24 in. (60 cm). Zone 3, maybe zone 2.

A. ptarmica. Useful spreading groundcover or a nasty weed, depending on where it is planted. It has pure-white flowers (usually double in the cultivated forms, which include 'Ballerina' and the more compact 'Nobelessa') over bright-green foliage. The cultivar 'Love Parade' is often sold under the incorrect name of *A. sibirica* ssp. *camtschatica.* Either way, it is a pretty clump-forming plant with large umbels of long-lasting baby-pink blooms. Not quite as tough or as drought tolerant as some yarrow species, but definitely worth trying. Reaches 12–24 in. (30–60 cm), blooming late spring through early summer. Zone 3.

Acidic and Alkaline Soils in the Garden

Northern sub-boreal soils are generally thought of as being more acidic than they really are, in part because their major organic component is a 10,000-year accumulation of dropped conifer needles, which are acidic. In fact the usual pH in our northern soils is around 6.5, barely on the low side of neutral, and this is as much the result of the parent material and climate conditions as it is the slightly acidic organic matter that has accumulated. This level of pH does not create a problem for northern gardeners, as it is the range in which most plants are happy.

The term "pH" has to do with the presence of hydronium atoms, or potential hydrogen, in the water molecules in soil—which still doesn't mean anything to most of us. In the gardening world, the pH is used to refer to whether a soil (or soilless mix) is on the acid or alkaline end of the pH scale. The scale runs from 1 to 14, with pure water designated as neutral at 7.

Trollius 'Yellow Queen.'

Dianthus allwoodii x 'Little Bobby' thrives in alkaline soil.

Gardeners might want to pay attention to pH because it affects which nutrients a plant can absorb, and the levels at which it can do so—and this varies from species to species. Blueberries starve in well-fertilized alkaline soils where lilacs thrive, and vice versa. A pH test is the cheapest and easiest type of soil examination (although by no means the only thing that can be tested for in soil) and may explain why some plants aren't doing well despite applications of fertilizer. Inexpensive pH testers are widely available either in the form of litmus paper, which comes with a colour-coded scale, or as digital probes.

Higher-pH soils are variously referred to as sweet, basic or alkaline, or as "chalk" soils in British gardening books. If you want to grow a plant that prefers these soils, the easiest way to raise the pH is with horticultural limestone or wood ash. The latter adds potassium as well, although with this or any other variable raw material it is hard to measure exactly what amounts of specific elements are being applied. Moderation is a good thing, in the application of wood ash as in much else in gardening and life. Many alpine plants prefer an alkaline root environment, and this can also be supplied by building a rockery out of limestone (which will leach lime) or by planting near a foundation, concrete blocks or a concrete sidewalk.

Low-pH soils are referred to as acidic or sour soils. Lowering the pH can be accomplished with sulphur, peat or a mulch of conifer needles. It is more difficult to make a significant and sustainable change downward in the pH than it is to raise it. If you are growing blueberries for fruit production, for instance, a soil amendment of a large bale (3.8 cu. ft. or .1 cu. m compressed) of peat for every 6 plants is recommended at planting time. The pH will tend to drift back up to the local norm over time, necessitating monitoring and additional measures.

The amounts of rainfall and watering also affect soil pH—deserts tend to be alkaline (hence the great salt flats of Utah) and the peat bogs of high-rainfall areas (such as in Ireland) tend to be acidic. So it also makes sense, in the absence of specific information, to assume that plants from very dry regions are more likely to be adapted to a higher pH, and plants from very wet regions are more likely to be adapted to a lower pH.

If you discover that you have a plant that, according to the books, prefers a low-pH soil, and it is thriving in high pH, or vice versa, remember Rayment's Rule—"don't mess with success." Plants don't read books, so they don't know any better; moving plants is just as likely to kill them as make them grow better.

Perennials that Live in the Extremes of Soil pH

PERENNIALS THAT PREFER ALKALINE SOIL AND/OR LIMESTONE ROCKERIES (PH OVER 7)

Baby's breath – *Gypsophila*
Bitterroot – *Lewisia*
Bone-set, Joe-Pye weed – *Eutrochium*
Candytuft – *Iberis*
Catchfly – *Silene*
Christmas rose – *Helleborus*
Edelweiss – *Leontopodium*
Garden sage – *Salvia*
Jupiter's beard – *Centranthus*
Mullein – *Verbascum*
New England aster – *Aster novae-angliae*
Pin cushion flower, butterfly flower – *Scabiosa*
Pinks, carnation – *Dianthus*
Poppy – *Papaver*
Saxifrage – *Saxifraga*
Skullcap – *Scutellaria*
Stonecrop – *Sedum*
Sunflower – *Helianthus*
Wallflower – *Erysimum*

PERENNIALS THAT PREFER VERY ACIDIC SOIL (PH OF 5–6)

Bleeding heart – *Dicentra*
Cinquefoil – *Potentilla tridentata*
Foxglove – *Digitalis*
Globeflower – *Trollius*
Meadowrue – *Thalictrum*
Sedge – *Carex*
Snakeroot, baneberry – *Actaea*
Turtlehead – *Chelone*

Left: *Aconitum cammarum* 'Eleonora'; right: *Aconitum x cammarum* 'Stainless Steel.'

Aconitum – Monkshood, Wolfsbane

Meadow | *Ranunculaceae*

Aconitum was the Medici family's poison of choice in the Italian Renaissance. People still occasionally make the news by dying after sampling small quantities of the foliage. Despite its potential deadliness, *Aconitum* is a popular garden plant and for good reason. The chemicals that make it poisonous protect it from pest damage, and it is a lovely tall late-blooming clump-forming plant that will adapt to any but the driest soils. It thrives in sun or part shade. I have seen some well-established clumps exceed 7 ft. (210 cm) in rich moist soil; mine usually top out around 5 ft. (150 cm). The spikes of flowers appear from midsummer on, usually in shades of dark blue and purple. There are a few paler-blue varieties, a soft pink, and a few pale yellows, all lovely in their own way. There is also a climbing variety, although more of a scrambler than a climber.

VARIETIES

Aconitum **cultivars and hybrids.** Most of the named varieties on the market are of mixed parentage, and it is not worth even trying to figure out their ancestry. It is best to choose plants in bloom, as the flower colours are variable and they are often mislabelled.

A. anthora. Pale yellow, shorter than most other varieties at 32 in. (80 cm). Zone 2.

A. cammarum 'Bicolor.' Two-tone flowers, white shading to blue around the back of the hood; this is quite a common plant

around old homesteads in northern BC, attesting to its toughness and longevity.

A. carmichaeli (*A. fischeri, A. wilsonii*). Variable, which is probably why it acquired so many different names. Light to dark purple blue.

A. hemsleyanum. Purple blue to wine red. This is the climber—mine scrambles up though an old globe cedar, to good effect.

A. kirinense. Purple blue, with distinct finely cut dark-green foliage—one of my favourites for that reason.

A. lycoctonum (*A. lamarckii, A. vulparia*). This suffers from some confusion in the naming. There seem to be both a pale-yellow and a dark purple-blue form.

A. napellus. There are many cultivars of this with most in various shades of blue to purple, in addition to several unspectacular pink forms ('Carneum,' 'Rubellum') and a white variation.

Actaea – Baneberry, Snakeroot, Bugbane, Black Cohosh

Meadow or Woodland | *Ranunculaceae*

Actaea now includes all those plants that used to be known as *Cimicifuga*—correct botanically but frustrating horticulturally. In the old days, the plants classified as *Actaea* were only those sprawling semi-woody perennials called baneberries, best known

Actaea simplex 'Brunette.'

for the colourful and poisonous berries. *Cimicifuga*, once you had mastered pronunciation, were tall stately perennials with even taller spiky flower heads. All the species in *Cimicifuga* have been moved into *Actaea*, leaving us with one genus instead of two—and much confusion.

Actaea, as in the old baneberry, is seldom seen in North American gardens, and even less seldom in garden centres, perhaps due to the poisonous qualities of so many of its parts. We grow many poisonous and toxic plants as a matter of course, but the danger of having pretty and deadly red, white or black berries at child level in the garden may be considered too great a risk. The North American wild variety, *Actaea rubra*, is part of the reason hikers are warned against eating any white berries, although that species can be found with either white ('Alba') or red ('Rubra') fruit.

Cimicifuga, on the other hand, despite many chemical and herbal qualities that should give it warning labels as well, is a sought-after garden treasure. Late blooming, the white or pink flower spikes can reach over 6 ft. (180 cm) by late summer, and it thrives in cool moist weather. Cultivars with dark purple-green and almost-black foliage have lately been introduced, and they are stunning planted with large blue- or gold-leaf hostas. They are slow to grow from seed, but reasonably easy from division done in early spring. The species and cultivars all seem to be equally hardy to zone 3.

VARIETIES

Used to be *Actaea* and still are:

Actaea pachypoda (**A. alba, A. rubra** and **A. spicata**). White flowers, black fruit, 20 in. (50 cm).

Used to be *Cimicifuga* and are now *Actaea*:

A. podocarpa (**C. americana**). Green foliage, white flowers tinged with red, 5 ft. (150 cm).

A. racemosa. Green foliage, white flowers, 6 ft. (180 cm).

A. ramosa '**Atropurpurea.**' Purple-red foliage, creamy-white flowers, 7 ft. (210 cm).

'Brunette': Brown-red foliage, pink flowers, 5 ft. (150 cm).

'White Pearl': Green leaves, white flowers, excellent variety, 7 ft. (210 cm).

'Hillside Black Beauty': Purple-black foliage, white flowers, 36 in. (90 cm).

A. simplex (**formerly C. ramosa**). Green foliage, creamy-white drooping flower spikes, 7 ft. (210 cm).

Adenophora – Ladybells, Lilybells

Meadow | *Campanulaceae*

Adenophora are closely related to *Campanula*, and it can be difficult to tell the two apart, especially with some of the taller bell-flowers (and notably so with the overly enthusiastic *C. rapuncu-*

Adenophora bulleyana.

loides, which often is shared between well-meaning gardeners as some other species are not so invasive). The two zone-3 hardy varieties, *A. bulleyana* (properly known as *A. khasiana*) and *A. liliifolia*, grow to nearly 36 in. (90 cm) tall, and have gently scented nodding lavender-blue flowers. They are a pretty contribution to a mixed natural border or meadow. Their tendency to self-seed probably makes them unsuitable for formal plantings, but they don't crowd out other plants and are easy enough to remove when necessary.

Aegopodium – Goutweed, Bishop's Weed

Woodland, Forest Floor, Meadow, Prairie or Rockery | *Apiaceae*

Aegopodium podagraria 'Variegatum' is the only variety that seems to find its way into gardens, and it is everywhere. Depending on who you are talking to and their growing conditions, *A. podagraria* is regarded as either a nasty weed or a valuable groundcover. The green and white foliage is very similar to that of the variegated dogwood shrubs, but this one is a spineless plant that crawls along the ground and roots wherever it

Aegopodium podagraria 'Variegata.' Photo Darwin Paton

Agastache – Anise Hyssop

Herb Garden | *Lamiaceae*

Agastache is a favourite of bees and herbalists, and makes a good cutting flower; unfortunately it doesn't do well in cool-summer climates. It thrives in hot sunny locations in well-drained soil, and probably likes more heat than most northern interior gardens get.

Many of the less hardy species and newer cultivars produce incredibly coloured flower spikes in desert sunset shades of red orange, orange, apricot and terracotta, while others play in the violet-blue shades. The only species I have had long-term success with is the light purplish-blue *Agastache foeniculum*. It has aromatic foliage and a subtle beauty. The cultivar 'Blue Fortune' is showier, but didn't last here in zone 3. Grows to 24 in. (60 cm). Zone 4.

Agastache 'Blue Fortune.'

touches down. Many new gardeners plant it, seduced by promises of "easy to grow, vigorous and hardy" and then are sorry. In the plant world of real estate as much as the human one, location is everything.

Around the base of an established tree with outward growth restricted by a mown lawn, or trapped between a sidewalk and a foundation, it is an attractive and fast-growing groundcover that prevents the incursion of other weeds. Well watered and with a bit of compost, it can look lush, and the summer clusters of small white flowers on upright stalks are a bonus.

In a mixed bed or around young trees or shrubs it quickly becomes a maintenance headache as it attempts to take over and the gardener struggles to keep it cut back. While it will survive in the poorest and driest of soils where little else will, it looks sparse and straggly under those conditions—hardly worth planting at all, but still difficult to eradicate.

The foliage grows to 12 in. (30 cm), less in poor soil, and the flower stalks can extend that much again. Zone 3.

Aggressive Spreaders

These are plants that spread by seed, rhizome or both. These are *not* officially classified as noxious weeds in BC, although some people think a number of them should be. The line between a useful groundcover (see Groundcovers) and a noxious weed is officially drawn when plants displace native-plant communities and have an economic impact, rather than simply multiplying with too much enthusiasm throughout the garden.

The species listed here are a nuisance in mixed borders, undoubtedly cursed by some gardeners, but useful in large semi-wild gardens and for stabilizing slopes. They tend to show up in abundance at fundraising plant sales, and are often given to novice gardeners by helpful friends. They are listed here by botanical name, as they have too many common names—a clue that they are a little bit too well-travelled. I don't include in this list those plants such as *Aquilegia*, *Armeria*, *Corydalis* and *Dicentra* (all of which I happen to be very fond of), which self-seed with some abandon but are short-lived and not hard to control if they happen to pop up in an inconvenient place.

Achillea millefolium – Yarrow, milfoil. There is variability of habit even within named seed strains; some individuals will spread with a little too much enthusiasm while others stay as polite clumps. Yarrow is native throughout Western Canada, and a valuable component in any natural or herbal garden.

Aegopodium podagraria – Ground elder, goutweed, bishop's weed. Like *Lamium* and *Lamiastrum*, this can be a pretty and useful groundcover, or a straggly nuisance. Location, location, location.

Ajuga – Bugleweed, carpet bugle. Famous for spreading into lawns, but a pretty plant and quite manageable under strong-growing shrubs and trees.

Centaurea montana – Mountain bluet, perennial bachelor's button. This ought to be banned—it is very aggressive by root and seed, and crowds out other plants both ways. The large bright-yellow thistle-like *C. macrocephala*, on the other hand, has never self-seeded in my garden. Most of the many species are somewhere in between, and overall no longer welcome in my garden. A few are indeed noxious weeds, including knapweed (*C. diffusa*).

Lamiastrum galeobdolon – Yellow archangel, false lamium. This is a useful low groundcover when grown between a rock and a hard place, and as a trailer in hanging baskets, but will root down everywhere it touches. In the north it doesn't have quite enough energy to expand into established native-plant areas, but in the southern parts of BC there is a move afoot to have it banned from nurseries and garden centres.

Lamium – Silver nettle, dead nettle. Spreads easily, above and below ground, and will grow in almost any soil. It can look terrible if grown in poor soil in a very dry location, or lush if given a bit of care in a similar situation where almost nothing else will grow. This is another one that southerners claim should be outlawed, yet it is a useful plant in the north.

Polemonium – Jacob's ladder, Greek valerian. Most of this genus are short-lived and self-seeding. The common garden *P. caeruleum* is the most prolific and most annoying to some people. The beautiful (and expensive) variegated leaf forms tend to produce solid-green offspring, so have to be propagated by division.

Sedum acre – Stonecrop, goldmoss stonecrop, goldmoss sedum, wallpepper. This fine-textured thug spreads and roots at the slightest provocation. There are many very nice *Sedum* species and varieties, and little excuse to grow this one. It spreads through turf grass in public places via commercial lawn mowers, which really should be cleaned between sites but usually aren't.

Viola – Pansy, violet, Johnny-jump-up. The worst are probably some of the little Johnny-jump-ups. A few popping up here and there are pretty, but those few seedlings can multiply exponentially, and a solid carpet of seedlings can choke out other plants.

Left: *Centaurea dealbata*; right: *Ajuga reptans*.

Ajuga genevensis 'Pink Elf.'

Ajuga – Bugleweed

Woodland, Meadow or Rockery | *Lamiaceae*

These are pretty and useful small groundcovers, with a mat-forming habit and upright flower spikes in early summer. The species and cultivars seem to vary in size and vigour more than in hardiness, all being able to survive in zone 3, with the tougher ones probably hardy to zone 2.

VARIETIES

Ajuga genevensis. The tallest, up to 16 in. (40 cm), and more mounding than spreading; flowers are usually purple blue, sometimes pink or white. Foliage is usually green.

A. pyramidalis. The parent of the dubious achievement known as 'Metallica Crispa,' which has small contorted leaves that look like they are under attack by aphids.

A. reptans. The most commonly available species, usually under 8 in. (20 cm) tall, but spreading up to 32 in. (80 cm). Cultivars range from the miniature dark-leaf 'Chocolate Chip' to the lush 'Catlin's Giant' with purple-green leaves. As a general rule of thumb, I have found the variegated forms (such as 'Burgundy Glow') to be not as vigorous or quite as hardy as the green-leaf forms, with the dark-leaf ones in between. They are shallow-rooted, and a useful groundcover under shrubs and at the front of perennial or mixed borders, where they will spread to fill any available space without overrunning other plants. Bugleweed will tough it out in poor soil and spread rapidly in good soil, and can be a nuisance in lawns if you care about your lawn being only turf grass. Myself, I don't see the problem with a flowering lawn—*Ajuga* will take some foot or paw traffic, although won't hold up to soccer games or the like.

Alcea – Hollyhock

Prairie or Meadow | *Malvaceae*

The hollyhocks of my childhood memory were the biennial *Alcea rosea*—towering (to a child) stalks with magical flowers that uncurled in slow motion to become brilliantly coloured ballet skirts. My fascination with seeds may have started there, because as good or better than the flowers were the precisely engineered rings of seeds that ripened over the weeks of summer, each seed tucked perfectly into the next inside a papery covering, the whole thing fitting together like a miniature shrimp ring. Years later, at university in Nova Scotia, I was delighted to find these growing half-wild in the alleyways of Wolfville, self-seeded in narrow gravel strips against buildings, blooming in all the same glorious mix of colours. A continent and a lifetime away, I have found that these will grow in the shorter season and heavier soils of northern BC, but seldom self-seed. Double-flowered forms are available, catering to some need for bigger, better and fluffier, but these do not meet my image of a hollyhock. Less seldom grown, more reliably perennial but still not long-lived, are several other species of

Alcea rosea unfurling. Photos Darwin Paton

Alcea, all reaching nearly 6 ft. (180 cm) in good conditions and hardy to zone 3.

VARIETIES

Alcea rosea **(hybrids).** Not surprisingly, efforts have been made to cross the several species, in a search for bigger better flowers on reliably perennial plants. Also not surprising, the best of these efforts have come out of German plant breeding programs. The 'Simplex' series includes a number of traditional colours; the 'Spotlight' series runs to colours of startling intensity, including the blazing red of 'Mars Magic.'

A. rosea **ssp.** *ficifolia.* Fig-leaved hollyhock. Single flowers in warm shades of yellow, pink, red and white.

A. rosea **var.** *nigra.* This is the coveted black hollyhock, a biennial.

A. rugosa. A bit taller than the others, with bright-yellow single blooms.

Alchemilla mollis. Photo Darwin Paton

Alchemilla – Lady's Mantle

Woodland or Meadow | *Rosaceae*

The most common member of this genus is lady's mantle (*Alchemilla mollis*), as popular in today's gardens as in our grandmothers'. The large grey-green leaves unfurl like fans or the folds of a cape (hence "mantle"), and trap beads of water for a most photogenic effect. The long-stemmed sprays of small yellow-green flowers are useful fillers in cut-flower displays, and at least one cultivar ('Select') has been bred especially for this quality. The more compact 'Thriller' is tidier and self-seeds less, if you prefer a neat garden.

Less common, but worth trying, are some of the smaller

species that are in most respects miniatures of the common species. These are all hardy to zone 3.

VARIETIES

Alchemilla alpina. Alpine lady's mantle. Growing to only 6 in. (15 cm), it has a mounding habit suitable for the shady parts of rockeries or in hypertufa troughs.

A. erythropoda. Darker foliage, sometimes tinged purple, growing to 8 in. (20 cm) and slowly spreading to make it a useful small-scale groundcover.

A. saxatilis. Nearly identical to *A. alpina* but more spreading in habit and said to be easier to grow in regular garden conditions. I haven't noticed any real difference in vigour in my garden.

Allium – Onion, Ornamental Onion, Chives, Garlic, Leek

Prairie, Meadow or Rockery | *Amaryllidaceae*

There are probably hundreds of different species of onions, ranging from miniature forms several inches high to towering globes on stalks taller than a child. Most need well-drained soil, and it seems to be a rule that the larger the flower, the more the need for sharp drainage. The bulbs rot over the winter in heavy clay soils, but thrive in rocky sandy soils even in bitter windswept locations. The delicate native species *Allium cernuum* flourishes on the windswept shores of Stuart Lake, although it is equally happy in the more Mediterranean climate of the Gulf Islands between Vancouver and Vancouver Island.

The onions all form globe-shaped flowers of one sort or another, from tight perfect spheres to looser sprays, in shades from yellow and white to the more common pinks and purples.

Left: *Allium cernuum*; right: *Allium senescens* seed heads.

Most have a tendency to self-seed, which makes it doubly practical to use them as cut flowers before this happens.

The flowers of all onions are very attractive to bees and other pollinating insects, and they are a great addition to the natural garden for that reason alone. Deer do not eat them, but voles are fond of the bulbs in the winter.

Given decent drainage, the following species are all hardy to at least zone 3.

Allium acuminatum, A. aflatunense, A. aflatunense 'Purple Sensation,' *A. angulosum* (mouse garlic), *A. caeruleum* (blue onion), *A. carinatum* ssp. *pulchellum, A. cernuum* (nodding onion), *A. christophii (A. albopilosum), A. fistulosum* (Welsh onion), *A. flavum, A. giganteum, A. hookeri, A. hymenorhizum, A. karataviense, A. libani, A. moly* (lily leek), *A. nutans* (nodding onion), *A. obliquum, A. oreophilum, A. ramosum, A. schoenoprasum* (chives), *A. senescens* (German garlic), *A. senescens* ssp. *montanum (A. lustanicum), A. sphaerocephalum (A. vineale), A. stellatum* (prairie onion), *A. tricoccum, A. triquetrum, A. tuberosum* (garlic chives), *A. ursinum* (wood garlic).

All are edible, and to some degree taste of onion. Most have been used for flavouring and/or medicinal purposes by the indigenous peoples of their homelands. These are a great group of plants to experiment with in a wild garden, and although they can be slow to form large clumps, they are easy and inexpensive from seed.

Althaea – Marshmallow

Meadow | *Malvaceae*

Althaea officinalis and *A. cannabina* (hemp marshmallow) are closely related to *Alcea* (hollyhock) but have smaller flowers and

Althaea cannabina. Photo Georg Ubelhart, Jelitto Perennial Seeds

are probably better suited to naturalizing because that makes them look more at home in the natural landscape. Traditionally used for medicinal purposes, they have summer blooms in shades of pink, and do best in deep well-drained soils. Hardy to zone 3, they can grow up to 6 ft. (180 cm) tall. They are short-lived perennials, but will self-seed in the right soil.

Alyssum scardicum.

Alyssum – Alyssum

Rockery | *Brassicaceae*

The perennial *Alyssum*, not as well known as the highly fragrant annual sweet alyssum, are small alpine plants, well suited to sunny rockeries or hypertufa troughs. The perennials *Alyssum montanum* and *A. saxatile* have been moved, and are now *Aurinia montanum* and *Aurinia saxatile*, respectively.

VARIETIES

Alyssum scardicum. Tiny alpine, bright-yellow flowers in early spring, 2 in. (5 cm). Zone 3.

A. serpyllifolium. Spring blooms in light yellow, to 2 in. (5 cm). Zone 4.

A. tortuosum. Bright-yellow, silver-green foliage, 4 in. (10 cm). Zone 2.

A. wulfenianum. Yellow-gold flowers for long period in spring, 6 in. (15 cm). Zone 4.

Amorpha – Lead Plant

Prairie | *Leguminosae*

Amorpha is hardy to zone 2, forming a sturdy, attractive clump in the landscape with blue-green foliage and sky-blue flowers. As a member of the legume family, it fixes nitrogen in the soil while adding beauty to the garden.

Amorpha canascens. Photo Georg Ubelhart, Jelitto Perennial Seeds

Anaphalis margaritacea.

Anaphalis – Pearly Everlasting

Prairie or Rockery | *Compositae*

This is the most common species of pearly everlasting, and native to much of BC. *Anaphalis margaritacea* is a mid-size spreading plant, reaching 30 in. (75 cm), with silver-grey foliage and clusters of papery white flowers in mid to late summer. As the common name suggests, it makes a good dried flower; it's also useful as a cut flower. Pearly everlasting can be used as a backdrop for showier plants in the garden or the vase, but is not unattractive in its own right in a mixed border.

The smaller and less common *A. triplinervis* tops out at 12 in. (30 cm), and the flower buds emerge with a pinkish hue before they open to white. It is more sprawling in habit than its cousin, and suited to the front of dry borders, or large rockeries.

Anemone – Windflower

Meadow or Woodland | *Ranunculaceae*

The hardy species and cultivars in this genus are often overshadowed by the not-so-hardy but showier Japanese or poppy anemones (*A. coronaria*) that bloom in a wider range of colours in late summer and fall but aren't hardy enough for zone-3 climates. The Japanese anemones can be grown as summer bulbs, lifted and stored over the winter along with gladiolas and dahlias and the like, or sacrificed as annuals. Very rarely they will surprise by overwintering in well-drained soil. *Anemone blanda*, the small Grecian windflower often sold as a bulb in the fall, has the same tendency.

The following hardy varieties are spring and early-summer blooming, in white, cream, ivory or pastel shades of red and blue, followed by interesting tufts of feathery seeds. They range in height from 12–24 in. (30–60 cm).

VARIETIES

Anemone sylvestris. Common in northern gardens, with pure-white flowers and a self-seeding habit that makes it standard fare at plant sales.

A. multifida. Available in white, pink and rose-red seed strains; tends to be short-lived.

Left: *Anemone multifida*; right: *Anemone sylvestris.*

A. altaica, A. baicalensis, A. canadensis, A. cylindrica, A. nemorosa, A. rivularis, A. rupicola, A. tomentosa and *A. virginiana.* These are all easy from seed, and naturalize well in a woodland environment without taking over; hardy to zone 3. My collection of these species grows happily under a mix of pink, mauve and purple lilacs, and bloom mostly at the same time for a pleasing effect. They vary in height and bloom time, but other than that there is not really much difference between them.

Anemone and Pulsatilla

The genus *Anemone* used to include many species that have been moved to *Pulsatilla*. Although the split was made on anatomical grounds, it worked out that those hardy species left in *Anemone* are more adapted to shade and those moved to *Pulsatilla* fare better in sunny conditions, which is more convenient than some of the other taxonomic changes that have been made.

Angelica archangelica. Photo Georg Ubelhart, Jelitto Perennial Seeds

Angelica – Angelica

Meadow | *Apiaceae*

The half-dozen or so common species of *Angelica* are all large striking herbs, with broad foliage and distinctive umbels that attract pollinating insects. They look enough like water hemlock to require an ID check before actually using them in the kitchen. The difference is in the chambered stem base of the water hemlock (*Cicuta douglasii*); angelicas have a hollow stem, except for the native species (*A. genuflexa*), which is even more similar to the very poisonous water hemlock and varies only in the leaf structure.

They tend to be biennials or short-lived perennials, but are worth growing for their architectural impact in the garden as much or more than for their purported herbal qualities. Rated as zone 3 or 4, it is usually the heavy soil that finishes them, not the winter cold. They like moist soil, but not wet feet.

VARIETIES

Angelica archangelica. Greenish-white umbels, green stems, 6 ft. (180 cm)—the root is used in traditional Chinese herbal medicine, seed strains offered differ in the estimated yield and concentration of essential oils.

A. atropurpurea. White flowers, purple stems, 6 ft. (180 cm)—striking garden plant, very attractive to beneficial insects. Stunning grown with the dark purple-leaf elderberry (*Sambucus*).

A. genuflexa. Northern BC native, found by stream-sides and in moist areas; white or pinkish-white umbels, green or purplish-green stems, to 36 in. (90 cm).

A. gigas. Deep-red umbels, purple stems, 48 in. (120 cm); the showiest in the garden.

Antennaria – Pussy-toes

Prairie or Rockery | *Compositae*

The cultivated species of *Antennaria* are all similar in habit, varying mainly in flower colour and size; they all seem to be hardy to zone 3. The pussy-toes are low-growing, spreading drought-tolerant plants with silver-grey or silver-green foliage, with small fuzzy flower heads (the "pussy toes") rising above the foliage and turning to a downy fluff as the seeds mature. They are lovely and functional at the front of dry sunny borders or filling in between

Left: *Antennaria dioica*; right: decorative seedheads of *Antennaria neglecta* var. *gaspensis*.

52

rocks in large or small rockeries. *Antennaria* is also a useful genus when planting "green roofs" because it is so tough.

VARIETIES

Antennaria carpatica. Cream flowers, sometimes purple tinged, 6 in. (15 cm).

A. dioica. White or pale-pink flowers, or deep pink in the variety 'Rubra', 4 in. (10 cm).

A. neglecta var. *gaspensis.* White flowers, 4 in. (10 cm).

A. rosea. Rose-pink flowers, 16 in. (40 cm).

There are also a number of native species—we are rich in native pussy-toes, with no less than nine listed in the invaluable reference book *Plants of Northern British Columbia* by MacKinnon, Pojar & Coupé.

Anthemis – Marguerite, False Chamomile, Dyer's Chamomile

Prairie | *Compositae*

Anthemis are mid-sized white, yellow or orange daisies, doing best in poor, well-drained soils. They can get excessively leggy and floppy in rich soil or if fertilized. While hardy to zone 3, they are short-lived; as with most fleeting plants they tend to self-seed, although not excessively.

VARIETIES

Anthemis carpatica (*A. cretica* ssp. *carpatica*). False chamomile. White ray flower with a yellow disc, over 6 in. (15 cm) with mat-forming aromatic foliage.

Aphids in the Perennial Garden

Aphids are especially attracted to the fresh lush growth produced by applications of high-nitrogen fertilizer (the "N" of N-P-K, and the first number in the three-numeral fertilizer formulas), therefore one way to control aphids is to not fertilize as heavily. Growing a diversity of plants, including many that attract and shelter beneficial insects, also helps. I had a long flower bed against an old wood snake fence that was packed with multi-coloured lupines, and it looked glorious for a couple of years. Once the aphids settled into it, though, it was a feast for them and rapidly became an eyesore for me. Now it is a mixed border, with self-seeded lupines popping up here and there, and no aphid problem. (Note that I say "no problem" rather than "no aphids." There will always be some bugs, as they are a natural part of any healthy garden.)

There are almost as many different kinds of aphids as there are plants for them to feast on—according to Wikipedia, 4,400 species of aphids. Usually green, they can also be darker coloured, depending on what plant material they are feeding on. They tend to congregate on the underside of foliage and on new growth—and are often exactly the same shade as that new growth, which makes them easy to miss unless you are really looking at the plant closely. It is the damage that is most often noticed first—curled-up leaves, lumpy-looking stem tips, and stunted growth. The aphids, in large numbers, literally suck the life out of plants.

Black aphids. Photo Darwin Paton

If action is necessary or desirable, the first line of control, useful mainly in home greenhouses and tiny gardens, and with small infestations, is to remove the beasties either by hand or with a stream of water. Only the first generation of aphids in the spring (which usually sneak in under our radar while we are busy with other chores) have wings, so the wingless later generations can be blasted off the plants and have no means of getting back from any distance (unless they are transported by ants, which happens).

Organic insecticidal soap sprays are widely available, and can be effective if used early and according to direction. These are "contact" sprays—the insects must be coated for the soap to work, and it is necessary to spray under the leaves and in all the hard-to-get-to places. Have you ever noticed that the first sign of aphid damage is usually the leaf edges curling under? This makes it difficult to get the spray on the aphids, which are under the leaves and protected by those curls. Regular dish or laundry soaps are no longer a good substitute for horticultural soaps, as it is difficult to find household products that are pure soap these days—they have too many other chemicals (dyes, perfumes and antibacterial ingredients) in them, some harmful to plants.

Trap crops can also be a useful part of any control strategy (again, note "control" and not "elimination"). A clump of sacrificial aphid-favourites in the back corner of the garden or greenhouse will at least keep all the aphids in one place, and the infested plants can be bagged up and disposed of in the garbage, bugs and all. I had some leftover purple basil plants in the greenhouse which inadvertently became my trap crop there. Perennial flowers that the aphids have been especially fond of here in the garden are lupines (*Lupinus*) and valerian (*Valeriana*).

Anthemis tinctoria 'Hollandaise Sauce.'

A. tinctoria. Dyer's chamomile. A leggy and somewhat woody-stemmed plant with named cultivars flowering in colours from white to a dark golden-yellow—it is the flowers that produce the yellow dye, which makes the white flowers rather useless, especially in a world already full of white daisies. (A pale green can be achieved from the aromatic foliage; mordants are required for either colour.) 24 in. (60 cm).

A. tinctoria var. sancti-johannis. Marguerite. The bloodlines have become obscured by time and trade secrecy, so these may be a species or a hybrid. It probably doesn't matter. 'Hollandaise Sauce' is a very pretty pale-yellow form, 'Kelwayi' is bright golden-yellow, seed-grown specimens tend towards golden-yellow or orange. There are some old Irish seed strains which are highly regarded in the British Isles, but never show up on this side of the ocean—more's the pity. They are all around 24 in. (60 cm) tall and clump-forming.

Aquilegia – Columbine

Meadow, Woodland or Rockery | *Ranunculaceae*
All of the columbines I have tried (dozens of species and probably a hundred varieties) have been hardy here in zone 3. The only complaint I have about columbines is that they finish blooming towards the end of July and then are done for the year. They are one flower I wouldn't get tired of.

Although the plants have traditionally been used for food and medicinal purposes in various areas of the world, some parts are poisonous (including the seeds). That said, hundreds of plants have coexisted quite happily in my garden with my dogs, who have chomped off a few shrubs here and there over the years but never shown any interest in the columbines or any other poisonous plants. I suspect whatever makes the plants poisonous

also tastes or smells bad enough to warn animals off. Columbines have few insect problems, other than an annoying but not fatal leaf miner, probably for the same reason.

The columbines vary in height, from miniature alpine varieties barely 4 in. (10 cm) high to outstanding tall species reaching to 36 in. (90 cm). They are all clump-forming, with graceful flowers over delicately lobed foliage in shades of green or blue green. The *A. vulgaris* group known as the Woodside Strain has foliage variegated in gold and green, like mottled sunlight on the forest floor. Some flowers have long sweeping spurs, while others are virtually spurless; the heirloom Granny's Bonnet varieties, also known as the Barlow series, are doubled in the corolla, while the "clematis-flowered" clementine types have double petals.

I have favourites, of course. The pure-white *A. caerulea* hybrid 'Kristall' (a.k.a. 'Crystal Star') is outstanding, and the clear yellow of the long-blooming *A. chrysantha* 'Yellow Queen' is a winner. The sky-blue tones of any of the species or series are always a wonderful addition to the garden or a vase of cut flowers. Any of the small fan-leaved *A. flabellata* varieties will grace a rockery with attractive foliage as well as flowers, and the taller ones are an essential component of natural gardens or meadows. They even grow well in containers. Fortunately they are easy from seed, whether purchased or wild or garden collected, so there's no reason not to have a variety.

What usually appears at garden centres are seed strains, such as 'Music,' 'Songbird' or 'Origami,' which are a blend of one type or another, uniform in size but offering a variety of colours. It's not a bad way to get started, but pick up more than one lonely plant—these are native to mixed meadows and don't look right rigidly planted as specimens.

Mixed *Aquilegia caerulea* cultivars.

Arabis alpina. Photo Darwin Paton

Arabis – Rock Cress

Rockery | *Brassicaceae*

Arabis are pretty and useful spring-blooming plants, commonly seen spilling over rockeries or retaining walls or at the front edges of dry sunny borders. They thrive in full sun with good drainage, and are adequately dense to discourage most weeds yet flexible enough to plant with large spring-flowering bulbs such as tulips and daffodils, which will push up through them. The most commonly found garden varieties flower in white, but pink forms are also available. The half-dozen or so native species (indeed, all New World species of *Arabis*) are now actually classified as *Boechera* rather than *Arabis*. They will be lumped together in most references.

VARIETIES

Arabis alpina (**formerly** *A. caucasica*). Evergreen foliage that grows to 6 in. (15 cm) with bright-white or pale-pink flowers that begin to bloom almost as soon as the snow is off. Several named cultivars exist, which seem to vary from each other only marginally in size; all seem to have "snow" in the common name. Zone 3.

A. blepharophylla. Slightly less hardy than the white varieties and short-lived, growing to 4 in. (10 cm) with bright-pink flowers. Zone 4.

A. procurrens. Not as vigorous as *A. alpina*, but probably still zone 3, with dark-green foliage and white flowers.

A. procurrens fernandii-coburgi '**Variegata**.' Very low growing, with dark-green and white foliage that has a tendency to revert to the solid green; keep that pulled out or it will overrun the less vigorous variegated parts. White flowers. Zone 3.

A. × sturii. The lowest growing, with foliage barely reaching 1 in. (2 cm) in poor dry soil, but incredibly tough and tolerant of some foot traffic. Delicate flowers on 6-in. (15-cm) stems; foliage turns purple red in the winter.

Arenaria – Sandwort

Rockery or Woodland | *Caryophyllaceae*

Arenaria montana forms a low-growing fine-textured mat covered with tiny white flowers in early summer. At only 4 in. (10 cm) it isn't really tall enough to choke out weeds, but makes a pretty groundcover in a sheltered spot. It needs well-drained soil, but can dry out in the middle and start looking ratty if it doesn't get sufficient moisture.

Arenaria montana.

Armeria maritima 'Splendens.'

Armeria – Thrift, Sea Thrift, Spanish Thrift

Rockery | *Plumbaginaceae*

Armeria are tough little plants, requiring only sunshine and well-drained soil to thrive.

VARIETIES

Armeria alpina. Bright carmine-pink flowers, short-lived in heavy soil, 6 in. (15 cm). Zone 3.

A. maritima. Sea thrift. This is the hardiest and most common, with the added bonus of being salt tolerant and very useful next to sidewalks or driveways where salt may be applied in winter. The low spiky mounds of foliage spread slowly, and can eventually hollow out in the middle, signalling time for division and rejuvenation. The globe-shaped brightly coloured flowers, sometimes white but more often in shades of lavender, pink or red, appear on relatively tall flower stalks in late spring. The whole plant gets to be 12 in. (30 cm) tall, but can spread to twice that. There are a number of named cultivars and seed strains.

A. maritima ssp. juniperifolia. Dwarf form of above, to 4 in. (10 cm), a tidy miniature with lavender flowers. Zone 3.

Arnica – Arnica

Meadow or Woodland | *Compositae*

Arnica is well known for its medicinal attributes, and both the native and introduced species have the active ingredient. As with any herb, if it contains a chemical compound that will have an effect on the body, there is also an amount that will be toxic or even fatal. It pays to know what you are doing before you start grazing in your garden. All the *Arnica* species that I have tried are hardy to zone 3, at least—the vigour with which some of them grow suggests they may be even hardier. With bright-yellow flowers, they are pretty in natural meadows or as mixed-border components in any moist humus-rich soil, blooming in early spring when little else does.

Arnica chamissonis. Meadow arnica, leafy leopard's bane. Dense spreading clumps, 20 in. (50 cm). Native to northern BC.

A. cordifolia. Heart-leaf arnica. The showiest of the ones I have grown, 24 in. (60 cm). Native to northern BC.

A. mollis. Hairy arnica. Spreading habit, 20 in. (50 cm).

A. montana. Mountain arnica, mountain tobacco. Clump-forming, 18 in. (45 cm). This is the species most often grown for medicinal use.

Artemisia – Wormwood, Sagebrush, Mugwort, Tarragon, Dusty Miller, Sweet Annie

Prairie or Rockery | *Compositae*

This is a large and useful genus, consisting of annuals, perennials and woody species, ornamental plants as well as medicinal and kitchen herbs, and hundreds of different species for a variety of habitats (although most prefer it hot and dry).

One of the hardy *Artemisia* species (*A. tridentata*) is known as buffalo sage and used in First Nations smudges; it is not to be confused with sacred sage, which is *Salvia apiana*. Several of the other hardy native species, including *A. glacialis* and the more common garden species *A. ludoviciana*, are also reported to be used ceremonially. Respect for the plant and the symbolic connection between man and earth may be more important than the exact species.

Cooks value the culinary qualities of tarragon (*A. dracun-*

Arnica cordifolia. Photo Darwin Paton

Artemisia stelleriana 'Silver Brocade.'

culus), discriminating imbibers are familiar with the tang of absinthe (distilled from *A. absinthium*), and gardeners everywhere are fond of the silvery mound of that so-well-named ornamental 'Silver Mound.' All of these thrive in poor dry soils, but there is even one *Artemisia* for those with only wet soil: *A. lactiflora* 'Guizhou' needs a consistently moist location.

Varieties

Artemisia absinthium. Wormwood. Greyish-yellow flower heads in late summer. To 36 in. (90 cm) tall. Zone 4.

A. campestris ssp. *borealis.* Northern wormwood. Silver-green foliage, unobtrusive flowers, to 12 in. (30 cm). Not especially aromatic foliage, but very hardy. Zone 2.

A. glacialis. Wormwood. Whitish flowers, finely textured grey-green foliage to only 6 in. (15 cm). Zone 2.

A. lactiflora. White mugwort. White flowers, good for use as dried flowers. Grows to 5 ft. (150 cm). Zone 2.

A. ludoviciana. Western mugwort. Undoubtedly a survivor in the wild, the named cultivars ('Silver King' and 'Silver Queen') have a tendency to try and take over in the garden. Tall, growing to 36 in. (90 cm) and spreading by rhizome, this is an aggressive beauty. Zone 3.

A. schmidtiana 'Nana,' 'Silver Mound.' This soft-textured silvery mound is the pick of the litter for dry garden use. It forms a tidy mound 18 in. (45 cm) high and slightly wider, and then just looks good all summer, as long as it gets lots of sunshine and heat. Cut it back first thing in the spring to encourage fresh new growth.

A. stelleriana 'Silver Brocade.' Beach wormwood, dusty miller. Not to be confused with the annual dusty miller plants that look similar but are in the genus *Senecio*. This is a sprawling silver-grey coarse-textured foliage plant, great in large rockeries or at the front of dry borders. It is evergreen (evergrey?) and can be cut back in the early spring to keep it from looking too straggly.

Aruncus – Goat's Beard

Woodland or Meadow | *Rosaceae*

Aruncus consists of three hardy species, in three distinct sizes.

Aruncus dioicus (*A. vulgaris, A. sylvestris*) is the largest. A northern BC native, it is—at its best—a glorious lush plant with tall plumes of white flowers. It is starting to show up in the backdrops of photos of European gardens, looking like an astilbe on steroids. It can reach 6 ft. (180 cm) in moist rich soil, and it spreads.

A. sinensis, native to China, as the name suggests, is smaller and more polite, topping out at 5 ft. (150 cm).

A. aethusifolius is a miniature Korean native forming a tidy mound 12 in. (30 cm) high and across. It is delightful at the front of a shady border where it can be appreciated, a compact contrast to ferns and hostas.

Aruncus dioicus with *Hostas.* Photo Darwin Paton

Asclepias – Milkweed, Butterfly Weed

Meadow or Prairie | *Apocynaceae*

Milkweed is famous as the flower of choice for monarch butterflies, but there are many other reasons to grow it. The summer blooms are vibrant in the warm shades of pink and orange usually lacking at that time of year, and the 2–6 ft. (60–180 cm) range in height allows them to fit into the middle or back of most planting schemes.

The many wild species are standard components of meadows and prairies across North America, and are a food source for a wide variety of beneficial insects despite the many defences the plants raise against predation. Some people react badly to the milky sap that gives this plant one of its common names, so use caution when handling it. It makes a good cut flower, but the use of gloves would be a wise precaution (and don't rub your eyes!).

The more commonly available species of *Asclepias* are hardy enough for most northern gardens, to at least zone 3, but they tend to be short-lived in my garden due to the heavy clay soil. Many of the species prefer moist conditions at least seasonally (in spring and early summer), and all need deep soil.

VARIETIES

Asclepias incarnata. In shades of pink or creamy white, flowers are vanilla scented. This will bloom the first year from seed, but tends to be short-lived, especially in dry soil. Several named cultivars are available, including the white 'Ice Ballet,' which did well here for four or five years before disappearing.

A. speciosa. Probably the hardiest, with dark-pink flowers. Reaches 30 in. (75 cm) and needs moist soil—would be a good candidate for the sides of a bog garden or the bottom of a rain garden. Zone 2.

A. syriaca. The tallest of the species, and needing moist deep soil to reach that height, this can get to 6 ft. (180 cm) but usually doesn't. Purple-pink flowers.

A. tuberosa. A variable species, and the subject of some breeding work recently; mid-sized at 24–36 in. (60–90 cm). A number of named varieties available in bright shades of orange and yellow bloom the first year from seed, although some are short-lived. The species form is pumpkin orange in colour, thriving in wet soils.

Asclepias speciosus. Photo Georg Ubelhart, Jelitto Perennial Seeds

Aster – Aster

Prairie or Meadow | *Compositae*

There are hundreds of species and probably thousands of cultivars of asters, but the hardy ones can be placed in one of three functional groups.

Aster alpinus 'Dark Beauty.'

Spring- and summer-blooming asters:

Aster alpinus – **Alpine aster.** Brightly coloured disproportionately large flowers in shades of blue, pink and lavender from June on, and growing to 12 in. (30 cm). There are both single- and double-flowered varieties—I disapprove of the doubles on environmental principles, as they do not provide nectar for pollinators. That said several clusters of them still survive in my garden, and they are pretty. 'Dark Beauty' remains my favourite.

Aster ptarmicoides (a.k.a. *Solidago ptarmicoides*) – **Arctic aster.** Low growing, and fits well into natural landscapes with clusters of small white flowers in summer.

Native asters:

There are eight or ten species of native aster in north-central BC, similar to each other but still different enough to rate separate species status. They are all relatively tall, at around 24 in. (60 cm), and flower in shades from pale lavender to dark purple in meadows and along roadsides in late summer. Since it is unlikely you will find any of these at your local garden centre, the best strategy would be to mark and then collect seed from an especially nice one, and then scatter this seed in your garden where you hope to establish it. These asters coordinate beautifully with wild and domesticated varieties of goldenrod (*Solidago*), and the muted tones of late summer and fall.

Fall-blooming asters:

This includes all the cultivated asters in the New England aster (*A. novae-angliae*—a.k.a. *Symphyotrichum novae-angliae*), Michaelmas aster (*A. nova-belgiae*), Indian aster (*A. tongolensis*) and wood aster (*A. dumosus*—a.k.a. *Symphyotrichum dumosum* var. *dumosum*) groups.

These and their many hybrids and named varieties are hardy enough to frustrate northern gardeners from coast to coast.

They overwinter, they bud up, they almost bloom—and then it snows and they are finished. They don't have the decency to just die so we can rip them out of our gardens and plant something better; they tease us by *almost* blooming every year (as with *Aster dumosus* 'Professor Kippenburg,' which buds up nicely, but has *never* bloomed for me in nearly ten years of variable weather).

Aster dumosus 'Professor Kippenburg,' covered in frost at the end of September.

Astilbe – Astilbe

Woodland or Meadow | *Saxifragaceae*

Astilbe have been popular garden plants for a long time, and it's not surprising there are so many different varieties available. With the exception of the *A. chinensis* group, they need consistently moist soil to do well. The more sun and heat they get, the more moisture they need; they will survive in a woodland garden with little or no additional watering, but will be miserable, if they live at all, in full sun with the same amount of water.

The *A. chinensis* group, also known as *A. rubra, A. chinensis pumila* or *A. taquetti,* can be distinguished by stiff upright magenta-purple bottle-brush flowers. Cultivars in shades of pink (i.e. lighter magenta-purple) are also available. These are definitely the workhorses of the group. To my surprise, I once saw them planted in a highway median in the middle of Smithers, and apparently doing quite nicely there. They are hardier (a solid zone 3, maybe even zone 2) and more drought tolerant than other astilbes.

Given all the breeding and cross-breeding that is going on, sorting out "who's who" in the astilbe world can be confusing. The short form of the story is that there are probably a thousand different named cultivars, in dozens of different series. They vary in height, from 8–48 in. (20–120 cm), and in colour, from pure

Top: A collection of *Astilbe* cultivars. Photo Darwin Paton.
Bottom: *Astilbe* 'Bronze Elegance.'

white to creamy white through shades of pink and lavender to darkest red. They tend towards the blue side of the colour spectrum; even 'Peach Blossom' is a cool shade of pink rather than the warm shade the name would suggest. The flower plumes can be upright or arching, feathery or dense, stiff or airy. Foliage colour varies as well, although some of that is seasonally influenced— some cultivars sport olive-green foliage, others bright-green, others are tinged with red or purple. Some turn spectacular red-purple shades in the fall.

Tags and signage tend towards more information about how to grow plants and less about their genetics, so it can be hard to tell what group any particular cultivar belongs to—and it may not really matter given the complexity of the bloodlines. Generally speaking, the *A. × japonica* hybrids are the first to bloom, in late spring or early summer. These are followed, or joined by, the *A. × arendsii* hybrids and the *A. × simplicifolia* hybrids, and then the rest. Given a sheltered location and well-drained soil rich in humus and watered occasionally, most *Astilbe* are probably at the sheltered end of zone 3, although with poorer conditions or more expensive plants a zone-4 rating would be a safer assumption.

Astilboides tabularis.

Astrantia major.

Astilboides – Astilboides

Woodland | *Saxifragaceae*

Also known as *Rodgersia tabularis*, *Astilboides tabularis* is a strikingly huge species of the saxifrage family, which thrives in moist humus-rich soils in partial shade. The more moisture, the bigger and better it gets—the leaves can reach up to 24 in. (60 cm) across under ideal conditions, even in a zone-3 garden; the whole plant in flower can be more than 6 ft. (180 cm) across and 8 ft. (240 cm) tall. The plumes of whitish flowers, appearing in midsummer, are almost an afterthought, but don't detract from the massive elegance of this plant. Not for every garden, but splendid when a perfect corner can be found for it.

Astrantia – Masterwort

Woodland or Meadow | *Apiaceae*

The many cultivars and hybrids of *Astrantia major* and *A. carniolica* don't seem to vary in hardiness, although some are slower to get established than others. They prefer moist, cool soil rich in organic matter, and can grow to be 18 in. (45 cm) tall, forming large clumps over time. The summer flowers range in colour from a pale almost-white to deep red; they actually consist of showy bracts surrounding a tight colour-coordinated umbel of florets. Their coarse foliage texture and habitat preference makes them the perfect foil for either ferns or hostas.

Astrantia plants tend to come relatively true from seed (the dark reds producing dark-red seedlings, and the lighter-pink ones producing pink seedlings), but are slow to establish. Many seed-grown varieties are available, with the newest ones tending to be touted as either lighter or darker than those currently available. They are all pretty, and easy to maintain once they get going.

Aubrieta deltoidea.

Aubrieta – Purple Rock Cress

Rockery | *Brassicaceae*

The masses of low purple flowers spilling over the edges of rockeries and retaining walls are always the first solid sign of spring in northern gardens. *Aubrieta deltoidea* and the hybrids derived from it bloom with the early-spring bulbs, soon after the snow is off. The foliage is evergreen and not harmed by cutting back after the bloom is finished; this tidies it up and keeps the plants from getting straggly. They can go dormant and look quite ratty if not watered during a dry summer, but will usually come back again the following spring anyway.

The available varieties differ mainly in colour, and are all lumped together as *Aubrieta* × *cultorum*; the polite Latin way of saying "we've been growing them so long we no longer know who the parents were." Although the variety names suggest significant colour differences ('Cascade Blue,' 'Cascade Red,' 'Royal Blue,'

'Royal Red,' etc.), in reality the blues are purple-blue and the reds are purple-red. The violets are a pretty shade of violet, and they all blend together in a very pleasing way, the colours fading a bit on older flowers and the whole effect a tapestry of warm rich colour.

There are variegated forms, but they don't seem to be as vigorous and the foliage tends to try and revert to solid green. When they do well they are eye-catching in a shady area close to a path where they can be appreciated.

Most of the larger and more vigorous spring-flowering bulbs will grow right up through the low-growing plants—to 6 in. or 15 cm—and they both thrive in well-drained soil, so it makes a good combination. The addition of a few late-leafing shrubs such as mock-orange (*Philadelphus*) would complete the picture and hide any summer straggliness that did occur.

Aurinia – Basket of Gold, Cloth of Gold, Gold Dust

Rockery | *Brassicaceae*

Aurinia was previously lumped in with the *Alyssum* genus, and is still often found there (and always will be in older books, of course). Its bright mustard-yellow flowers set it apart from the related *Alyssum* and rock cress cousins with which it blooms in the spring. *Aurinia montana* sports yellow-gold flowers earlier in the spring than the similar *A. saxatilis* cultivars, and grows to only 6 in. (15 cm), spreading to three times that. *Aurinia saxatilis* grows to 10 in. (25 cm) and has grey-green "evergreen" foliage that can get straggly-looking by early summer. Cut it back by a third or more after it is finished blooming to tidy it up and control the spread. There are a number of named cultivars that vary in

Aurinia saxatilis.

size and habit (some are more compact); the cultivar names and the common names are frequently confused, making it a bit of a challenge to know what you are buying.

Baptisia – False Indigo, Wild Indigo

Meadow | *Leguminosae*

The one tested and reliably hardy member of this genus is *Baptisia australis*, false indigo, which isn't grown as often as it should be for perhaps understandable reasons. It grows to be a magnificent clump of more than 36 in. (90 cm) tall and wide, but takes several years to achieve this status. Very drought tolerant because it is taprooted, it doesn't transplant well for the same reason. For those who have the patience to start with a seed or a seedling, *Baptisia* is

Bear Problems

The bears probably think that they have a human problem, and they may be right. Compost piles containing meat or dairy products (or the remains of caught fish, which I have seen done, as thoughtless as that may seem), and fruit left to rot on or under trees will attract bears. Bears that have thus been trained to hang around humans and human habitations may have to be shot, as they become too dangerous. Bears who wander into cities and towns and don't find food wander out again and usually don't bother coming back. The situation is ours to manage intelligently.

I have had bears attracted to the ripe fruit on my fruit trees, to a bag of bone meal left out in the carport, and to bird feeders. It took me a while to figure out that refilling the bird feeders and putting them back up wasn't the answer. I had a poky little bear one year who overturned nursery containers and bit holes in the hoses, presumably just exploring his world. Nowadays, with two loud dogs and no bear treats left out, I rarely see the bears up close. I'm hoping they are still out there, poking around and doing bear things.

The thickness of a screen door…
Photo Darwin Paton

Baptisia australis.

Bergenia crassifolia.

a beauty, with attractive blue-green foliage and stunning pure-blue pea-like flowers in early summer. The flowers are followed by the seed pods, which give away its membership in the legume family.

Lesser known but possibly as hardy are *B. alba* (*B. leucantha*, *B. pendula*), white flowering, and *B. tinctoria*, with yellow flowers. The latter yields a dye, once processed. I have also recently seen several hybrid cultivars, with names such as 'Purple Smoke' and 'Solar Flare,' with hardy parents so most likely hardy.

They all need fairly deep soils (and sulk in my heavy clay) but other than that seem to be undemanding and beautiful.

Bergenia – Elephant's Ear, Pig Squeak

Woodland or Meadow | *Saxifragaceae*

There is a healthy clump of *Bergenia* growing under a hedge out at the old Dominion Experimental Farm site by the Prince George Airport; it has been there, growing in solid Pineview clay, for 50 years or so. That kind of longevity is reassuring.

Bergenia crassifolia (*B. cordifolia*) will grow in clay or well-drained soil, in shade or sun (as long as it has some moisture), and spreads slowly enough so as not to pose a threat to the garden. It can take a bit of time to establish, but makes up for that in longevity. It is evergreen, taking on deep, rich shades of red and burgundy in the fall. In the north it is covered by snow all winter, of course, but will emerge from the snow still green, and begin flowering soon afterwards. New foliage emerges in late spring after the flowers are finished.

The flowers range in warm shades from pale pink to deep red. A number of cultivars are available, which vary in size as well

as colour—'Baby Doll' is the most compact and has light-pink flowers, 'Winter Glow' claims the best fall colour. A few varieties are advertised to have long enough stems to be useful as cut flowers, but mine have never shown that tendency.

Brunnera – Bugloss, Siberian Bugloss

Forest Floor or Woodland | *Boraginaceae*

The small blue forget-me-not flowers give away *Brunnera*'s relationship to the familiar annual or biennial forget-me-not (*Myosotis*), but everything else about it is quite different.

The plain green form of *Brunnera sibirica* is rarely seen in gardens or garden centers, with heart-shaped leaves and a ground-covering habit. That and its tough drought- and shade-tolerant character make it a nearly perfect plant (cont. on p. 64)

Brunnera macrophylla. Photo Darwin Paton

Beneficial-insect Attractors

The natural world is far more complex than we can know, and that's probably a good thing. A little humility might keep us from destroying it. The plants listed in this section are a small number of those that offer food and/or habitat to various pollinators and predatory insects at different stages of their lives.

We have probably all heard the factoid that something like 90 percent of the insects in our gardens are either beneficial or "neutral" to human purposes. Most of the thousands of insects in our gardens use different plants at different times in their life cycles for different purposes— as food for larvae or adults, shelter, overwintering, laying eggs on, etc. Given that most of us are unable to identify the majority of bugs in our gardens, along with what plants they need at which stage of their lives, the sensible approach is to grow as wide a diversity of plants as possible, and hope for the best. Sterile "improved" double forms of flowers do not offer pollen, but still have leaves to eat and lay eggs on.

Most insects need water or moisture in some form, and some—including many butterflies—thrive in the presence of a mud puddle where they can access minerals as well as moisture. A small mud puddle underneath the edge of a bird bath, where the overflow from one feeds the other, can be aesthetically pleasing and environmentally sound at the same time.

Some Beneficial-insect Attractors

Bergamot – *Monarda*
Catmint or Catnip – *Nepeta*
Columbine – *Aquilegia*
Culver's root – *Veronicastrum*
Delphinium, Larkspur – *Delphinium*
Foxglove – *Digitalis*
Globe thistle – *Echinops*
Ironweed – *Vernonia*
Jacob's ladder – *Polemonium*
Lavender – *Lavendula*
Leopard's bane – *Doronicum*

Lungwort – *Pulmonaria*
Lupine – *Lupinus*
Mallow – *Malva moschata*
Milkweed – *Asclepias*
Mint – *Mentha*
Onion (ornamental or edible varieties)
   – *Allium*
Oregano – *Origanum*
Poppy – *Papaver*
Primrose – *Primula*
Purple coneflower – *Echinacea*

Rock cress – *Aubrieta, Aurinia, Arabis*
Sage – *Salvia*
Speedwell – *Veronica*
Sunflower (perennial and annual varieties)
   – *Helianthus*
Thyme – *Thymus*
Tulip – *Tulipa*
Valerian – *Valeriana*
Vervain – *Verbena*
Yarrow – *Achillea*

Echinops provides a globe-shaped landing platform.

The presence of ladybugs suggests a healthy garden. Photo Darwin Paton

Malva in bloom attracts pollinating insects such as bees.

for the dry shade under conifers. It should be no surprise that this type of habitat is where it evolved. *Brunnera macrophylla* is also fairly drought tolerant, but has largely been overshadowed by its higher maintenance but spectacular offspring. Both species' forms are zone-3 hardy.

The first variegated *Brunnera*, 'Jack Frost,' took the gardening world by storm, and by now, even with a number of cultivars on the market at reasonable prices (and new "improved" ones coming out very year), they still get quite a bit of attention. The variegated leaf cultivars all tend to be clump-forming rather than spreading, and seem to need a bit more moisture than the species—more Woodland in nature than dry Forest Floor. Other cultivars include 'Looking Glass,' 'Dawson's White,' 'Hadspen Cream,' and 'Langtrees.' These all seem to be more zone 4 than 3.

Unlike most variegated "mutants," these seem to come rela-tively true from seed, which is interesting—I have several volun-teer seedlings virtually identical to their parents; this brings the whole issue of plant protection licensing into question. I'm sure the seedlings are not genetically identical (they are not clones), and their habit may be slightly different (one seems to have a bit of a tendency to spread, which its parent doesn't) and only vegeta-tive propagation is prohibited in this case. (You can't stop plants from doing what plants do, after all.)

Buphthalmum – Yellow Ox-eye Daisy

Prairie | *Compositae*

Buphthalmum salicifolium (willow-leaved ox-eye daisy, sunwheel) produces bright golden-yellow daisy flowers on stems reaching to only 24 in. (60 cm), a welcome change from some of the

....

Biennials

Biennials are plants with two-year life cycles. The first year they put their energy into forming a rosette of leaves and a strong root system (usually a taproot), which allows them to survive over the winter. In their second year, they switch strategies and put all their energy into flowering and then setting seed, usually with tall showy flower stalks to catch the attention of pollinators.

Alcea rosea.

The abundant flowers are useful in attracting beneficial insects to the garden. The biennial Queen Anne's lace, the cousin of our domestic carrot, is a popular weed in some places for that reason. Many of our garden vegetables, including carrots, parsley and cabbage, are biennials that we harvest at the end of the first year; we are taking advantage of this tendency to store energy in the first year by cutting their life cycle short. To save seed, some northern gardeners store the roots or heads over the winter, and replant them in the spring to go to seed. The plants will sometimes but not always overwinter outside without protection.

In the ornamental garden, biennials can be a nuisance. In the good old days of bedding-plant schemes and garden staff, the biennials were grown in a plot behind the shed and moved into place the year, if not the month, they bloomed, usually replacing the early annuals that were finished by then. These days most of us have trouble planting our gardens once, let alone growing a second garden's worth of replacement plants. In a tidy garden, these prolific self-seeders get weeded out; in a wilder garden they can have a tendency to take over. They are seldom found in garden centres, because consumers want to buy plants that are in bloom, yet these are almost finished by the time they are blooming.

To further confuse the issue, plants are not as keen on being pigeon-holed as people are of classifying them. Many of the *Verbascum*, for instance, can't make up their minds whether they are biennials or short-lived perennials, or even annuals. There are *Verbascum* species in each group, as well as the indecisive ones. Many of the showy new named varieties of *Verbascum* have been created by crosses of perennials with annuals and biennials, so are beautiful but not long-lived, especially in the north. Life in the garden is full of compro-mises. The following are clearly biennial:

Dame's rocket – *Hesperis matronalis*
Forget-me-not – *Myosotis sylvatica*
Foxglove – *Digitalis purpurea*
Hollyhock – *Alcea rosea*
Mullein – *Verbascum bombyciferum, V. densiflorum, V. nigrum* and

probably any hybrids created using these (the perennial species tend to be short-lived, but survive to a third summer often enough to avoid this classification)
Sweet William – *Dianthus barbatus*

Buphthalmum salicifolium 'Alpengold.'
Photo Georg Ubelhart, Jelitto Perennial Seeds

towering mid- to late-summer yellow daisies. While the compact size makes it useful in smaller gardens, it is still long-stemmed enough to make a good cut flower.

Cactus: *Escobaria* and *Opuntia*

Prairie or Rockery | *Cactaceae*
While cacti, like orchids, are not popularly believed to grow in the north-central interior of BC, this myth is proved wrong by at least two specimens that have been successfully grown here, in two separate locations. If one person (or two) can grow them, anyone can, given the right location and a bit of luck.

Escobaria vivipara is a small ball cactus native to southeastern Alberta. There is a specimen growing and blooming (outdoors,

not in a greenhouse or on a windowsill) in the Goodsir Nature Park, 30 minutes north of Prince George. It appears to be perfectly happy.

Opuntia, prickly pear cactus, is well known to anyone who has run barefoot through the hills around the Okanagan lakes. There are many species, cultivars and named varieties floating around in the nursery trade, and hobbyists have been collecting, breeding and trading specimens for decades, if not centuries. Several of those specimens have made their way to Mackenzie, BC, where they live in a sunny flower bed tucked in with an assortment of other rare and common plant varieties. They have not flowered yet, to my knowledge; the two plants came labelled as "pink flower" and "yellow flower."

Calamintha – Calamint

Meadow | *Lamiaceae*
Calamintha is closely related and similar to the mints (*Mentha*) and catnips (*Nepeta*), except that it is slightly less hardy, probably only to zone 4. It is a pretty meadow plant, suitable for naturalizing and attracting beneficial insects, with deep-green foliage and clusters of pink flowers. It grows to 12 in. (30 cm) high, and doesn't spread as much as the family connections might suggest.

Opuntia hybrid and friend.

Calamintha grandiflora. Photo Georg Ubelhart, Jelitto Perennial Seeds

Calla palustris. Photo Darwin Paton

Calla – Water Arum

Pond & Water Garden | *Araceae*

This beautiful small native pond plant is rarely used in water gardens, perhaps because it is seldom available. *Calla palustris* can be grown from seed, but the seed must be sown fresh, and never allowed to dry out. Few seed companies have the technology to handle it correctly, and very few gardeners are in the right place at the right time to collect seed. (Trying to germinate dead seed is frustrating, trust me.) Digging up plants in the wild would be unethical even if there was a chance of them living, which there isn't.

This *Calla* is only distantly a relative of the calla lily (*Zantedeschia*), which is a tender bulb or a houseplant in northern climates.

Campanula – Bellflower

Prairie, Meadow or Rockery | *Campanulaceae*

Campanula has to be one of the largest and most varied genera that northern gardeners have to play with. There are bellflowers for sun, shade, rockery, pond edge, wild meadow or container. There are annuals, perennials and biennials. There are groundcovers and accent plants, aggressive weeds and delicate alpines. There are tall ones, mid-size ones, and low-growing mat-forming ones. There are even double-flowered forms of many species. While there isn't a wide range of colour—the majority bloom in some shade of blue or purple (not a bad thing), with the occasional white or pink—the blooms begin in mid to late spring and continue on right until fall.

The following list barely taps the wide variety of species that may show up in specialty catalogues or at sales, with over 500 species in the genus. *Campanula* are relatively easy to grow from seed, so it could be worth risking a few dollars to try a new one.

The low-growing varieties from mountain regions are probably going to be happy in the Rockery Habitat (needing drainage); the taller ones in the Meadow Habitat (needing more organic material in the soil and moisture).

VARIETIES

(Common names are omitted except in those cases where it isn't "bellflower."

Campanula × 'Birch Hybrid.' Purple-blue flowers. To 4 by 24 in. (10 by 60 cm). Rockery, zone 4.

C. alliariifolia. Ivory bells. Ivory-white flowers. 18 in. (45 cm) tall and wide. Meadow, zone 3.

C. carpatica. There are a number of different cultivars of this popular mounding plant, in white and shades of blue; also double forms. 14 in. (35 cm) tall and wide. Meadow or Rockery, zone 3.

C. cochleariifolia. Fairy's thimbles. Delicate tiny blue or white flowers, perfect up front somewhere it can be appreciated. 4 by 8 in. (10 by 20 cm). Meadow or Rockery, zone 3 or 4.

C. garganica. Small starry blue flowers. 4 by 8 in. (10 by 20 cm). Rockery, zone 4.

C. glomerata. Clustered bellflower. Deep-purple flower clusters on upright stems, also a white version. Easy to grow, spreading, will naturalize (not quite a weed). Numerous named cultivars exist, ranging from 12–24 in. (30–60 cm). Meadow, zone 3 or even 2.

C. lactiflora. Pale-blue to white flowers, one of the taller species at 5 ft. (150 cm), with a number of named cultivars and seed strains. Short-lived, will usually self-seed. Meadow, zone 4.

C. lasiocarpa. Violet or white flowers. Mounding to 10 in. (25 cm). Several named cultivars exist. Rockery, zone 4.

C. latifolia. Milky bellflower. Tall, variable species, with flowers in white and every shade of blue and purple. Several named cultivars exist. 36 by 18 in. (90 by 45 cm). Meadow, zone 3.

C. medium. Canterbury bells, cup and saucer. A number of different cultivars are available in white and shades of blue, both single and double forms. Clump-forming biennial to 30 by 12 in. (75 by 30 cm). Meadow, zone 4.

C. persicifolia. Peach leaf bellflower. This is one of my favourites in the garden. Sky-blue or pure white, nodding bells on tall 36 in. (90 cm) stems, from early summer sporadically through to freeze-up. It self-seeds enough to pop up throughout the garden in sunny spots, but never tries to take over, and is a great cutting flower. A number of named cultivars exist; it is also easy from seed. Meadow, zone 3, maybe even zone 2.

C. portenschlagiana. Dalmatian bellflower. (No, it's not spotted.) White, violet or deep-purple flowers, mounding habit to 8 in. (20 cm) tall and somewhat wider. Rockery, zone 4.

Campanula alliariifolia.

Campanula glomerata.

Campanula persicifolia.

C. poscharskyana. Serbian bellflower. Lavender blue with a white eye. There is also a double flowered cultivar. To 8 in. (20 cm) and up to 24 in. (60 cm) across. Rockery, zone 3.

C. punctata. Spotted bellflower. Large nodding bells in pinkish-white to deep pink, often spotted and mottled. Named varieties vary in depth of colour. Grows to 12 in. (30 cm) and spreads by rhizome; can be aggressive in lighter soils; reasonably well behaved in heavy clay soil. Meadow, zone 3.

C. pyramidalis. Chimney bellflower. Large flowers in light blue or white, on tall stems that can reach 6 ft. (180 cm). Short-lived, but does better in dry well-drained soils. Prairie, zone 3 or 4.

C. rapunculoides. Rampion. Think "rampant." This one is an aggressive spreader and the bane of many northern gardens. Pretty lavender-blue flower on 36-in. (90-cm) stems. This spreads by both root and seed, and can be distinguished from its polite cousins by the fleshy tuberous roots (pieces of which stay in the ground to regrow every time you pull the plant out). Unfortunately, hardy to at least zone 3.

C. rotundifolia. Harebells, wild bluebells. Delicate-looking blue bells, occasionally white. This is a native and circumpolar species that self-seeds in a naturalizing kind of way without trying to take over the whole garden. Beautiful and easy to control. Forms a loose mound 12 in. (30 cm). Meadow or rockery, zone 2 (although hardiness will vary with seed source).

C. takesimana. Mottled pinkish-white flowers over glossy foliage. A great groundcover or a horrible weed, depending on who you talk to (and where it was planted). Great under large shrubs or trees, not so good in mixed perennial beds. Meadow, zone 3.

C. trachelium. Bats-in-the-belfry, throatwort. You know anything with common names like these has been around English gardens for a while! Flowers in blue or white; double forms of both are available. Upright plant to 36 in. (90 cm) does best in drier soils and partial shade, so at the back edge of the Meadow border, perhaps, or the front edge of the Woodland.

Carex – Sedge

Bog Garden or Pond & Water Garden | *Cyperaceae*

Carex are a huge group of plants adapted to varying degrees of moist and wet soils, somewhat similar to grasses in appearance but quite different botanically. As the rhyme goes, "Sedges have edges, rushes are round, and grasses have nodes all the way to the ground." The "nodes" are the lumps on the stems where new leaves start, and sedges don't have them; also grass stems are perfectly round in cross-section at the base, while sedge stems have that "edge."

I wish I could say that sedges are better behaved than grasses in gardens, but most of them aren't. Like grasses, their ecological mission is to cover ground, in this case wet ground, and they do it well—and diversely. There are dozens of species of native sedges in northern BC alone; they are valuable filters in wetland habitats, important as migratory bird food and spring bear grazing and useful for restoration work. Many of them will grow outside of wetlands in heavy acidic soils, and they are used as an indicator for poor-quality pasture because of this. Any of them (identification is tricky, and can take a microscope) could be usefully transplanted or seeded in a large natural pond or sizeable ditch.

There are many non-native species and cultivars starting to show up in the nursery trade and in garden centres, following on the success of ornamental grasses. This includes a number of striking yellow, bronze and variegated forms, most of which aren't hardy, probably a good thing as we have enough introduced weeds as it is.

During my sedge phase, I collected dozens of different ornamental sedges, and only one has survived the test of time. The others either died out or tried to take over. The only one not voted off the island was *Carex muskingumensis,* a hardy species with sturdy yellow-green foliage. It grows to nearly 36 in. (90 cm) and produces fairly large 2-in. (5-cm) bronze-brown seed heads in summer. It needs a moist location to do well; mine sits in a small drainage ditch where it is always moist and occasionally very wet. It self-seeds a bit, only into the ditch and not onto dry land. (The runoff from the ditch is filtered through a rain garden before it drains anywhere, so I don't have to worry about seed going downstream to the Fraser delta.) I wouldn't want to plant it near a native wetland because of this tendency to self-seed.

As container plants in urban gardens, the sedges are quite striking, and maybe no hazard—although seeds will wash into storm sewers, and the spent plants and seed heads will be disposed of at the end of the season somehow, possibly into a compost pile or over a fence into a green belt. Let's take this opportunity to avoid introducing another weed.

Carex muskingumensis.

Centaurea montana.

Centaurea – Knapweed, Star Thistle, Cornflower, Mountain Bluet, Persian Cornflower, Lemon Floss

Meadow or Prairie | *Compositae*

Centaurea montana hit the provincial noxious weed watch list 15 years too late for my garden. It is a hardy—very hardy—perennial, producing masses of pretty and long-lasting starry blue flowers. The first-cousin relationship to the even worse (officially on many noxious weed lists) diffuse and spotted knapweeds (*C. diffusa* and *C. stoebe*) might have been a warning, but I have never considered it fair to tar all species in one genus with the same brush. Every species (in this case, all *Centaurea*) is not necessarily a thug just because one is.

Even in this genus of ruffians, many of which share common names of knapweed and star thistle, there is one perennial species (there are also a number of annual species) that doesn't spread and that I wouldn't want to do without in my tall Prairie Habitat border. That is the statuesque yellow *C. macrocephala* (Lemon Floss) which I will continue to encourage—it is holding its own but not spreading. Reaching 48 in. (120 cm), this stately plant has flower heads reminiscent of oversize yellow thistle flowers.

On the other hand, *C. montana*, *C. dealbata* and *C. phyrgia* continue to cause me grief, and I am reduced to the goal of control rather than outright elimination. These plants all self-seed with abandon and have tough spreading root systems that make them difficult to pull up. These are well-designed weeds—the extensive root system not only makes them harder to eradicate, but also renders it more likely that a piece of root will be left in the ground to regrow.

Most of these species continue to be available as seeds and plants through reputable seed companies and at garden centres, so beware. Different-coloured cultivars of the perennial cornflower or mountain bluet are also hitting the market, which is disturbing as they will attract even more gardeners to this pretty weed. A new white-flowered version of *C. montana*, attractively named 'Amethyst in Snow,' was released several years ago, and although at first I had hoped that it might be sterile, even its promoters suggest that you deadhead it to prevent self-seeding. Targeting the trend towards almost-black flowers, 'Black Sprite' is a dark-purple and dwarf form—which again should be deadheaded to keep it from seeding.

There are so many different plants available that will grow well in northern gardens that we really don't need to be planting ones that are known to cause problems. For the extent of the damage that can be done by weed species, see the Northwest Invasive Plant Council website at *www.nwipc.org*.

Maybe the plant world needs some version of Smokey the Bear to persuade people not to plant weeds, as well as not throw burning cigarettes into the forest. These invasives can do as much damage, although without the headlines.

Centranthus – Jupiter's Beard, Valerian

Prairie | *Valerianaceae*

Jupiter's beard grows best in well-drained alkaline (lime) soils, but survived a number of years in my heavy clay anyway. It can look stunning if well grown, an upright plant with large rounded flower heads, each consisting of hundreds of small florets that are attractive to insects as well as humans. *Centranthus ruber* blooms in early summer, usually dark red; is also found in white ('Alba') and occasionally 'Coccineus,' a similar red shade but a more compact habit. It grows to 24 in. (60 cm) and is hardy to zone 4.

Centranthus ruber is only one of several species that goes by the common name of valerian. The one used by druggists and herbalists is *Valeriana officinalis*. *Centranthus* is reported to be edible but not particularly palatable, and to have none of the sedative qualities of its cousin.

Cephalaria gigantea.

Cephalaria – Giant Scabious, Yellow Scabious

Meadow or Prairie | *Caprifoliaceae*

The scabious of common name are closely related to the *Scabiosa* of Latin name, and the relationship can be seen in the similarity of the flower structure. The *Cephalaria* plants themselves, as least in the hardy varieties, are supersized, towering over their cousins. They produce relatively small flowers on long wiry stems, blooming from midsummer on. They are an interesting addition to the natural or wild garden, especially if you like to boast a perennial that will grow to nearly 10 ft. (3 m) tall. Hardy to at least zone 3, they have the added benefit of being clay tolerant.

VARIETIES

Cephalaria alpina. Alpine scabious. Pale-yellow flowers, on stems to 36 in. (90 cm).

C. gigantea. Giant scabious. Soft-yellow flowers towering over everything in the garden at close to 10 ft. (3 m). The stems are wiry and do not need staking—this adds some airy height and interest without adding maintenance.

Centranthus ruber. Photo Stan Shebs*

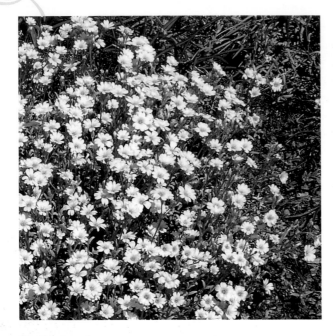

Cerastium tomentosum.

Chelone obliqua.

Cerastium – Snow-in-Summer, Mouse Ear

Rockery or Meadow | *Caryophyllaceae*

Snow-in-summer is aptly named, with its tiny white flowers covering silver-grey foliage—a common sight in northern gardens. *Cerastium tomentosum* (snow-in-summer) grows to 4 in. (10 cm) and blooms from late spring to midsummer, spreading over several years to form a mat up to 20 in. (50 cm) across. It has a slight tendency to self-seed, which results in small pockets here and there throughout the garden. It isn't hard to control, and using it as a filler in a dry sunny garden isn't such a bad idea. In lusher conditions the weeds will out-compete it.

Cerastium alpinum (C. lanatum), commonly called mouse ear, is an alpine with grey-green foliage and white flowers, reaching only 2 in. (5 cm) tall and 8 in. (20 cm) wide. Another small species of mouse ear, *C. arvense*, reaches 4 in. (10 cm) tall and 12 in. (30 cm) across and is more at home in a Meadow Habitat, spreading happily around trees or shrubs in filtered light or partial shade. It is shallow rooted, and not as drought tolerant as the silver-foliage species.

Chelone – Turtlehead

Woodland or Meadow | *Plantaginaceae*

The individual flowers of the *Chelone* species do look like little turtle heads, without too much squinting necessary. They bloom in late summer and are clay tolerant, forming large clumps over time but not self-seeding in my garden.

VARIETIES

Chelone glabra. White or white tinged with pink, to 24 in. (60 cm).

C. lyonii. Purple-pink flowers, to 30 in. (75 cm).

C. obliqua. Dark-pink flowers, to 24 in. (60 cm).

Clematis – Clematis

Meadow | *Ranunculaceae*

Most clematis are woody vines, but some of them are perennial in habit (dying back each winter), and a number of these are completely hardy to zone 3. As true perennials, they can be cut back in the early spring of every year, to the ground or at least back to any healthy growth that has overwintered. Not as common, perhaps overshadowed by the flashier vines, these are tough, clay-tolerant beauties that could be used far more often.

VARIETIES

Clematis heracleifolia. Sprawly perennial with fragrant mid- to dark-blue flowers that appear in midsummer. It grows to 36 in. (90 cm) if supported, or will spill down a rockery.

C. integrifolia. Boasts slate-blue flowers in midsummer and a number of cultivars have recently been released in a wider range of blue as well as lavender pink. This is the hardiest of the perennials, and at 20 in. (50 cm) compact enough to be grown in a peony ring for support if that is placed over the plant early in the spring. (Jamming the plant into it in midsummer after it has already collapsed does not yield an attractive result. Trust me on this.) (cont. on p. 72)

Clay-tolerant Perennials

There are two approaches to clay soil (three if you count giving up on gardening entirely). You can amend it, or you can plant species that are clay-tolerant. A patchwork approach, amending some areas but not others, can also work but be wary of creating "buckets" of good soil that will collect all the water that can't drain through the surrounding clay.

Amending the soil can greatly extend the range of plants that can be grown. Clay soils are rich in many minerals but low in organic matter, so opening them up so that they drain and roots can get through them can result in very productive soils. The first impulse always seems to be to add sand, but this is not recommended as it cannot be added in large enough quantities to do anything other than turn the mix into something resembling concrete when it dries out. Compost and/or peat, in large enough quantities, will help to modify the soil structure and add that essential organic component, but can also change the pH and may add too much of some nutrients—soil testing on an annual basis until you have reached an equilibrium is a good idea if you are taking this approach.

If the clay is the kind that ought to be used for pottery it can be very difficult to work the amendments into it, and the best solution for this is the addition of gypsum. This is important even if you build raised beds on top of the existing clay soil, as the roots of almost anything you plant will sooner or later need to go farther down than the layer of topsoil that was added.

Raised beds are one solution. Photo Darwin Paton

Gypsum (the naturally occurring material that drywall is made of) re-bonds with clay molecules, and opens the soil up so that it drains and roots can get down into it. Gypsum works best (and most quickly) if it can be mixed into the soil by digging or rototilling. It will wash down through soil by itself in time—watering expedites this process. Existing lawns can be top-dressed with gypsum, with the added benefit of that material neutralizing the damaging effect of female dog urine.

In garden areas where the soil can be worked (as opposed to lawns), adding and working in large amounts of finished compost, peat and/or aged wood chip is still necessary. Once the gypsum has started to react with the clay, the soil becomes more friable (but still clay) and the amendments can be dug or tilled in to create both improved texture and a reasonable level of organic matter, necessary to create good soil that the widest possible variety of plants will thrive in.

Agriculturally, gypsum is added at 5–10 tons per acre; less than this is not terribly effective, more is a waste of money. In the home garden, one 50-lb. (22-kg) bag is sufficient to amend from 100 to 200 sq. ft. (10–20 sq. m) roughly, depending on how bad the clay is. This is not instant, as it takes time to work, but is a one-time application that will not need to be repeated.

Some eastern-based garden references advise against gypsum, but eastern clays have a different mineral composition than western; what doesn't work back east does work in the west.

Many of our native plants are, of course, well adapted to our heavy clay soils, as are some plants from other parts of the world. The native perennials are seldom if ever available at garden centres, but can be started from wild-collected seed or young plants (of non-threatened species) moved into the garden from wild areas. New subdivisions are a good source of plant-rescue material, as the usual approach is to bulldoze everything before the building starts. No one has to feel guilty about getting in there before the machines (unless you are contemplating the broader implications of our collective role in a mad consumer culture, where flattening whole plant communities and animal habitats for shopping centres and subdivisions makes sense), but obviously you must get permission to harvest plants on privately owned land.

Aster (some) – *Aster*	Eastern columbine – *Aquilegia canadensis*	Lupine – *Lupinus*
Bellflower (some) – *Campanula*	False indigo – *Baptisia*	Meadowsweet – *Filipendula*
Black-eyed Susan, coneflower – *Rudbeckia*	Fleece flower – *Polygonum*	Milkweed – *Asclepias incarnata*
Blazing star – *Liatris*	Globeflower – *Trollius*	Prairie coneflower – *Ratibida*
Burnet – *Sanguisorba*	Goldenrod – *Solidago*	Shasta daisy – *Leucanthemum*
Culver's root – *Veronicastrum*	Iris (Arctic, Siberian) – *Iris*	Vervain – *Verbena*
Daylily – *Hemerocallis*	Joe-Pye weed, bone-set – *Eupatorium, Eutrochium*	Yarrow – *Achillea*

Clematis seed heads. Photo Darwin Paton

With a vine-like habit, *C. recta* is definitely in need of a trellis or shrub to hang onto. It blooms in midsummer with sprays of small white fragrant flowers. The cultivar 'Purpurea,' variable from seed, has purple stems and a purple tinge to the new foliage. These are both hardy to zone 2, although not as vigorous as *C. integrifolia*.

Two other vining semi-herbaceous species are seldom available but pretty in a natural or wild garden. *Clematis terniflora* var. *mandshurica* grows to 36 in. (90 cm); *C. potaninii* to 6 ft. (180 cm). Both produce umbels of delicate white flowers in early summer, and will scramble up through shrubs or small trees, or along the ground and down over rockeries. They have a subtle beauty not found in the large-flowered types, and are easy from seed. Both can be pruned if they die back or just left alone to grow wild and take care of themselves. The dead bits break off, fall to the ground, rot and become soil: this is the cycle of life and death in the garden, not something that we the gardeners need to put on our "to do" lists.

Codonopsis – Bonnet Bellflower

Meadow | *Campanulaceae*

Codonopsis clematidea produces beautifully sculptured bells in pale blue or white, both colours marked with tangerine and black rings inside the throat. The flowers become reminiscent of clematis flowers as they age and open. At 30 in. (75 cm), this upright clump-forming plant is a worthy addition to the sheltered meadow garden, and is rated hardy to zone 4.

Unfortunately it is very taprooted and difficult to transplant past the seedling stage; it also does not tolerate clay soil. If buying container-grown stock, check to see that it is not rootbound, as those thick coiling roots can't be untangled without breaking them and killing the plant. Go with a small plant that is barely rooted, or grow your own from seed.

Codonopsis clematidea. Photo Georg Ubelhart, Jelitto Perennial Seeds

The bonnet bellflower's cousin *C. pilosula* is a widely used Chinese herb, known as poor man's ginseng; nibbling on any part of it (or any other garden plant of unknown chemical properties) is not recommended.

Convallaria – Lily-of-the-Valley

Woodland | *Asparagaceae*

Convallaria majalis, better known as lily-of-the-valley, has been a part of gardens and posies for centuries, and for good reason. The 6-in. (15-cm) stalks of exceptionally fragrant white flowers scent the air in late spring, and were effective in covering up

Convallaria majalis.

the lack of regular baths and deodorant in Victorian days. It has also been valued as an ornamental plant, including the variety ('Rosea') with light-pink flowers, and the recently released variegated version (although this has not been tested in the north and there are suggestions it is not quite as hardy.

One problem with lily-of-the-valley in northern gardens, specifically gardens in the dry central interior plateau, is that although it is hardy to zone 2, the foliage suffers in the summer from the dry air. The leaves start going brown around the edges and looking ratty, and it can become a bit of an eyesore, annoying if it has been planted up close and personal so the fragrance can be appreciated.

The other problem is that it spreads like a weed, popping up farther and farther from the original planting every year, apparently determined to take over the whole garden. Under strong-growing shrubs this isn't a problem, but mixed in with other perennials it can be too aggressive—it overran several small hostas in my garden before I got it back under control. I'm not quite sure what to do with it at this point. The lily-of-the-valley growing in my garden came to me from a friend who had received her original plants from my mother some 40 years ago, shortly after the friend's marriage, so it doesn't seem right to dig it all out and turf it in the compost pile. Maybe it needs to be planted between a large rock and, for example, a mature Savin juniper (*Juniperus sabina*) where it has more shade and not many places to go to cause trouble.

Coreopsis – Tickseed

Prairie | *Compositae*

Coreopsis are summer-blooming North American prairie natives that are annoyingly short-lived in short-season cool-summer climates. Although rated as zone 3, and surviving quite happily in that zone on the prairies, they seem to need the long summers and extended hot days (and nights) that come with that location. They also need well-drained soil; clay can be the final death blow for these plants.

VARIETIES

Coreopsis grandiflora. Large dark-yellow flowers, some cultivars have maroon centres; variable in height up to 24 in. (60 cm). Blooms first year from seed so can be grown as an annual.

C. lanceolata. Dark-yellow or gold flowers, with at least one double form available. Slightly hardier than the species above, but still temperamental. Cultivars vary in size from 16–24 in. (40–60 cm).

C. rosea. This fern-leaf pink-flowered cultivar is the parent (or at least one parent—no one is handing out the secrets of their breeding programs) of the many new pink and "red" named

Coreopsis verticillata. Photo Darwin Paton

cultivars so popular in recent years. None have even tried to overwinter in my zone-3 garden.

C. verticillata. Fern-leaf coreopsis. This is worth growing for the foliage alone; it lives up to its common name. Delicate ferny foliage can reach 30 in. (75 cm). There are several cultivars available, usually in golden-yellow, but including the highly coveted light-yellow 'Moonbeam.' They are all short-lived and/or borderline hardy, but worth trying in a sheltered spot with good drainage.

Cortusa – Cortusa

Woodland | *Primulaceae*

Cortusa are small relatives of primroses, and similar in many ways. These are small spring-blooming treasures that need to be planted somewhere they can be seen and appreciated—a difficult thing when they are only 4–8 in. (10–20 cm) tall at best. They need that famous moist, well-drained soil, and partial shade or

Cortusa matthiola 'Alba.'

filtered sunlight. Clump-forming, they produce delicate flowers in either a purplish-red (magenta) or white, and are perfectly hardy in the right locations, which includes hypertufa troughs in the shade.

Corydalis – Fumitory, Fumewort, Yellow Bleeding Heart

Woodland | *Papaveraceae*

Corydalis look rather like their cousins, the bleeding hearts (*Dicentra),* and prefer much the same habitat, but can be found in a wider range of colours including some tantalizing and almost hardy pure-blue species and hybrids. There are at least three native species, an introduced perennial that is very hardy and bright yellow, and a dozen or more named selections and hybrids that are borderline hardy but beautiful enough to make them worth a try or two. At best the *Corydalis* are short-lived, but they also tend to self-seed, as do many fleeting species.

I went through a *Corydalis* phase some years ago, as I am wont to do, and tried every species I could get my hands on—which turned out be a dozen of the more than 400 that exist worldwide. They are all beautiful but few are tough enough for northern gardens.

Some *Corydalis* are alpine species and some are woodland species—the alpine ones won't grow here at all, or at least not in the conditions I was prepared to give them. Most of the perennial species that do well in northern gardens need a sheltered location with moist, well-drained soil in semi-shade or filtered light.

VARIETIES

Corydalis aurea. Annual with bright-yellow flowers in spring, and very pretty until the plant starts falling apart. Not to be confused with the much better yellow *C. lutea.* Zone 3.

C. cava (C. bulbosa). Dull-magenta or violet-purple flowers, occasionally white, in early spring. Up to 6 in. (15 cm). This grows from a small tuberous bulb, which makes it one of the easiest to transplant. Will self-seed and naturalize under trees if happy. Zone 4.

C. elata. The named selections of this are not common but worth looking for, flowering in a shade of incredible blue that is usually only seen in the Himalayan poppies. They are short-lived but self-seeding. A small planting of 'Sapphire' survived here for many years, with a new seedling or two every year, before finally dying out after the surrounding pines had to be removed. A cluster in a sheltered garden in town is still going strong and eliciting gasps when people see it for the first time. They have a mounding habit, growing to 18 in. (45 cm) tall and wide. Zone 3 or more reliably 4.

C. flexuosa. This is the parent of most of the gorgeous sky-

Corydalis lutea. Photo Darwin Paton

blue cultivars. More are coming on the market all the time, including varieties with golden foliage or purple flowers, but the blue-flowered ones are hard to beat. 'Blue Panda' is probably the best, with 'China Blue' not far behind. Zone 4.

C. lutea. This golden-yellow beauty isn't as spectacular as the blue species, but it is the workhorse of the family. (Unfortunately, this may really belong to a different family—*Pseudofumeria lutea.* Same plant, different name.) The foliage is bright-green and emerges early in the spring. It is covered with flowers from early summer on, forming a tidy mound up to 24 in. (60 cm) tall. Zone 3.

C. semperviren (Capnoides sempervirens). Annual or biennial with pink and yellow flowers, airy open habit to 24 in. (60 cm). Native to northern BC and a common colonizer after burns and disturbances, this self-seeds with enthusiasm but is very shallow rooted and easy to control. I don't have a problem with it popping up here and there throughout the garden.

Delphinium – Delphinium, Larkspur

Meadow | *Ranunculaceae*

Delphiniums are among those plants that excel in northern gardens, loving the cool summer nights. If fewer people than expected grow them it might be because the tall varieties need to be staked, and more gardeners are moving away from this kind of high-maintenance plant. Fortunately there are many compact forms that are just as beautiful but less needy. The sprawling small species *D. grandiflora* is the solution for anyone who wants that brilliant blue at the front or mid of a border without any staking.

Delphiniums, tall or short, tend towards shades (cont. on p. 76)

D

Deer-resistant Plants

Deer-resistant plants have in common such traits as being prickly or fuzzy, and having dry fibrous stems and leaves or strongly scented foliage. I have seen a great many lists of supposedly "deer-proof" and "deer-resistant" plants over the years, and they all become meaningless when there is a dry year and the deer are hungry.

An 8-ft. (240-cm) fence will stop most deer (although moose will walk right through it), but inevitably someone will leave the gate open and a hungry deer will slip in. They can jump high or wide, but not both, so two shorter fences 48 in. (120 cm) apart would work, if the cost wasn't prohibitive. Deer will also not, I am told, jump when they cannot see where they are going to land, so a solid screen of shrubbery on the far side of the fence would deter them by making it a blind landing.

The best solution I have found is a good 6-ft. (180-cm) fence and a couple of dogs—the fence keeps the dogs in, the dogs keep the wildlife out. There is a fellow in the eastern United States running a nursery-protection business, leasing large "rescue" dogs out to nursery owners who have properly fenced orchards or fields. The dogs have a good life running the property, interacting with staff during the day, and keeping four-legged interlopers from eating the crops. In return they are supplied with proper housing, food and water, regular veterinary care and a job to do. Here, the dogs are pampered members of the family, but do the same job with enthusiasm.

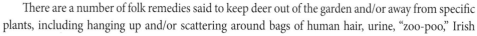

I have effectively used makeshift barriers (such as a pile of wire tomato cages over succulent Martagon lily sprouts) to deter the deer while the plants were particularly tasty and susceptible. In this case, the wire frames were piled over the chewed-down nubs of my treasured lilies early in the spring, as soon as I noticed the damage. They were left on for a month and taken off when the lilies were starting to grow through them. The deer had lost interest by then, so it worked well. If I remember, I will build a chicken wire cage this winter, and drop it over those lilies as soon as the snow is off; they were the only plants in that bed that the deer were interested in, given a veritable smorgasbord from which to choose.

Deer don't seem interested in the leathery foliage of *Bergenia*.

There are a number of folk remedies said to keep deer out of the garden and/or away from specific plants, including hanging up and/or scattering around bags of human hair, urine, "zoo-poo," Irish Spring soap, flashing metal or plastic "scare" strips, ad infinitum. The deer will get used to any of these measures after a while when the scare is not reinforced by a real danger, so to be effective the methods have to be changed every couple of weeks.

There are several commercial sprays (Scoot, Plantskydd, Liquid Fence) available, organic and non-organic, as well as any number of recipes for homemade sprays. They either act as area repellents by smelling bad (something you may not want in your garden—the garlic, blood and raw-egg mixes I can live without, although the dogs would probably enjoy them) or are distasteful to the deer, which mean the deer have to be sampling the plant for them to be effective. The bad-tasting treatments work by training the deer to avoid those particular plants, and they will pass this knowledge on to their offspring. This is, however, a learned behaviour, so you will find that any deer new to your area will have to be "trained" as well.

The commercial sprays have to be used regularly and as directed to be effective; most have to be sprayed on during rain-free periods, and when the temperatures are above freezing. The commercial sprays are usually developed for one species (deer or elk); their effectiveness against the whole range of warm-blooded plant predators (from voles to moose) has not been proven. They are one more tool in the kit, not the sole answer to the problem. As with so many things in life, there is no single solution.

Deer-resistant Plants

Barrenwort, bishop's hat, fairy wings – *Epimedium*	Lavender – *Lavandula angustifolia*	Silver mound – *Artemisia schmidtiana*
Crane's bill – *Geranium*	Lungwort – *Pulmonaria*	Stonecrop – *Sedum*
Elephant's ear – *Bergenia*	Lupine – *Lupinus*	Thyme – *Thymus*
Hen and chicks – *Sempervivum*	Pinks, carnation – *Dianthus*	Yarrow – *Achillea*
Iris – *Iris*	Sage – *Salvia nemerosa*	
	Shasta daisy – *Leucanthemum*	

Delphinium elatum 'Guinevere.'

Delphinium grandiflorum.

of blue, along with white, lavender pinks, mauve, lavender and deep purple. The blues are spectacular—every shade of pure blue from palest sky- blue to rich cobalt. The stamens and pistils in the centre of each blossom form a cluster that looks like, and is called, a "bee." This is especially appropriate as the delphs are favourites of the bees and other pollinators. The floral "bees" come in either white or black, adding an extra dimension to the colour range and making it even harder to pick favourites. The pure-white with a white bee is elegant, the white with a black bee even more so. The black bee deepens the colours of the darker hues, but the white snaps them into contrast. It is hard to just have one delphinium; fortunately, growing your own from seed can give you a range of colours at an affordable cost.

All the delphiniums, including the annuals and biennials known as larkspurs, do best in deep soils, although too rich a soil can lead to excessive height in the tall varieties and more of a tendency to fall over in the first windstorm of the summer.

VARIETIES

Delphinium belladonna. This is a group rather than a pure species, although the wild one may still exist somewhere. While closely related to *D. elatum*, and even placed in that group by some authorities, they are quite different in character so I chose to keep them separate here. The Belladonnas are available in the whole range of delphinium colours, and fairly compact in height at less than 5 ft. (150 cm). The flower spikes are loose and more natural looking than some of the densely packed *D. elatum* cultivars, making them more suitable for the natural garden. They also have less of a tendency to fall over at the first sign of bad weather. The whites are particularly clean, and the

'Summer Sky' mix of mid blues is very much worth growing.

D. elatum. This group includes most of the familiar top-heavy garden delphiniums. There are a number of series, including Guardian (to 5 ft./150 cm), Magic Fountain (to 36 in./90 cm), Pacific Giants (to 6 ft./180 cm)—these include the reliable Round Table sub-series—and most recently the New Millennium hybrids out of New Zealand. The latter are quite simply the most stunning delphiniums I have even seen. The colour range is incredible, the stems literally packed with huge florets. Although advertised as not needing support, they can still fall victim to wind and rain, so staking (or large tomato cages) is advised.

D. grandiflorum. Bright cobalt-blue flowers like flocks of unlikely butterflies cover these all summer. Reaching only 12 in. (30 cm) and short-lived but self-seeding, they are perfect in the more natural garden.

Dianthus – Pinks, Carnation

Rockery | *Caryophyllaceae*

The pinks and carnations are a large family of popular plants, both annuals and perennials that have been bred and grown in gardens for centuries. The result is hundreds, even thousands, of different hybrids and cultivars, and a splendid confusion of nomenclature (there has been some duplication of effort as well as a little plant piracy over the years, I'm sure).

Although many in this genus will grow in heavy soils, they thrive in well-drained alkaline soils, so have been placed in the Rockery Habitat. The low-growing varieties are popular at the

Mixed *Dianthus* cultivars.

front of sunny borders, in part due to their fragrance, and they usually do well in those narrow south-facing strips between the sidewalk and the house where backfill against the foundation ensures good drainage.

Carnations are a favourite of florists and cut-flower enthusiasts, again due to the fragrance but also because they last so well. The tendency, in some schools of design, to turn the subtle natural colours into gaudy unnatural shades with vegetable dyes is beyond reason. Carnations are not supposed to be blue or green.

Most carnations and pinks are, not surprisingly, pink, or shades from white to red. Some are dark enough to be called burgundy, and many are bi-coloured, with contrasting eyes or fringes or picotee edges. There is at least one species that has to be the exception—*D. knappii* blooms in a pretty butter yellow, although it is unusual rather than stunning, and the plant itself is a bit of a leggy thing.

Most *Dianthus* are summer-blooming and scented. Not all are fragrant, however, as this has been sacrificed in some modern cultivars—sniff before you buy, if this is important to you. Many are short-lived, especially in heavy soil; some tend to self-seed but not excessively.

Varieties

Dianthus alpinus. Mid to dark pink, to 4 in. (10 cm). Zone 3.

D. arenarius. Sand pink. Fringed white flowers, some with pink shading, to 8 in. (20 cm). Zone 3.

D. armeria (D. × allwoodii, D. hybridus 'Allwoodii'). Shades of pink, to 4 in. (10 cm). Zone 4.

D. barbatus. Sweet William. Biennial. Wide range of named cultivars and seed strains in solids and bi-colours, to 16 in. (40 cm). Zone 3.

D. carthusianorum. Cluster-head pink. Deep-rose pink, to 16 in.

(40 cm). Plant has a tendency to collapse outward from the centre as it finishes blooming. Zone 3.

D. deltoides. Maiden pink. Wide range of colours, mostly solid, over a long bloom period. Mat-forming to 8 in. (20 cm). One of the more reliable species for northern gardeners, although the flowers are not as large as some others. 'Nelli' is a nice deep red with dark foliage; there are many good cultivars and seed strains. Self-seeds. Zone 3.

D. gratianopolitanus. Cheddar pink. Flowers are usually dark pink or red and very fragrant; a large number of cultivars are available. 'Firewitch' was the 2006 Perennial of the Year. Mat-forming with blue-green foliage, 6 in. (15 cm). Zone 3.

D. knappii. Sulphur pink. Yellow flowers, upright habit to 16 in. (40 cm). Zone 3.

D. petraeus. Rock pink. Single white flowers, very fragrant, 6 in. (15 cm). Zone 3.

D. plumarius. Border pink. Flowers in a wide range of colours, singles and doubles. Usually available in mixed colours. Very fragrant. 16 in. (40 cm). Zone 3.

D. repens. Pink flowers, grey-green foliage, to 8 in. (20 cm). Arctic species. Zone 1.

D. serotinus. White or off-white fringed flowers, blue-green foliage to 12 in. (30 cm). Zone 4.

D. superbus. Purple-pink flowers, to 16 in. (40 cm). Zone 3.

D. sylvestris. Light- to rose-pink flowers, to 16 in. (40 cm). Zone 3.

Dicentra – Bleeding Heart

Woodland | *Papaveraceae*

The nomenclature in this genus has been amended, to the annoyance of many gardeners who don't like Latin names to start with. *Dicentra eximia* and *D. formosa*, along with the seldom-seen *D. canadensis*, remain where they are as *Dicentra*; but the large bleeding heart, formerly known as *D. spectabilis*, is now classified as a *Lamprocapnos spectabilis*. Gardeners may eventually get used to this nomenclature split (instituted in 1845).

Dicentra and *Lamprocapnos* have similar flowers, but varying habits and very different preferred growing conditions. The small species that remain *Dicentra* favour moist soil and light shade, and are woodland creatures, with an exceptionally long bloom period from spring on. *Dicentra eximia* and *D. formosa* are very similar to each other, and both are valuable in the shady garden.

The bigger species of bleeding heart, now properly referred to as *Lamprocapnos* (which is not actually that hard to pronounce, once you get used to it) is a spring bloomer that loves sun and is quite drought tolerant, although it goes dormant when it has finished blooming if allowed to dry out.

The *Dicentra* start flowering in my garden in the spring even before the daffodils are finished. Their self-seeding habit means that they pop up with delightful abandon throughout a large bed of mature lilacs. This is a pretty mix, as the blooms tend to a dusty or lavender pink that goes well with lilacs. The white-flowered form is a very nice milky white; pinks range from a pale pink pearl to a dark rose that is almost red. The foliage tends towards greyish-green, but can also be found in shades ranging from dark green to chartreuse.

VARIETIES

Dicentra eximia. Fringed bleeding heart. As the common name suggests, this has ferny foliage in shades of blue green to dark green, mounding to 24 in. (60 cm). It is very long-blooming from early summer on, with flowers ranging from ivory and pale pink to almost true red.

D. formosa. Western bleeding heart. The western species, native to southwestern BC, is slightly smaller, at only 18 in. (45 cm), but spreads more, reaching up to 36 in. (90 cm) wide. The flowers are usually a soft dusty pink, with many named cultivars as well as hybrids between the two species that make the parentage of some named cultivars open to question. They are all pretty, so it probably doesn't matter.

Dicentra formosa 'Langtrees.'

Digitalis grandiflora. Photo Darwin Paton

Digitalis – Foxglove

Meadow | *Plantaginaceae*

Foxgloves come in both biennial and perennial forms, but it is probably the biennials that most people recognize. The tall spikes of speckled pink and purple flowers are a familiar sight in coastal gardens and along roadsides, where they are approaching weed status. Northern gardeners only wish they would reproduce so enthusiastically. Foxgloves are an iconic part of the English meadow garden, suggestive of fairies and toadstools and Beatrix Potter animals.

The hardy perennial varieties have their own quiet beauty, although there are several almost-hardy species that are quite striking. They might be worth trying in sheltered microclimates in deep soils.

VARIETIES

Digitalis grandiflora (**D. ambigua**). Perennial. Tall spikes of pale-yellow flowers early to midsummer, good cut flowers. The named selection 'Carillon' is more compact and has darker yellow flowers. To 24 in. (60 cm). Zone 3.

D. × mertonensis. Short-lived perennial similar to the biennial species, with large strawberry-pink flowers to 30 in. (75 cm). Zone 3.

D. purpurea. This is the popular biennial. A variety of mixed

colour seed strains and single colour selections are available, including a pure white and a white with black spots. They vary in height from 32–60 in. (80–150 cm). They are all rated zone 4, and will sometimes overwinter and bloom in zone 3, but don't have the same tendency to self-seed in short-season gardens, which is a pity.

Dodecatheon – Shooting Stars

Woodland | *Primulaceae*

The flowers remind some people of small shooting stars, with the petals flowing back in the solar wind behind the glowing gold tip. Like many small woodland plants, they bloom in early summer and go dormant in a dry summer. The largest is barely over 12 in. (30 cm) to the top of the flowers; they don't spread, self-seeding only occasionally in the north, and are best planted in groups for more impact—a galaxy of shooting stars.

Dodecatheon meadia. Photo Darwin Paton

Drainage

There are two kinds of drainage, or rather two different uses of the word, which gardeners, especially northern gardeners, have to worry about. The most common use applies to the texture of the soil itself, and whether or not water runs down through it. Sand and gravel drain really well, clay does not; this is obvious. If in doubt, dig a hole in your garden and fill it with water. The other fast way to make a diagnosis (especially if you are buying a rural property in the winter time) is the existence of a sewage lagoon rather than a septic field; lagoons mean clay.

For ways to modify and improve clay soil, as well as plants that are clay tolerant, see that section.

Whatever your soil type, your choices include modifying your soil, building raised beds (great on a small scale) or limiting yourself to plants that will grow in that type of soil. There are plants that will grow in anything—there probably was a whole complete and complex forest ecosystem growing where your house is before it was bulldozed to make room for progress. The inch or two of genuine topsoil was most likely destroyed and the rest compacted, creating the terrible soil that you are now trying to improve.

The second aspect of drainage, which doesn't get enough attention until the flooding starts, is that of grade. Grade is the way the surface of the land is shaped—the way that surface water is directed. Almost every northern gardener has to deal with this in early spring when the snow melts, early rains fall and the ground is still frozen; it doesn't take too much of a depression or lack of correct grade for this to become a problem. Water forms puddles and pools that freeze, or it runs across sidewalks and then freezes, turning them into skating rinks every morning. Even sandy-gravelly soils can be impervious early in the spring. Standing water can kill some plants

Dryas octopetala. Photo Darwin Paton

when their crowns are submerged for only a few days. These are the plants that are (or should be) labelled, "Will not tolerate wet feet." Their death is often wrongly attributed to winter kill, but it wasn't the cold that was the killer.

Grade-related drainage becomes immediately obvious when it occurs on a large scale and a lake appears in your yard, but it is not so apparent when it is on a micro scale. An otherwise well-drained rockery or hypertufa trough can trap a small pool of water early in the spring when the soil is frozen solid, which will be the end of any sensitive alpine plants sitting in it. I lost a few *Lewisia* before I finally learned this lesson.

HARDY VARIETIES

Dodecatheon alpinum, D. clevelandii, D. hendersonii, D. meadia, D. pulchellum (D. macrocarpum) and *D. tetrandrum (D. jeffreyi).*

Doronicum – Leopard's Bane

Woodland | *Compositae*

The leopard's banes have fine-textured bright-yellow ray flowers, blooming in late spring or early summer. They prefer partial shade or filtered light, doing well in moist humus-rich soil. Not drought tolerant, they get straggly if allowed to dry out after blooming. They live up to their common name very well, as they have totally kept leopards out of my garden.

HARDY VARIETIES

Doronicum austriacum, D. columnae (D. cordatum) and *D. orientale (D. caucasicum).*

Doronicum grandiflorum.

Dracocephalum – Dragon's Head

Meadow or Woodland | *Lamiaceae*

Dracocephalum blooms in summer over a fairly long period, usually with short spikes of purple-blue flowers. The individual florets each look like a miniature dragon's head, in the same way that turtle-head flowers look like that animal. They grow well in most soil types, being clay tolerant but doing better in well-drained soils.

VARIETIES

D. nutans (D. grandiflorum). Abundant spikes of purple-blue flowers in early summer, up to 12 in. (30 cm) tall. This self-seeds, but is shallow-rooted, so is easy to manage. There is a large area in my garden that looks like it is shrouded in a

Dracocephalum ruyschiana.

purple haze when this is in bloom, around and under a mix of evergreen and deciduous shrubs and small trees. Zone 3, maybe 2.

D. ruyschiana. Upright clumping habit, little tendency to self-seed, with rich blue-purple flowers. Hardy here in zone 3, but I'm told not hardy on the prairies, which is odd—it's usually the other way around. Maybe it likes heavy clay?

D. tanguticum. Almost everything from the Tangut area of Tibet does well in north-central BC—the lovely yellow clematis, *Clematis tangutica,* is from the same region. This is very similar to the more common *D. nutans* but with a tidier habit and less tendency to self-seed. Zone 3.

Dryas – Mountain Avens

Rockery | *Rosaceae*

The mountain avens are small alpine sub-shrubs with woody stems, but it is unlikely that the gardener would look for them in the shrub section, so here they are. They vary radically in habit and habitat from that other genus (*Geum*) that also goes by the common name of avens. It wouldn't do to confuse the two.

Mountain avens thrive on well-drained mineral soil—soil containing little or no organic matter. I have seen them growing happily on gravelly roadsides and on rocky cliffs. I fought with them constantly in the nursery until conceding defeat and growing them the way they wanted—in a fine and perfectly drained gravel-sand mixture. The slightest hint of coddling with compost, mulch or fertilizer, and they rot.

There are two native species, one sub-species and one hybrid that are hardy enough for northern gardens. They all have feathery "bad hair day" seed heads. An acquaintance who works in site reclamation and habitat restoration tells a great story of collecting the light fluffy seed by the side of a highway in the most efficient way possible—with a shop vacuum. It not only worked well, it made the day for a busload of Japanese tourists who stopped to take pictures. Just look at these clean Canadians, vacuuming the side of their road!

VARIETIES

Dryas integrifolia. At 4 by 6 in. (10 by 15 cm), the smallest species, with white flowers.

D. octopetala. 4 by 30 in. (10 by 75 cm). White flowers.

D. octopetala ssp. drummondii. 6 by 30 in. (15 by 75 cm), bright-yellow flowers in early summer.

D. × suendermannii. A cross of garden origin between the white-flowered *D. octopetala* and its yellow subspecies, with the larger size, and flower colour variable, ranging from ivory to pale yellow. They bloom from late spring through to early summer.

Dryas integrifolia. Photo Darwin Paton

Drought-tolerant Perennials

Drought-tolerant plants have various methods of achieving that condition, but in almost all cases they are "drought tolerant once established." In the wild, they grow slowly from seed, adapting to the existing conditions; if placed into the garden as half-grown plants used to moist well-drained potting mix, they will need watering at least the first summer. A good deep drenching weekly is better than daily light watering, as the latter just encourages the plant to establish a shallow root system that will always be dependent on supplemental irrigation.

Achillea millefolium 'Weser River Sandstone.'

Drought-tolerant Perennials for Full Sun

Baby's breath – *Gypsophila*
Bearded iris – *Iris*
Beardtongue – *Penstemon*
Bitterroot – *Lewisia*
Black-eyed Susan, coneflower – *Rudbeckia*
Border stonecrop – *Hylotelephium*
Cactus – *Opuntia*
Carnation, pinks – *Dianthus*
Catchfly – *Silene*
Cinquefoil – *Potentilla* (some)
Crane's bill – *Geranium* (some)
Creeping phlox – *Phlox subulata*
Daylily – *Hemerocallis*
Globe thistle – *Echinops*
Grasses – many ornamental grasses
Hen and chicks – *Sempervivum*

Lamb's ear – *Stachys*
Lavender – *Lavandula*
Mountain avens – *Dryas*
Mullein – *Verbascum* (some)
Ornamental onions – *Allium*
Pearly everlasting – *Anaphalis*
Perennial sunflower – *Helianthus*
Pussy-toes – *Antennaria*
Rock cress – *Arabis*
Roseroot – *Rhodiola*
Russian sage – *Perovskia*
Sea holly – *Eryngium*
Sea lavender – *Limonium*
Shooting star – *Dodecatheon*
Silver mound, sagebrush, wormwood, mugwort – *Artemisia* (most)
Snow-in-summer – *Cerastium*

Stonecrop – *Sedum*
Thrift – *Armeria*
Thyme – *Thymus*
Wallflower – *Erysimum*
Yarrow – *Achillea*

Drought-tolerant Perennials for Shade or Semi-shade

Barrenwort, fairy wings – *Epimedium*
Beardtongue – *Penstemon* (some)
Bleeding heart – *Dicentra*
Cinquefoil – *Potentilla* (some)
Crane's bill – *Geranium* (some)
Dead nettle – *Lamium*
Goutweed, bishop's weed – *Aegopodium*
Stonecrop – *Sedum* (some)

Duchesnea indica.

Echinacea purpurea 'Ruby Star.'

Duchesnea – Mock Strawberry

Woodland | *Rosaceae*

Mock strawberry, *Duchesnea indica*, is not to be confused with barren strawberry (which used to be *Waldsteinia* but is now *Geum fragarioides*). It is a low-growing spreading groundcover, happy in a lightly shaded location in any but the heaviest clay. Not dense or tall enough to choke out weeds, this attractive small plant also doesn't overwhelm other ornamentals, being happy to weave its red-stemmed runners around the bases of more upright perennials and shrubs. It has small bright-yellow flowers and red fruit, which only look like strawberries. They are unpalatable, but not poisonous.

Echinacea – Coneflower, Purple Coneflower

Prairie | *Compositae*

Echinacea has long been a popular genus of plants for both its ornamental and herbal qualities. The horticultural industry, never one to leave well enough alone, has set about to improve this already good plant, and recent years have seen the introduction of dozens of brightly coloured hybrids and selections. The classic purple coneflower, once considered a novelty when it was offered in white, is now available in a whole range of colours, not to mention double and oddly contorted double-decker forms, some looking like poodles with bad haircuts.

Echinacea can be slow to establish in the cool short summers of north-central BC, but the survivors eventually become splendid large clumps, blooming in late summer and right until the first snowfalls.

VARIETIES

Echinacea angustifolia. This is the species most valued medicinally. Pink or pale lavender-purple flowers, to 36 in. (90 cm), zone 4.

E. purpurea. The classic purple coneflower, growing to 48 in. (120 cm) in ideal conditions, more likely 36 in. (90 cm). The purple-pink selection 'Magnus' was the 1998 Perennial Plant of the Year, and still hard to beat, although 'Ruby Star' is equally as good, in a brighter carmine-red. Double and "mophead" versions, in purple, pink or white (even a lime-green version named 'Coconut Ice') have joined the trend towards bigger, better and fancier, but don't seem to be as hardy. The simple pure-white forms are elegant and do as well as the single purples. The dwarf single forms are reliable, at half the size but sometimes twice the price.

E. tennesseensis. This seldom-seen eastern native has been important in the breeding programs that have produced so many new and different coneflowers. Unfortunately, it is only hardy to zone 5, which may be part of the problem with all the new hybrids.

Echinacea **hybrids.** There are dozens of them now, and more every year. Northern gardeners, myself included, got quite excited when the first of these was released with great fanfare, but our excitement dimmed when the new sunset-hued cultivars either failed to overwinter or straggled through a season or two before fading expensively away. In the meantime, my clumps of 'Magnus' and 'Ruby Star' just keep getting bigger and better every year, no matter what the weather. I feel like I have to apologize to them for having been untrue. (That doesn't mean I won't try the next generation of new and improved. . .)

E

Echinops – **Globe Thistle**

Prairie or Rockery | *Compositae*

The globe thistles produce large spiny globes in mid to late summer, each consisting of hundreds of tightly packed florets. A rich pollen source for many different insects, a flower in late summer looks very much like a busy airport, with a constant stream of flights coming and going.

All of the globe thistles are taprooted plants that need deep soil, and they thrive in hot dry gravel soils in full sun. Surprisingly, they also do fairly well, although not reaching the same size, in heavy clay soil. They make good cut or dried flowers if snipped before they fully open; the globes can disintegrate after cutting if they are too ripe. Using them this way also doubles in purpose, preventing self-seeding, which can be a bit of a problem with some varieties. All seem hardy to at least zone 3.

VARIETIES

Echinops bannaticus. Spiky globe-shaped blue flower heads, long stalks, large floppy leaves that are deeply serrated and spiny-looking. This tends to be the most common at plant sales, as it self-seeds with enthusiasm. Pure-blue and pure-white named selections are available; volunteer seedlings tend to be dull blue. To 36 in. (90 cm).

E. ritro. This is probably the most common variety in garden centres, with several nice named cultivars available, the best of them ('Taplow Blue') being a brilliant blue with contrasting woolly-white stems. Up to 36 in. (90 cm).

E. sphaerocephalus. The wild form is tall, reaching 5 ft. (150 cm) with large grey-blue flowers. A more compact 24-in. (60-cm) white-flowered form is also available, with startling burgundy-red stems. (Plant some purple-red heuchera around the base for a stunning effect.)

E. tianshanicus. Uncommon and architecturally striking, the Chinese globe thistle reaches well over 6 ft. (180 cm) in good soil, with silver-white globes and a strong presence in the garden. It needs large strong-textured and/or coloured plants around it to look at home.

Epimedium – **Bishop's Hat, Fairy Wings, Barrenwort**

Forest Floor | *Berberidaceae*

It is the rather unattractive archaic name of barrenwort that gives the best clue as to the real character of this attractive plant. "Wort" simply means plant, but "barrens" are raw areas with little soil or plant life. This is where the *Epimedium*, with their exquisite and delicate flowers, are found in nature, so it should be no surprise that they thrive in poor, dry, well-drained soils. The foliage is

Echinops tianshanicus.

Epimedium versicolor 'Sulphureum.' Photo Darwin Paton

tough and papery; many of the varieties have interesting red tones to the leaves or leaf edges as well.

They form loose mounds up to 18 in. (45 cm) tall and slightly wider, and add a pleasant contrast in shape and texture to the shade garden. They show no signs of self-seeding or being invasive, which is a bonus.

Several varieties have successfully overwintered in my zone-3 garden without any protection other than snow cover. These include *E.* × *rubrum, E.* × *versicolor* 'Sulphureum,' *E.* × *youngianum* 'Niveum,' and *E.* × *youngianum* 'Roseum.' We planted half a dozen more varieties this year, so time will tell.

Erigeron speciosus 'Azure Fairy' with *Adenophora*.

Erigeron – Fleabane Daisy

Meadow | *Compositae*

The fleabanes are a large group of small daisy-type plants, excellent as a supporting cast rather than showstoppers. It was believed that the foliage, strewn around the home, would help keep fleas away; pet fleas are another pest that is not a problem in the north, so it's hard to tell if this would work.

Whether North American or European species, they are all clump-forming summer-blooming plants that prefer moist fertile soils, and will not tolerate drying out in the heat of summer. They are clay tolerant.

VARIETIES

Erigeron compositus. There are selections of this in white, pink, or pale lavender blue. They grow to 6 in. (15 cm) and will self-seed a bit, which is good or bad depending on the location. Zone 3.

E. grandiflorus (E. simplex). White, lavender-pink or lavender-blue flowers; native to eastern North America, grows to 12 in. (30 cm). Zone 3.

E. philadelphicus. Pretty lavender flowers with gold centres. It is widely distributed all over the middle latitudes of the continent, including northern BC. Short-lived but self-seeding. Zone 2.

E. speciosus. This is probably the most ornamental, and the one on which the most breeding work has been done. There are several named cultivars (seed grown and therefore variable) that are showier than the native species, which has the classic small lavender daisies. 'Azure Fairy' and 'Pink Jewel' have done well in my garden. The cultivars vary in height, but can grow to 24 in. (60 cm). Zone 2.

Eryngium – Sea Holly

Prairie or Rockery | *Apiaceae*

The sea holly species are striking additions to any dry sunny garden, with spiny leaves and flowers, and silver-blue to steel-blue colouration. They actually do their best in poor sandy soil and can get straggly in rich or well-fertilized soil. They won't overwinter in soil high in organic matter, rotting away beneath the ground. Their preferred growing conditions and subtle colours make them ideal companions to the more brilliantly hued Oriental poppies (*Papaver orientale*) and daylilies (*Hemerocallis* cultivars).

The flowers, borne from midsummer on, consist of a central cone surrounded by papery or spiny bracts, and are highly favoured in some circles in fresh or dried flower arrangements.

VARIETIES

Eryngium alpinum. Sea holly. Steel-blue or silvery-blue bracted flower heads, to 28 in. (70 cm). Several named selections are available, varying in foliage colour.

E. amethystinum. Amethyst sea holly. Bright steel-blue flowers with spiny toothed bracts. To 28 in. (70 cm). Zone 4.

E. bourgatii. Bright-blue flowers, to 22 in. (50 cm). Zone 5.

E. giganteum 'Miss Wilmott's Ghost.' Large ghostly off-white flowers and bracts, to 28 in. (70 cm). Zone 4.

E. maritimum. Sea holly. This is the most salt tolerant, having originated near some ocean (hence "maritimum"). Very blue holly-like bracts. To 16 in. (40 cm). Zone 4.

E. planum. Small light-blue flowers with spiky bracts, to 36 in. (90 cm). This is the hardiest of the species and the easiest to grow, even in clay soil. A number of named cultivars, differing in size as well as colour, are available. It has a tendency to self-seed. Zone 3.

Eryngium planum. Photo Darwin Paton

Erysimum helveticum.

Eupatorium cannabinum.

Erysimum – Wallflower

Rockery | *Brassicaceae*

Wallflowers are biennials and short-lived perennials that need well-drained slightly alkaline soil and full sun. The biennials used to be classified as *Cheiranthus*. As the common name suggests, in their native land they are found growing in between rocks in walls. If you don't have an old rock wall, a rockery or south-facing gravelly slope would be fine.

VARIETIES

Erysimum × cheiri. Wallflower. Short-lived perennial usually grown as a biennial. Cultivars are available in hundreds of shades of rich yellow, orange, bronze and red, similar to the colours marigolds come in. They grow to 30 in. (75 cm) and start blooming in early summer.

Erysimum helveticum. Wallflower. Perennial with bright sulphur-yellow flowers in summer. It is a sprawling plant to 8 in. (20 cm) high and several times that wide. This habit would make it perfect in a rockery or at the top of a retaining wall.

Erysimum × marshallii (**a.k.a. *E. × allionii*).** Siberian wallflower. A bright-orange biennial growing to 12 in. (30 cm).

Eupatorium – Hemp Agrimony, Hardy Ageratum

Meadow | *Compositae*

The two most popular species in this genus have been removed to another, and it's hard not to feel bitter about that. They all look the same, all do well in the same growing conditions, yet gone

they are. Formally *Eupatorium fistulosum* and *E. maculatum* are now in the genus *Eutrochium*, at least having taken their second names with them.

The species that remain are large vigorous plants that do well in moist heavy soils. They are slow to get started in the spring, but spectacular by late summer.

VARIETIES

Eupatorium cannabinum. Hemp agrimony. Loose corymbs of light purplish-pink, to 5 ft. (150 cm). One of the least showy, but the stems are a good source of fibre if you wish to experiment with spinning or paper making. Zone 3.

E. perfoliatum. Bone-set. White flowers, sometimes with a lavender tinge, to 5 ft. (150 cm). Zone 3.

E. purpureum. Purple-red flowers, occasionally white, on a vigorous plant to 6 ft. (180 cm). This one prefers alkaline soil. Zone 3.

E. rugosum. White flowers, nettle-like foliage, 36 in. (90 cm). Zone 4. The cultivar 'Chocolate' has strangely attractive brownish-red foliage, but unfortunately is less hardy. Probably zone 5.

Euphorbia – Spurge

Rockery, Meadow or Prairie | *Euphorbiaceae*

The *Euphorbia* genus consists of one very tough and useful hardy perennial, one fairly hardy perennial, one very popular and very tender perennial, over two hundred species of annuals, perennials, shrubs and even trees, about one thousand named selections and cultivars that aren't hardy enough for most northern gardens, and a handful of very noxious weeds. This is one genus you'd think the "splitters" in plant nomenclature could get to work on, but instead the opposite is true, with more groups being added to it as the genetic relationships are clarified by DNA testing.

All of the *Euphorbia* have in common some degree of succulent foliage, and a milky-white sap that is extruded when the succulent foliage or stems are scratched or broken, which can cause severe rashes. It is strongly recommended to wear gloves, long-sleeved shirts and eye protection when working with the plant, or even weeding around it.

The useful hardy variety is *Euphorbia epithymoides* (formerly *E. polychroma*). This cushion spurge puts on an early show in the spring, alongside the daffodils. The bright yellow of the emerging flower heads comes from the cyathium, a quasi-flower arrangement, and the bracts that surround it. There isn't actually a flower to get pollinated and then fade, so there is the illusion of a long bloom period. At the other end of the growing season it takes on

Euphorbia epithymoides. Photo Darwin Paton

variable red and orange hues in the fall, adding to its garden value. Some gardeners in southern climates think of it as a weed, but in the heavy clay and short growing season of the north it is one of my more reliable workhorse plants. This grows to 16 in. (40 cm), is clump-forming and spreads by seed. It prefers well-drained soil but tolerates clay, and is hardy to at least zone 3. The almost-hardy (zone 4) species is *E. myrsinites*, which overwinters often enough to encourage me before dying out.

Probably the best-known and bestselling member of this genus is the poinsettia (*E. pulcherrima*). Some marketing genius has convinced most of North America that Christmas wouldn't be the same without a pot or two of this flamboyant but tender Mexican tropical plant sitting on the windowsill slowly drying out and dying.

As for the thousands of other *Euphorbia* varieties, whole books have been written on them, and most species and cultivars are not hardy enough to include here. A few that are borderline hardy make it onto the noxious-weed lists in various North American locations on a regular basis, including the common *E. cyparissias*. The pretty 'Fens Ruby' and the standard green form show up regularly around Prince George. Every gardener that I know who has one of these allegedly weedy plants defends their particular little colony as not being aggressive, although each colony has quite obviously been spreading through the garden or along the gravel bank where planted. The only *Euphorbia* listed as an official noxious weed in BC is the leafy spurge, *E. esula*. If you are thinking of experimenting with some of the borderline hardy species (many of which are not at all invasive), do your research first so you are at least aware of the possible consequences as well as the required conditions. A heated but still cool solarium would be a good place for a collection of these architecturally diverse plants.

Eutrochium (formerly included in *Eupatorium*) – Joe-Pye Weed, Bone-set

Meadow | *Compositae*

Two of the species that we are all used to calling *Eupatorium* are now *Eutrochium*. Under either name, they are splendid plants. Their one drawback is that they are slow to get started in the spring. We used to have trouble selling them at the David Douglas Botanical Garden plant sale each spring (under any name) as they were barely stocky noses poking out of the soil at that time of year. Although people who knew what they were would snap them up, the plants were a hard sell against anything in bloom already. By the end of summer, all those fleeting beauties of spring are looking ratty, and the *Eutrochium* are heading for 6 ft. (180 cm) and the centre of attention. The flowers are large flat corymbs that

F

Eutrochium maculatum purpurea.

Ferns

Ferns are a whole addiction unto themselves, as the many books written just about them testify. They have never become trendy the way grasses have, yet in many ways they are a lot more rewarding to play with, allowing gardeners to create lush havens in any degree of shade. For the most part they are easy to grow once the correct habitat has been established, and the biggest drawback may be that other than a few common varieties they are not locally available. There are a number of perfectly good native species that are relatively easy to transplant, and common enough that it can be done (with permission, or on prospective construction sites) with a clear conscience.

There are ferns for sun or shade, for moist or dry, for average soils and for growing on rotting tree trunks. They come in at least a hundred shades of green and a thousand different textures, and present an interesting challenge to anyone who wants to expand their horizons and grow them from spores. VanDusen Botanical Garden (*www.vandusengarden.org*) includes fern spores in their online seed sales, with 13 varieties currently listed on their website, many of them hardy or at least worth trying.

Try a fern—you'll like it.

Athyrium filix-femina × nipponicum 'Pictum.' Photo Darwin Paton

attract a wide variety of insects.

Eutrochium definitely need moist soil to do well, and would be happy at the edge of a natural pond, or a man-made pond without a liner. (With a pond liner, the soil is very dry around the water's edge; the opposite of natural conditions.)

Quite apart from changes (or corrections, as the case may be) in the nomenclature, there has always been confusion in the classification of these and probably always will be; these are worth growing any which way they are labelled.

VARIETIES

Eutrochium fistulosum. Joe-Pye weed. Ivory-white flowers, grey-green stems. To 6 ft. (180 cm), half of that the first year from seed. Zone 4.

E. maculatum, E. maculatum purpurea. Red-purple umbels, dark-purple stems to 6 ft. (180 cm); best growth is achieved with regular moisture in a warm summer. Several cultivars exist, including the compact 'Gateway,' which doesn't seem to be as hardy, and the white 'Alba.' Zone 3.

Adiantum pedatum. Photo Darwin Paton

Ferns – *Adiantum* – Maidenhair Fern

Woodland | *Adiantaceae*

Adiantum pedatum is a pretty and graceful mid-sized fern, growing to 12 in. (30 cm) and looking more delicate than it is. Soft-green fronds adorn wiry black stems, the whole thing attaching to a rhizomatous root system that can spread the plant quite widely in the right conditions. It needs humus-rich moist soil to do well. There are scattered wild populations of it through the north, but it is more common—in gardens and in the wild—in the south and coastal locations. It is officially hardy to zone 3, although so variable that individual specimens could easily be more or less hardy than that.

Adiantum aleuticum, formerly classified as a subspecies of *A. pedatum*, is hardy to zone 2 and undemanding to grow. There are also any number of selections and hybrids, all different from each other in one way or another, not to mention over 300 species of *Adiantum* worldwide.

Ferns – *Athyrium* – Lady Fern

Woodland | *Woodsiaceae*

Athyrium filix-femina, the lady fern, is among the best known and easiest to grow of the hardy ferns. It is circumpolar, native to northern BC, hardy to zone 3 and grows up to 5 ft. (150

Athyrium filix-femina.

cm) high and wide. Responding well to compost and watering in the garden, it is happy in moist shady locations, or even in a fair amount of light given enough moisture. The fiddleheads are edible and quite tasty when young and small (up to 4 in./10 cm).

Thanks to the popularity of ferns during the Victorian era there are dozens of cultivars in different sizes, shapes and frond configurations. A lot of them have crested, congested or dissected tips to the fronds, which give a lacy effect; others have narrower or elongated fronds. They are rather like hostas in that the wide selection starts to wear thin after a while, but nevertheless it is nice to have some different choices, and they add texture to the shade garden. The fronds are diamond-shaped overall, being narrower towards the base, broader in the middle and then tapering towards the tip. This distinguishes them from their male-fern partners (*Dryopteris*), which are more triangular in shape, being broad at the base and narrowing towards the tip.

The popular Japanese painted fern, *A. filix-femina × nipponicum* 'Pictum,' is closely related, and just as hardy although slow to establish. I have a number of specimens of that variety growing here, after planting them in the humus-rich moist shady location they wanted instead of the close-to-the-house-where-I-could-see-them place I wanted. (VanDusen offers spores of this through their website seed sales; they are open-pollinated and variable, but attractive.) A number of other similar but closely related hybrids and selections with interesting colouring are becoming available, as species and sub-species long separated by continents are grown together in gardens and hybridize naturally. Their hardiness has not been tested, of course, but they would be worth trying.

These are physically delicate ferns, unlike the tougher male ferns (*Dryopteris*), so don't place them in the way of human or pet traffic.

F

Ferns – *Dryopteris* – Wood Fern, Shield Fern, Buckler Fern

Woodland | *Dryopteridaceae*

The *Dryopteris* species are a useful group of medium to large sturdy ferns, native to woodland habitats around the globe, including northern BC. They prefer the moist, humus-rich soil of woodlands with full to partial shade, and applications of compost along with regular watering. They can be distinguished from the somewhat similar lady ferns (*Athyrium*) by their triangular fronds, broad at the base and narrowing to the tip. The fiddle-heads are edible when small, and the rhizomes are a traditional food of some First Nations groups. Not surprisingly, there are a number of crested, contorted, dwarf and otherwise unusual varieties of these available through specialty nurseries. A keen observer in the woods could probably add to that number.

Gymnocarpium dryopteris.

Dryopteris expansa.

Ferns – *Gymnocarpium* – Oak Fern

Woodland | *Woodsiaceae*

Gymnocarpium dryopteris is a delightful small carpeting fern that will tolerate some sun but not survive drying out. It blankets a section here in my garden under some clumps of large lilac bushes. As it is not dense enough to prevent weeds and self-seeding garden plants from popping up through it, I have to keep it weeded manually to prevent it from being overrun; not a high

price to pay. Reaching 8 in. (20 cm), it is hardy to at least zone 3. A slightly larger version, *G. robertianum*, is named limestone poly-pody, and needs the high pH soil that name suggests—it would do well on the shady side of a limestone rockery, perhaps under some birch trees there.

Ferns – *Matteuccia* – Ostrich Fern, Shuttlecock Fern

Woodland | *Woodsiaceae*

Matteuccia struthiopteris is an outstanding tall native fern, up to 6 ft. (180 cm), which will grow with its feet in the water or in

Matteuccia struthiopteris. Photo Kropsoq*

ordinary garden soil, tolerating full to partial shade. It sends out stolons to create colonies a yard or more away, so is best planted where this won't be a problem. In the wild, I have seen it growing on the low side of a beaver dam in constant seepage, and quite happy. In my garden, it grows in a low area of heavy soil, with a few small trees and large perennials, and just pops up wherever it wants to. The location is protected enough that the bright-green fronds stay fresh-looking all summer. It responds well to compost and watering, as do many of the big ferns. The young fiddleheads are edible when they emerge in the spring, being the largest and tastiest of any of the native ferns. If you happen to have a black walnut tree (*Juglans nigra*), this is one of the few plants that is juglone-tolerant and will grow under that species.

Osmunda regalis.

Polystichum munitum.

Ferns – *Osmunda* – Cinnamon Fern, Royal Fern

Woodland | *Osmundaceae*

The two hardy members of this genus are large ferns, not as vigorous or as spreading as the native ostrich fern (*Matteuccia*) but still hardy to zone 3. They both do well in moist, organically enriched soil in partial shade, and spread slowly by rhizome. *Osmunda cinnamomea* (cinnamon fern) gets its name from the colour that the fertile fronds take on as they mature, rising from the middle of the dark-green sterile fronds. It grows to 36 in. (90 cm) and has an upright habit. *Osmunda regalis* (royal fern) is also upright, but reaches the more regal height of 6 ft. (180 cm). Several crested forms of this are available (although not common).

Ferns – *Polystichum* – Sword Fern, Christmas Fern, Holly Fern, Shield Fern

Woodland | *Dryopteridaceae*

The evergreen sword ferns are familiar to anyone who hikes the coastal rainforests, but less common in the drier interior. The hardiest species are rated zone 3, which means there is a good chance for them in northern gardens, especially in sheltered corners. VanDusen Botanical Garden offers spores of several of these species through their online seed sales.

Filipendula – Meadowsweet

Meadow | *Rosaceae*

Meadowsweet species vary from towering giants to ferny ground-covers, but they all have sprays of tiny flowers on relatively long stems, and do best in moist soils and full sun. This is a decorative and useful group of plants in formal or wild gardens. Growing in damp meadows and stream-sides in their natural habitats, they look at home in similar situations in the garden. The arching foliage can trail attractively over rocks at pond edge, and any flower petals they shed into the water are tiny. Blooming midsummer on, they are a great plant genus to experiment with if you have heavy and/or moist soils, as much for their pest-free vigour and texture as their frothy flowers.

VARIETIES

Filipendula palmata. Siberian meadowsweet. Pale- to dark-pink flowers, with a white form sometimes popping up. Vigorous clump-forming plant, to 48 in. (120 cm). Zone 2.

F. purpurea. Japanese meadowsweet. Carmine-red blooms, to 48 in. (120 cm). Zone 4.

F. rubra 'Venusta.' Martha Washington's plume, queen of the prairie. Huge football-size flower corymbs in candy pink.

Up to 8 ft. (240 cm), with a spreading habit that can be either useful or annoying, depending on whether or not you have planted it in the right place. I have never seen the species form offered, only this lovely cultivar. Zone 2.

F. ulmaria. Meadowsweet. This is a mid-sized plant, at 30 in. (75 cm), with a more formal clumping habit than many of its cousins. It has dark-green foliage and creamy-white flowers. Selections are also available with double flowers ('Florepleno'), golden foliage ('Aurea'), and a striking variegation pattern ('Variegata') that is the best of all. The gold-leaf form tends to burn a bit in the sun; the others do best in full or filtered sun with reliable moisture. Zone 2.

F. vulgaris (F. hexapetala). Dropwort. This is the lowest of the species, with most of its 20 in. (50 cm) in the flower stems; low-growing ferny foliage sprawls out from the centre. It has frequently been mistaken for a fern in my garden. The flowers are usually white; there are also double-flowered forms. Zone 3.

Filipendula ulmaria. Photo Darwin Paton

Flood-tolerant Perennials

Some perennials cannot tolerate standing in water at all (see Drainage), but many can survive short periods underwater. This was brought quite keenly to my attention several years ago, while helping a friend recover her riverside garden after a horrible winter of ice-jams and floods. A small glacier had ground its way across her garden, driven by the force of the backed-up ice and river water behind it. We expected devastation, but were astonished by the multitudes of perennial plants that were starting to emerge from the thawing ground.

It turns out that winter dormancy is a good strategy in an uncertain world. Small treasures such as *Erythronium* popped up out of the debris, as did other spring bulbs and early foliage. As we worked through the yard cleaning up, it became apparent that most of the physical damage had been suffered by the woody shrubs (and the house, which unfortunately wasn't as flexible).

A good part of the reason for the resiliency lies in the fact that the plants were dormant and the ground frozen by the time the river banks overflowed; it would have been a different story during the growing season. Some plants evolved on flood plains, and can tolerate saturated soils and the lack of oxygen in the root zones; others can't. As with any habitat situation, having some understanding of where plants come from helps in deciding where to put them.

Many plant species native to stream or river banks are no strangers to flooding, and suitable for low-lying areas in the yard or for gardens beside rivers that may overflow. These are not necessarily plants that need to be wet all the time, as do most species native to wetlands or bogs.

Iris pallida tolerates occasional flooding.

This list is far from exhaustive, but my most likely candidates include many of the irises (the non-rhizomatous ones)—Siberian and Setosa irises, along with a dozen or so lesser-known species. Most meadow plants can also tolerate some flooding, which is why I find it useful to classify plants by habitats such as Meadow (which may flood) or Prairie (which doesn't tend to flood). Many of the hardy geraniums (*Geranium*), meadowsweet (*Filipendula*) and meadowrue (*Thalictrum*), and most members of the Ranunculaceae family (buttercups, monkshood and delphiniums, among others) come from meadows and stream banks. Perennials that grow from a bulb or deep taproot are more likely to survive that kind of scouring and/or flooding than shallow-rooted or woody-stemmed varieties.

In flood-prone gardens as in any other kind, diversity in plant species will ensure that at least some plants survive the worst that can happen; keeping notes will ensure that you will remember those and benefit from experience.

Fragaria – Strawberry, Wild Strawberry, Ornamental Strawberry

Woodland or Meadow | *Rosaceae*

Cultivated strawberries are a favourite food of people, deer and birds. If you plan to grow them for the fruit, consider how to protect them long enough to enjoy the harvest. (My dogs are no good here—they love strawberries, too.)

There are numerous named cultivars, hybridized and selected over centuries from two wild varieties. The wild ones (*F. vesca* and *F. virginiana*) are pretty little groundcovers in their own right, with classic small white flowers and tiny red fruit that have incomparable "wild" flavour in a berry a tenth the size of the garden varieties.

The named cultivars sold for ornamental use still have edible fruit, just not as much of it as those developed for fruit production. The *F. vesca* selection 'Yellow Wonder' has a mounding habit (with few if any runners), white flowers and edible yellow fruit,

Fragaria vesca 'Pink Panda.'

Foliage Favourites

Some perennials are grown solely for their foliage; with many others the foliage is every bit as important as the flowers. This is as it should be, if you think about it—few of them are in bloom all season, and it is their foliage we have to live with the rest of the time. I can forgive a plant for having nondescript flowers, but not for having ratty leaves and an awkward growth habit. The following are a few that have truly outstanding foliage.

Filipendula ulmaria 'Variegata.'

Avens – *Geum borissii.* Fresh green foliage emerges right out of the snow.

Cinquefoil – *Potentilla tridentata.* Evergreen circumpolar groundcover, with dark-green foliage turning tomato red, orange and gold with frost.

Culver's root – *Veronicastrum.* Fascinating radial leafing pattern, regularly spaced up tall straight stems.

Ferns – I never met a fern I didn't like.

Geranium – *Geranium.* Many of the hardy geraniums have textured and deeply lobed or serrated foliage that adds a subtle interest to the garden.

Lady's mantle – *Alchemilla.* All of the species have fan-shaped foliage that holds drops of rain and always looks fresh.

Meadowrue – *Thalictrum.* Feathery grey-green leaves uncurl from the ground and look good right through the year, even as they turn interesting shades of gold in the fall.

Peony – *Paeonia.* The bright-red stalks are amazing in the spring, and many varieties have sturdy foliage that stands well into the fall with good dark-red colours. The 'Itoh' hybrids that I have tried seem to be especially good for this. The seed pods are also architecturally interesting, on the plant or in dried-flower arrangements.

Silvermound – *Artemisia schmidtiana.* Soft, silver foliage that lives up to its name.

Variegated Jacob's ladder – *Polemonium reptans* 'Stairway to Heaven.' The best of the variegated *Polemonium*, in my opinion.

Variegated meadowsweet – *Filipendula ulmaria* 'Variegata.' The yellow variegation swirls around the stems on the dark-green foliage, and is eye-catching without being gaudy.

Windflower – *Anemone richardsonii.* Vigorous rich-green foliage first thing in the spring.

which some people find disturbing. It can get up to 8 in. (20 cm) tall and twice that in width.

Hardy to at least zone 3, the low-growing ornamental 'Pink Panda' has large bright-pink flowers, small edible red fruit, and spreads rapidly by runner. This is good if you want a groundcover and a nuisance if you don't. It is perfect for adding a splash of colour under small open trees or shrubs, and it doesn't mind a bit of shade. This and 'Pink Lipstick,' similar in flower but not quite as vigorous and with a mounding rather than running habit, may be hybrids between *Fragaria* and one of the closely related perennial *Potentilla*. The plant breeders tend to be vague on these matters, considering them trade secrets. This group would be an interesting challenge for the amateur plant breeder or the bored gardener (if there is such a thing).

Gaillardia – Blanket Flower

Prairie or Meadow | *Compositae*

Gaillardia are native to a large part of North America, across the plains and prairies, and up the broad river valley systems of British Columbia. The species map for *Gaillardia aristata* on eflora (*www.eflora.com*), the electronic native-plant database for BC, shows the wild distribution at a glance; the northern tip of the population just barely reaches Prince George. Blanket flowers are also found growing wild in the marginally gentler climate of the Robson Valley; please leave them and their seed where it is, and look in garden centres or online for the readily available seed of domestic varieties.

Blanket flowers are short-lived perennials, self-seeding as many of those are inclined to do. Late blooming, they need a long hot summer to complete the cycle of flowering and ripening seed. They bloom the first year from seed, and can be grown as an annual, which they will be unless situated in deep well-drained soil.

The native type has a dark central cone, surrounded by ray flowers that are burgundy red in the centre and liberally tipped with yellow for a halo effect. Cultivars vary somewhat in height but mostly in colour and pattern. The dwarf cultivar 'Goblin,' at 12 in. (30 cm), is a compact version of the wild one, and the most reliably hardy of any of the cultivars I have tried in my heavy clay soil. The other named selections tend to grow up to 30 in. (75 cm). There are solid colours ranging from butter yellow, to orange, to dark mahogany or purple brown, some with dark or light central cones.

Galium – Bedstraw, Lady's Bedstraw, Sweet Woodruff, Woodruff

Meadow or Woodland | *Rubiaceae*

The *Galium* species are fine-textured groundcovers that do well in moist humus-rich soils, in sun or shade. The native *G. boreale* is somewhat clay tolerant. Galium bloom in late spring and early summer.

Galium odoratum. Photo Darwin Paton

Gaillardia aristata 'Goblin.'

VARIETIES

Galium boreale. Northern bedstraw. Sprays of tiny white flowers, fine-textured foliage. This spreads happily under trees and shrubs, and we need not fear it displacing native plants because it too is native. To 24 in. (60 cm) but usually less. Zone 2.

G. odoratum (formerly *Asperula*). Sweet woodruff. Starry white flowers over bright-green foliage, slightly invasive but very pretty where it will grow. It needs a sheltered location and moist soil to do well. 18 in. (45 cm). Zone 4.

G. vernum. Yellow bedstraw. Sprays of tiny yellow flowers over fine-textured foliage, 12 in. (30 cm). Zone 3.

Gentiana – Gentian

Meadow | *Gentianaceae*

Gentians, with a few exceptions, bloom in the hues of rich true blue that gardeners always covet but so rarely find. They have sturdy pest- and disease-free foliage, and ask nothing more than moist well-drained humus-rich soil, in filtered light or partial shade. My collection is on the east side of a row of small open deciduous trees, where they get morning sun and then light shade the rest of the day, and they are all thriving.

There are varieties of gentian that bloom in spring, summer and late summer, so it is possible to have one for every season. I don't know why we don't see them more often—they will grow anywhere the hardy *Primula* will, and are excellent companions for them.

VARIETIES

Gentiana acaulis. Stemless gentian. Blue flowers in late spring and early summer. Low growing, to 4 in. (10 cm). Zone 3.

Gentiana dahurica.

G. affinis. Gentian. Deep-blue flowers in summer, 12 in. (30 cm), upright habit. Zone 4.

G. asclepiadea. Willow leaf gentian. Blue flowers with white throats, upright habit, to 24 in. (60 cm). Zone 4.

G. cruciata. Cross gentian. Dark-blue flowers from midsummer on, 16 in. (40 cm). Zone 3.

G. dahurica. Daurican gentian. Deep-blue flowers in late summer, 16 in. (40 cm). Zone 4.

G. septemfida. September gentian. Bright-blue flowers in late summer, 12 in. (30 cm). Zone 3.

G. tibetica. Tibetan gentian. White flowers in late summer, 10 in. (25 cm). Zone 3.

G. verna. Spring gentian. Sky-blue flowers with white throats, late spring. Zone 4.

Geranium – Crane's Bill, Hardy Geranium, Shepherd's Warning

Meadow, Prairie, Woodland, Forest Floor or Rockery
Geraniaceae

Geranium (crane's bill) is a huge genus, with species adapted to habitats from dry shade to wet open meadows. Many of the varieties make fine border and groundcover plants; a few self-seed enthusiastically and should be used with caution in a mixed border. Many (but not all) that are rated as zone 4 or 5 in the references and catalogues are turning out to be reliably hardy in zone 3—there are far too many (probably hundreds) for any one person to test. What follows is merely a cross-section of the hardy species and varieties; all are hardy to zone 3 unless noted otherwise.

VARIETIES

Geranium bicknellii. Crane's bill. Small pale-mauve flowers, open sprawling plant habit, to 12 in. (30 cm) tall. Native plant found in disturbed areas. Prairie, Meadow or Rockery Habitats.

G. bohemicum 'Orchid Blue.' Crane's bill. Violet-blue flowers. Short-lived perennial or biennial with a nasty self-seeding habit. Grows to 36 in. (90 cm). Meadow Habitat.

G. × cantabrigiense 'Biokovo,' 'Cambridge,' 'Karmina.' Crane's bill. Magenta or pink flowers on compact evergreen plants to 8 in. (20 cm), good groundcover with red fall foliage colour. Meadow Habitat.

G. cinereum 'Ballerina.' Crane's bill. Pink flowers with purple-veining, evergreen, mounding habit to 6 in. (15 cm). Meadow or Rockery Habitats.

G. clarkei 'Kashmir Purple,' 'Kashmir White.' Crane's bill. Purple-blue or white flowers, spreading habit, to 20 in. (50 cm) tall. Prairie or Meadow Habitat.

G. endressii. Crane's bill. Bright pink, spreading, to 20 in. (50 cm) tall. Zone 4. Meadow Habitat.

Clockwise from top left: *Geranium maculatum, Geranium phaeum* 'Album,'
Geranium pratense, Geranium sanguineum 'John Elsley.'

G. erianthum. Crane's bill. Pale violet. Clumping habit, self-seeds with enthusiasm, to 24 in. (60 cm). Native, Meadow or Woodland Habitats.

G. himalayense. Crane's bill. Light purple, to 18 in. (45 cm). Spreading, shade tolerant. Woodland Habitat.

G. ibericum 'Johnson's Blue.' Crane's bill. Blue purple, to 18 in. (45 cm) spreading. There seem to be several different clones sold under this same name. Meadow Habitat.

G. macrorrhizum. Crane's bill. The species form has small magenta flowers, others are pink or white. Aggressively spreading groundcover—very useful in the right place, but does not share nicely. Grows to 18 in. (45 cm) tall, and spreads to infinity. Zone 2. Meadow, Woodland or Rockery Habitats.

G. maculatum. Crane's bill. Magenta-pink or pink flowers. Clump-forming, to 24 in. (60 cm). Meadow Habitat.

G. × magnificum. Crane's bill. Large violet-purple flowers. Clump-forming. Zone 4. Meadow or Woodland Habitats.

G. nodosum. Crane's bill. Lilac-pink flowers, glossy mid-green foliage, spreading habit, 18 in. (45 cm) tall. Forest Floor or Woodland Habitats.

G. × oxonianum. Crane's bill. One of the more variable hybrid groups, in size, colour and hardiness. Most seem to be zone 4, but worth sampling if you have run out of reliably hardy varieties to try. Woodland or Meadow Habitats.

G. palustre. Crane's bill. Magenta flowers, white in centre of flower. To 18 in. (45 cm). Meadow Habitat.

G. phaeum. Mourning widow. Dark-maroon flowers, or occasionally white. Leaves are sometimes decorated with dark splotches. To 24 in. (60 cm). Clump-forming, self-seeds. Woodland Habitat.

G. platypetalum. Crane's bill. Violet-blue flowers. Clump-forming, to 18 in. (45 cm). Meadow or Woodland Habitats.

G. pratense. Meadow crane's bill. Variable light to dark purple-blue flowers, up to 48 in. (120 cm) tall. There are several purple-leaf forms with pale-violet flowers that come true from seed, prolifically. They tend to be around 24 in. (60 cm). I like having this dark contrast pop up amidst the green-leaf coral bells (*Heuchera*), windflowers (*Anemones*) and Jacob's ladder (*Polemonium*) that populate that part of the garden. *G. pratense* is one of the most enthusiastic species for self-seeding; great in a meadow, a disaster in a mixed border. Many tall named cultivars of unspecified heritage have this as a parent, and take after it in that regard. Meadow Habitat.

G. sanguineum. Bloody crane's bill, shepherd's warning. Flowers are in light to dark shades of violet pink. Clump-forming, spreading enough to make a good groundcover if closely planted. Selections range from 'Nana' at 2 in. (5 cm) and half

that again wide, to sprawling types 18 in. (45 cm) tall and proportionately wide. Foliage gets good fall colour. Meadow or Woodland Habitats.

G. sylvaticum. Wood crane's bill. Variable flowers, from white to pale pink, pinkish purple and blue purple. Clump-forming, to 36 in. (90 cm) tall. Zone 4. Woodland Habitat.

G. versicolor. Crane's bill. White flowers with maroon veins, to 18 in. (45 cm). Clump-forming. Zone 4.

Geranium hybrids. There are hundreds—perhaps thousands—of hybrids and cultivars of unspecified or complex parentage and varying size and hardiness. Some do splendidly in the north, others less so. The 2008 Perennial Plant of the Year 'Rozanne' is more of a zone 4 than the zone 3 it was rated. As with everything else, microclimate is important, as is pure blind luck.

Geum – Avens

Meadow or Prairie | *Rosaceae*

Geum (avens) are mounding semi-evergreen perennials, usually found at meadow's edge or on stream banks. They are relatively clay tolerant and surprisingly drought tolerant. The following species are zone 3 unless noted otherwise.

VARIETIES

Geum aleppicum. Yellow avens. Dark-yellow flowers, to 12 in. (30 cm).

G. borissii. Boris is a winner, with bright-orange flowers over a long period from mid-spring on. One of the best of the genus here in my garden, with foliage that emerges (cont. on p. 98)

Geum borissii. Photo Darwin Paton

Glacial Heritage

They say that you have to understand where you have been to know where you are going. In the case of gardeners, this means understanding your soil, which both tells the past and predicts the future. Too often I have asked customers and clients about their soil type, and had them tell me that they have great soil—they just brought in 6–8 in. (15–20 cm) of it. That's not soil—soil is a living breathing organism, with layers and texture and structure, and a million microscopic organisms living in each cubic foot of it. That stuff the dump truck just dropped off is a start, but nothing more. The soil that it was dumped on top of is really more important in the long run.

There are sections in this book on Clay Soils and Gravel Soils that have more information. And please invest in any one of a number of good basic books on soils targeted to the gardener (these tend to be practical rather than technical). The phrase "Soil Science" tends to scare off a lot of gardeners, self included. It doesn't have to be that complicated.

The take-home message here is that more of our gardening problems in northern BC are related to the soil than the weather (which isn't great either). The soil is easier to fix. Most of the soil-related problems in northern gardens have to do with a lack of organic matter and nutrients (especially nitrogen). Glacial activity ten thousand years ago stripped off much of the existing soil, and in our short-season cool climate, it rebuilds at something like an inch every thousand years. The depth of the existing soil can be easily observed at any roadside cutbank—that thin dark layer on top is what passes for topsoil. Treasure it!

The layers underneath the topsoil were left by glaciers and glacial lakes, and by the patterns those forces leave on the surface of the earth. Our famous eskers are post-glacial relics, as are the broad scoured river valleys. Glaciers left the morainal deposits of rocks and gravel that create drainage a little too perfect in some areas, and the settling out of silt in glacial lakes created the huge expanses of solid clay that now don't drain at all. If nothing else, know how well your soil drains, as that will establish to a great extent what you can best grow. This is easy to determine by the simple expedient of digging a hole and filling it (or trying to fill it) with water. Gravel will not fill up, clay will not drain or drains very slowly, the loam soils are in between with regard to texture and particle size.

Whether clay, gravel or that fine sandy-loam, they all have in common the lack of any organic content. To improve it, and make the existing mineral content available to plants, add organic matter of any and all kinds. This includes peat (whether baled or from local pits), leaf mulch, wood-chip mulch, bagged amendments and manures from the garden centre, and compost made from leaves, hay, straw, manure, wood chip, garden waste and/or kitchen waste. Almost any kind of organic matter, in moderation, is good, although each has an environmental cost associated with it, in harvesting, packaging and transporting.

The history of the land, written in layers. Photo Darwin Paton

I once had a Hydro brushing crew dump off a load of "wood chips" during my absence, and was horrified upon my return to find raw, very coarsely shredded wood and bark—not the pretty chips I had imagined. This stringy haystack of half-chipped half-shredded material was impossible to shovel and hard to move even with a pitchfork. Now, 15 years later, the area it was spread over (in a layer 8 in./20 cm thick) has very nice humus-rich soil, and no longer looks like the disaster I thought it was. Nature works miracles, indeed, given time.

Each type of soil amendment is different in nutrient composition, texture and rate of breakdown; diversity here as in everything else is a virtue. Moderation is also important—it's not a good idea to add too much of one thing or, conversely, too many different elements at once. The organisms that break matter down in the soil and make it available to plants take time to build up populations, plus they don't like landslides and earthquakes (on their scale) any more than we do (on ours).

from the snow fresh and green. It is a more compact plant in heavy clay, half the size of those grown in more open soil, but still healthy and thriving. From 8–16 in. (20–40 cm). This is sometimes listed as a species of its own, sometimes a hybrid, sometimes a cultivar of *G. coccineum*. Any way you find it, it is a great little plant.

G. macrophyllum ssp. perincisum. Big-leaf avens. Bright-yellow flowers on tall gangly stems that reach to 36 in. (90 cm) over a mound of foliage half that height. Native species with a tendency to weediness, great in wet meadows and shallow bogs.

G. montanum. Used to be classified as *Sieversii montana*, although it looked for all the world like a *Geum*. It was a relief to move it into the *Geum* genus. Now, however, it has been moved again, and it really is (or should be) *Parageum montanum*. It is a tidy and compact "nearly avens" (which is what "para-geum" means) with bright-yellow flowers and feathery seed heads. 12 in. (30 cm).

G. quellyon (G. chiloense). Garden avens. Cultivars such as 'Mrs. Bradshaw' and 'Lady Stratheden' are pretty, producing brightly coloured double or semi-double flowers in red, orange or yellow. They are not as vigorous or as clay tolerant as some of the unimproved species. Mounding habit to 16 in. (40 cm), tall. Zone 4. (There are a number of new cultivars, most of them double-flowered, that haven't been tested for our climate as far as I know. They are probably also in the zone 4 range.)

G. rivale. Water avens. Variable species, with a number of cultivars and subspecies; flowers in pink, pink red, orange, white or yellow. Grows from 12–24 in. (30–60 cm), very tolerant of wet soil.

G. triflorum. Prairie smoke, old man's whiskers. This prairie native is in a class by itself. It has subtle maroon flowers, followed by the feathery seed heads that suggested the common names. The ornamental seed heads persist right into winter or until eaten by birds. It grows to 8 in. (20 cm), and tolerates drier soil than most other species; it is hardy to zone 1. This would be suitable, even lovely, in a small rockery or trough.

Glechoma – Ground Ivy, Creeping Charlie

Woodland | *Lamiaceae*

This is another one of those plants southerners keep telling us we shouldn't grow because it is invasive, when in fact we can have trouble overwintering it and rather wish we could grow it better. *Glechoma hederacea* (also known, incorrectly, as *Nepeta hederacea*) is a low-growing and only slightly ivy-like ground-cover with small violet-blue flowers in early summer. There is

Geum rivale 'Icelandica.'

Glechoma hederacea.

a variegated form, *G. hederacea* 'Variegata,' with green foliage edged in white, commonly used as filler in hanging baskets.

Glechoma is useful under small shrubs, especially in that type of narrow shrub border found between a house and a sidewalk. Shallow rooted, *Glechoma* spreads slowly in poor heavy soil. It roots wherever it touches down, making it a good solution for a slope but a bad idea for mixed flower borders.

Some people object to it getting into lawns; I think a lawn that bloomed in violet blue would be an improvement. Either form grows to 4 in. (10 cm), half that in the north in heavy clay. They are hardy to zone 3, better in zone 4. I do acknowledge that it can be invasive in the rich soils and mild climate of the BC Lower Mainland area or Vancouver Island. If this or anything else is invasive where you live, don't grow it.

Grasses

Grasses are classified in at least two ways, apart from the botanical nomenclature.

Grasses tend to be either clump-forming in habit or running. It doesn't take much thought to figure out that only the clump-forming varieties are welcome in gardens. (And, even then, they can seed with enough abandon to make themselves unwelcome.)

The running, spreading varieties are well suited to pastures and turf grass, and to stabilizing banks, but not to being polite garden accents.

Grasses are also classified as warm season or cool season, depending on whether their annual growth cycle is triggered by heat or daylight hours. The former do not fare well in cooler climates, even though winters in zone 2 or 3 won't faze them: warm-season grasses don't really start putting on growth until it warms up in the summer, by which time the growing season is mostly over.

The cool-season grasses start growing early in the spring when the days lengthen, with little regard to actual temperatures, and are a better bet for short-season northern gardens. Unfortunately, most of the splendid large grasses are warm-season—they may overwinter, but don't thrive and seldom set flower or seed.

Grasses should be cut back in the early spring to allow both gardener and wildlife alike the benefit of the ornamental seed heads over the winter. If you are growing a species that is a malicious self-seeder, on the other hand, cutting off every single seed head and disposing of it all very carefully double-bagged in the garbage (not on the ground as mulch, not in the compost) is a better idea. (I admit that I am getting paranoid about grasses, and their tendency to try and take over the world.)

Bluestem Nursery (*www.bluestem.ca*) in Christina Lake, BC, has established itself as the authority on grasses, and the website is a wealth of information for gardeners and those working in reclamation.

Grasses – *Arrhenatherum* – Bulbous Oat Grass

Meadow | *Poaceae*
Cool season, clump-forming.

Bulbous oat grass (*A. elatius* var. *bulbosum* 'Variegatum') is one of the few grasses safe to grow in the mixed ornamental

Lucy in the garden with diamonds. Photo Diane Sales

Arrhenatherum elatius var. *bulbosum*. Photo Jerzy Opiała*

garden. It spreads outward as a clump, but slowly, undoubtedly hindered by its borderline hardiness in zone 3. Striped green and white, the foliage forms a loose mound up to 24 in. (60 cm) high and wide, and stays where it is put. Slightly shade tolerant, it does best in moist soil, and is pretty as a companion to large-leaved perennials or massed under a small tree.

Grasses – *Calamagrostis* – Reed Grass, Feather Reed Grass

Meadow | *Poaceae*

Cool season, clump-forming.

Calamagrostis is a large genus of good-sized grasses, most of which are either not well enough behaved for garden use or not hardy enough for short seasons. The notable exception is the outstanding hybrid cultivar 'Karl Foerster,' named after the man who first popularized the use of ornamental grasses in gardens. Under ideal conditions it can reach 6 ft. (180 cm) and the feathery seed heads persist over the winter, doing what the big grasses are

Calamagrostis 'Karl Foerster.' Photo Darwin Paton

supposed to do. Originally rated as hardy to only zone 5, everyone now seems agreed on what northern gardeners discovered right away, namely that it is fully hardy to zone 3. It thrives in deep moist soils, and sulks in my heavy clay, but still survives.

There are a number of native species of which *C. canadensis* is the most spectacular but it is also an aggressive colonizer, so best not brought into the garden.

Grasses – *Deschampsia* – Hair Grass, Tufted Hair Grass

Meadow | *Poaceae*

Cool season, clump-forming.

Deschampsia cespitosa is an attractive mid-sized grass with delicate foliage and airy seed heads. It is hardy to at least zone 3, and would be ideal for northern gardens except that it puts dandelions to shame in its ability to self-seed. There are few things I am sorrier to have planted. It behaved itself for a few years, long enough to lull my suspicions, and then took off, seeding merrily in all directions. I have no hope now of ever eradicating this from my garden; I can only try to control it. The named varieties, with foliage in mediocre shades of gold or bronze, are not outstanding, and revert to the species form in seeding.

Deschampsia cespitosa. Photo Darwin Paton

Grasses – *Festuca* – Fescue, Blue Fescue

Meadow or Rockery | *Poaceae*

Cool season, clump-forming.

Members of the *Festuca* genus are probably some of the most successful small grasses domesticated by man. Part of every turf-grass mix, they have also become popular as small blue-toned

Festuca amethystina with stonecrops.

clump grasses, dotting landscapes across North America and Europe. The turf grass selections are running types, the named ornamental selections are clump-forming.

Festuca amethystina (a.k.a. *F. glauca*, a.k.a. *F. ovina*) – Sheep's fescue, blue fescue. Blue-green foliage, varying in colour between cultivars, and not coming true from garden-collected seed. They range in size from 12–24 in. (30–60 cm) high and wide, and do best in well-drained soil. Flower stems and heads turn to an attractive golden-tan as they mature. The plants fall apart and become ratty-looking very quickly, needing dividing every few years to keep them looking attractive, which rules them out in my garden.

Helictotrichon sempervirens. Photo Darwin Paton

Grasses – *Helictotrichon* – Blue Oat Grass

Prairie or Meadow | *Poaceae*
Cool season, clump-forming.

Helictotrichon sempervirens is one ornamental grass that I don't have any trouble recommending to northern gardeners (which is a relief, because I can sound like a grass-hater). The spiky-looking blue-green foliage is evergreen, and grows to around 24 in. (60 cm). The flower/seed heads can rise that much again over the plant, turning to golden tan as they mature. It is an attractive mounding grass that looks good singly or grouped, and blends well with almost all other perennials in creating prairie or meadow looks.

There are several cultivars available, which vary a bit in colour. None have shown much tendency to self-seed, and division is the recommended method of propagation.

Grasses – *Hierochloe* – Sweet Grass, Vanilla Grass

Meadow | *Poaceae*
Cool season, running habit.

Hierochloe odorata is known as vanilla grass or sweet grass for its distinctive pleasant fragrance. It is popular in First Nations smudges and was traditionally used in basket weaving, so it's a pity it can't be given any room in the ornamental garden. It is a mid-size grass with ambitions to take over the world by means of aggressive runners. It would be a splendid grass for stabilizing a

Isolepsis cernua.

Hierochloe odorata. Photo Georg Ubelhart, Jelitto Perennial Seeds

miniature landscape where I saw it, or perhaps a shaded trough garden. It thrives on lots of moisture, so would make an interesting addition to a half-barrel or glazed-clay mini-bog garden. It is probably hardy to at least zone 4.

Grasses – *Miscanthus* – Silver Grass, Chinese Silver Grass, Silver Banner Grass, Japanese Silver Grass, Eulalia Grass

Prairie or Meadow | *Poaceae*

Warm season, both clump-forming and running types. This is probably the most popular group of grasses in more southern

Miscanthus sinensis 'Early Hybrids.' Photo Georg Ubelhart, Jelitto Perennial Seeds

sandy gravel bank. Here I keep it confined to a large tub, where it grows leggier than it would in poor soil but at least doesn't travel, except for persistent attempts to sneak out the drain holes at the bottom of the pot.

Grasses – *Isolepsis* – Fiber-optic Plant

Bog Garden | *Cyperaceae*

I had written off the lovely little ornamental *Isolepsis cernua* as another tender curiosity best grown as an annual in a container—and therefore of little interest to me. Visiting a friend's garden, I was surprised to see several plants of this tucked into a shady corner of a small stream, artfully decorating a tiny waterfall. I was assured that they had overwintered there for several years. Wonders never cease. This member of the rush family, usually rated to zone 8, is called "fiber-optic plant" because each stem has a tiny tuft of flower head (and then seed head) on its end, making it look like one of those trendy lamps. It is cute, but at 6 in. (15 cm) high and wide not outstanding except in the kind of climes, and also the most likely to start arguments in the native-plant versus invasive-plant debate. Northerners can avoid the fight because most of the species and cultivars simply aren't hardy enough to grow in short-season zone-3 climates (although they do well on the prairies in zone 3 with a long growing season and summer heat). If you can ripen wheat where you live, this would do well. We can't here. *Miscanthus sinensis* 'Purpurea' is the only cultivar I have tried that does at all well, and it doesn't live up to its potential—it is merely alive.

Grasses – *Molinia* – Moor Grass

Meadow | *Poaceae*

Cool season, clump-forming.

Molinia caerulea (a.k.a. *M. arundinacea*, *M. caerulea* ssp. *arundinacea* or *M. altissima*) most often appears in gardens in the variegated form as a pleasing and well-behaved (thankfully) mound that doesn't spread or seed. This compact (up to 24 in./60 cm) grass is somewhat shade tolerant, and grows best in moist soils. The green and cream lengthwise variegation on the arching leaves is well-balanced, and the whole effect is an understated

beauty that works well with dark-leaved *Heuchera* (coral bells) and *Ajuga* (bugleweed).

The species form has solid-green leaves, and is seldom if ever seen in garden centres, but I have noticed the recent introduction of several attractively named cultivars ('Skyracer,' 'Fountain of Rays,' 'Moor Flame,' etc.), said to be taller, more graceful or more bronze or silver or gold (there is definitely a metallic theme in the description of grasses), or better in some other way. While they may be, sadly, outside of urban settings they just look like more of the grasses that cows eat.

Grasses – *Phalaris* – Ribbon Grass, Gardener's Gaiters

Meadow | *Poaceae*

Cool season, running habit.

Phalaris arundinacea is usually found in gardens in the variegated forms, assorted unidentified varieties that travel through garden sales and gifts from friends. Two common cultivars are 'Feesey,' a.k.a. 'Strawberries and Cream,' with a pink streak to it, and 'Picta,' clear green and white. I have seen these grow right underneath a sidewalk and pop up on the other side, although as many gardeners swear *by* these as swear *at* them. If you don't mind having to beat your plants back and dig out whole beds to get rid of them, they are very pretty, and can even be spectacular if grown in moist well-drained soil (which they seldom are). I don't mind maintenance, but do not have time to police the over-enthusiastic plants I already have, so have avoided planting this one. That said I would consider it if I had somewhere between a rock and a hard place (or a driveway and a building) to contain it.

Molinia caerulea. Photo Georg Ubelhart, Jelitto Perennial Seeds

Phalaris arundinacea. Photo Lilly M*

Sandy Soils

are the remnants of old glacial moraines, whether these be the ...ines of roughly sorted rock and gravel along the edges of the broad va... the unsorted jumble of the terminal moraines that mark where the glaciers came grinding to a halt. The good news is that they drain beautifully; the bad news that they drain too beautifully.

You can, of course, simply grow only those plants that thrive in well-drained gravel soils, but gardeners tend to be perverse by nature. It would make sense to collect pine trees or alpine perennials with a soil like that; instead gardeners lust after roses and peonies and tomatoes. See Glacial Heritage for thoughts on how to enrich the soil.

Perennials for Well-drained Gravel and Sandy Soils

Anise hyssop – *Agastache*
Aster – *Aster* (introduced cultivars especially)
Baby's breath – *Gypsophila* (especially the tall ones)
Bitterroot – *Lewisia*
Border stonecrop – *Hylotelephium*
Candytuft – *Iberis*
Catchfly – *Silene*
Grasses – many grasses – but they also spread rapidly in loose soils, so beware
Jupiter's beard – *Centranthus*

Lily – *Lilium*
Mugwort – *Artemisia*
Mullein – *Verbascum*
Ornamental onions – *Allium*
Pin cushion flower – *Scabiosa*
Poppy – *Papaver* (especially the large Orientals)
Sage – *Salvia*
Sagebrush – *Artemisia*
Stonecrop – *Sedum*
Sunflower – *Helianthus, Helianthoides, Heliopsis*
Wallflower – *Cheiranthus, Erysimum*

Post-glacial soil. Photo Darwin Paton

Groundcovers

We grow many plants that come advertised as being groundcovers, and to some extent that is what all plants do—they cover the ground, in small or large increments. Some, however, are better at doing it than others, and not all of those are noxious weeds.

To be effective, a weed-suppressing groundcover should grow to at least 12–18 in. (30–45 cm) tall. At this height, the weeds germinate underneath the plant canopy but don't generally have enough energy to get above it, so they die off. Many low plants, such as creeping thyme (*Thymus*) and creeping speedwell (*Veronica*), that we tend to classify as groundcovers grow so low that weeds can easily get above them in the initial spurt of growth. They cover the ground, but don't suppress many weeds. This doesn't mean they aren't useful to deter weeds in some locations; they are clearly far better than bare soil. And they are still very pretty small things, of course, functional almost anywhere in the front of a garden bed or rockery.

"Groundcovers" don't necessarily have to be low-growing plants. The criteria, really, is that they spread, choke out weeds and look attractive. This can include some taller plants, which serve the same function of spreading enthusiastically while preventing the growth of weeds. I was surprised to see *Filipendula ulmaria* (meadowsweet) listed in this category by one garden writer, but upon reflection it would—in the right location—serve the purpose quite nicely. That location would have to have moist soil, and no bordering flower beds where the spreading rhizomes would cause a problem. I can picture it at the bottom of a slope, between a road and a path for instance, where some height was wanted in summer but snow removal issues eliminated the use of shrubs.

Very Low Perennial Groundcovers:
(foliage under 4 in./10 cm)

Cinquefoil – *Potentilla*
Creeping Charlie – *Glechoma*
Creeping Jenny – *Lysimachia
    nummularia*
Creeping phlox – *Phlox stolonifera*
Creeping speedwell – *Veronica*
Pussy-toes – *Antennaria*
Sandwort – *Arenaria*
Stonecrop – *Sedum*
Strawberries – *Fragaria*
Thyme – *Thymus*

Low Perennial Groundcovers:
(foliage under 8 in./20 cm)

Bugleweed – *Ajuga*
Cinquefoil – *Potentilla*

Creeping and moss phlox – *Phlox*
Dead nettle – *Lamium*
Fleece flower – *Polygonum affinis*
Yellow archangel – *Lamiastrum*
Mother-of-thyme – *Thymus*
Snow-in-summer – *Cerastium*
Stonecrop – *Sedum*

Mid-height Perennial Groundcovers:
(foliage under 24 in./60 cm)

Arnica – *Arnica*
Bedstraw – *Galium odoratum, G. vernum*
Catnip – *Nepeta*
Elephant's ear – *Bergenia*
Goutweed – *Aegopodium*
Silver brocade mugwort – *Artemisia
    stelleriana*
Speedwell – *Veronica*
Yarrow – *Achillea*

Tall Perennial Groundcovers:
(foliage over 24 in./60 cm)

Loosestrife – *Lysimachia punctata*
    'Firecracker'
Meadowsweet – *Filipendula ulmaria*
Mugwort – *Artemisia*
Pearly everlasting – *Anaphalis*

Ajuga reptans 'Burgundy Glow.' Photo Darwin Paton

Gypsophila – Baby's Breath

Rockery or Prairie | *Caryophyllaceae*

There are two distinct types of baby's breath, for different places in the garden. The low-growing species are great in rockeries or at the front of dry sunny borders, the tall ones (favourites of florists) are best in the middle or back of dry borders, or in dedicated cutting beds (but they are also considered noxious weeds in the southern part of BC). They all prefer deep, well-drained alkaline soils.

VARIETIES

Gypsophila cerastoides. Mounding baby's breath. Pale-pink flowers with a long bloom period, and a low mounding habit to 2 in. (5 cm). This is suitable for rockery or trough, and seems to do better in filtered light or perhaps just a sheltered location. It grows here in my garden, but doesn't really thrive—a soil problem rather than a climate one, I think. I need to work on finding the right location, as it is a beautiful little plant. Zone 3.

G. pacifica. Tall baby's breath. Sprays of pinkish-white flowers, 36 in. (90 cm). Zone 4.

G. paniculata. Baby's breath. Sprays of white or pinkish-white flowers, with single and double forms, to 48 in. (120 cm). Many named cultivars are available. This is the one beloved of florists and hated by the Northwest Invasive Plant Council. I am torn—I would love to be able to grow this for the light airy white flowers that can tie whole beds of mixed flowers

together, not to mention the beneficial-insect factor. The problem is that it won't overwinter here, which I find insulting since it is considered a noxious weed further south. Somewhere between the heavy clay soil and the cold wet spring and fall weather, this just gives up the ghost. In the drier, more alkaline soils south of Quesnel, it can be a problematic weed, so if you can grow it you probably shouldn't.

G. repens. Creeping baby's breath. White or pale-pink flowers, on low mat-forming plants 6 in. (15 cm). Finely cut foliage, similar to an alpine-type *Dianthus* until it blooms. Long bloom period in summer. Great in rockeries, in sun or partial shade. Zone 3.

Helenium hoopesii.

Helenium – Helen's Flower, Sneezeweed

Meadow or Prairie } *Compositae*

Helenium are prairie natives that thrive with little or no care in moist soil and full sun. Clay tolerant, they are useful for attracting beneficial insects and pollinators, and also last well as cut flowers.

VARIETIES

Helenium autumnale. Helen's flower. Cultivars and mixes are available in a rich autumn range of bright gold, orange red, rust red and maroon. While they grow up to 5 ft. (150 cm) high, many of the named cultivars are a bit more compact. They are popular in Europe, as part of that prairie group of plants that were subject to a lot of breeding and selection work. Much of

Gypsophila repens 'Rosea.'

this was done in Germany, which explains the proper names of many cultivars ('Kugelsonne,' 'Feuersiegel,' etc.). Those are sometimes (incorrectly) translated into an English version for the English-speaking market, or given a totally different marketing name in the United States—this makes it possible for one clone to have up to three different cultivar names. Zone 4; zone 3 with a warm location and well-drained soil.

H. bigelovii. Bright golden-yellow ray flowers with a domed dark-brown disc centre. This grows to 24 in. (60 cm). Zone 4.

H. hoopesii. A simple unpretentious pumpkin-pie orange daisy that blooms early in the summer, just as the early flowers have finished and the midsummer wave is starting. I love the unusual warmth of this colour, which looks good with the early blue-purple and lavender irises. It forms solid clumps to 24 in. (60 cm) tall. Zone 3.

Helianthus – Sunflower, Perennial Sunflower

Prairie | *Compositae*

All of the annual sunflowers also belong to this genus, and these are similar in height and colour range. They are rated as zone 4, and thrive in the long hot summers on the prairies, but will not do so well in northern BC in those years when summer consists of three days in August. On the other hand, instead of dying out, they just tough it out, as is typical of many "unimproved" native plants, and when they do well they are spectacular. I grow them in zone 3, in a large enough garden that everything doesn't have to perform every year, for just that reason.

The sunflowers, perennial and annual, all consist of a central

Helianthus laetiflorus.

cone or disc (in which the seeds will develop), surrounded by brightly coloured ray flowers that attract the pollinators.

VARIETIES

Helianthus laetiflorus. Bright-yellow flowers, 6 ft. (180 cm).

H. maximiliani. Golden-yellow flowers, 7 ft. (210 cm).

H. × microcephalus 'Lemon Queen Strain.' (Or, if you prefer, *Pappobolus microcephalus* var. *microphyllus.*) Clear bright-yellow flowers with small dark centres, to 6 ft. (180 cm).

H. occidentalis. Orange-yellow flowers, 48 in. (120 cm).

H. tuberosus. Jerusalem artichoke, sunchoke. Large bright-yellow flowers, with a tuberous root system that can be hard to eradicate once established. The small potato-like tubers are edible. This can grow to 8 ft. (240 cm). It is not an artichoke and not from Jerusalem.

Heliopsis helianthoides 'Scabra.'

Heliopsis – False Sunflower, Yellow Ox-eye Daisy

Prairie | *Compositae*

The one common name of this is a mystery, as there is nothing false about these sturdy prairie natives. They bloom bright golden-yellow from late summer until hard frost, and the flower heads persist over the winter to provide bird food in the form of seeds. They make good cut flowers. The clumps grow slowly, are not aggressive and haven't been self-seeding at all here—I almost wish they would.

Heliopsis helianthoides is golden-yellow and grows to 5 ft. (150 cm); the naturally occurring subspecies 'Scabra' is shorter and more variable with flowers in golden- to lemon-yellow with darker centres. Several new selections out of various European breeding programs have come back to North America, with both 'Summer Sun' and 'Summer Nights' beautiful but not as long-lived as the species form in my garden. Zone 3.

Helleborus – **Christmas Rose, Hellebore**

Woodland | *Ranunculaceae*

Hellebores are one of those plants that are made more attractive by their difficulty. Gardeners who don't relish a challenge—and the rewards of having success with a plant that few of their peers have—won't bother with these early-blooming beauties. For some gardeners, they become an addiction.

Helleborus orientale. Photo Darwin Paton

Hellebores don't, of course, bloom at Christmas in northern climates, but wait until the snow comes off. They form flower buds deep in the crown of the plant the summer before, which is why they can bloom so early. It also means that if that crown or the buds in it suffer from freezing, drought or physical damage anytime after they begin to form, there will be no flowers. As soon as they have some daylight in the spring, hellebores send up flower stems and open exquisite flowers. The sepals, not the petals, are the showy coloured bits, and they are usually white, sometimes pink, purple or mottled, solid coloured or speckled, sometimes pale apple green. A whole new generation of hybrids is available in a wide range of colours, and there are no ugly ones.

Most of the plants that I know of growing in the Prince George area are either *Helleborus niger* (the hardiest species), or *Helleborus orientale* hybrids (this being the most popular species

to play around with hybridizing, due to the colour variations that can result). So much breeding work has been going on (and some breeders tend to be reticent about their trade secrets) that any plant that is a named cultivar could be anything, and has about a 50/50 chance of being hardy. Your best guarantee of hardiness lies in getting a clump from someone already growing it. Large clumps of hellebores divide up easily; this is usually done in spring just after they finish blooming.

If you are patient, and start from fresh viable seed, you can grow your own. It isn't hard (nature does this all the time), but you do need the right growing conditions, and a couple of years. Hellebores are native to the deciduous forests of the eastern United States, and require well-drained humus-rich soil in a shady or semi-shady location. They are evergreens, and because of this do not tolerate exposure to drying winds, winter or otherwise.

The survival of hellebores, as with many plants, may have more to do with soil conditions than with actual hardiness. The deep humus-rich soils of deciduous forests have little in common with the young sandy loams or heavy clays of northern BC, even if a bale of peat has been added. Start developing a woodland area now, with the continuous addition of layers and layers of partially decomposed leaves—do not disturb these layers by turning or tilling the soil, and definitely refrain from cleaning up the area every fall by removing dead leaves! Hellebores grow under decid-uous trees, therefore it is a fairly safe bet that hellebores like fallen leaves. If you start your plants from seed, they will be ready to go to their new homes at about the same time the soil is becoming suitable. Keep them watered, not often but deeply, so that the soil never dries out 6 in. (15 cm) below the surface. The next spring, you should be rewarded with flowers.

Hemerocallis – **Daylily**

Meadow or Prairie | *Xanthorrhoeaceae*

Hemerocallis are as popular for their beauty and diversity as for their tough nature. They are adaptable to most sunny locations, being clay, drought and salt tolerant. The old "ditch lily" species had a bad (but well-deserved) reputation for spreading too aggressively; the new cultivars don't do this. Evergreen varieties are slightly less winter-hardy than those that go fully dormant, especially where there is not reliable snow cover; apart from that, most cultivars seem to be reliably hardy in zone 3. My rule of thumb is the bigger and fancier the flower (and more fanciful the name!) the less vigorous the plant. This is not entirely an unfounded prejudice, as plants—like most people—can only do one thing at a time. We can't expect a daylily to have 6-in. (15-cm) frilled double blooms that repeat all summer, and still be as tough as the beautiful old single clear yellows.

Left to right: *Hemerocallis flava*. Photo Darwin Paton; *Hemerocallis* 'Canyonridge Sunrise' – a BC-bred beauty. Photo Canyon Ridge Daylily Farm

My favourite orange, blooming in the mid-range of daylily season and glowing from across the garden, is 'Tuscawilla Tigress.' You couldn't get too much more orange, and the flowers are large and strong.

'Salieri' is hard to beat in the purple-brown colour range, although the taller 'Sweet Hot Chocolate' comes close (and that name is a winner).

The old 'Hyperion' is still unbeatable for a pure yellow on a tall graceful plant.

There are a fair number of whites and creamy whites, but I haven't found any that are both hardy and vigorous enough for my garden—yet. With so many yellow, gold, peach, apricot, pink, mauve, lavender, purple, wine-red and almost true-red colours available, the whites never seem to hit my "must-try" list.

The only one that I can really live without is the much over-used 'Stella d'Oro.' There is nothing much wrong with it, but despite the claims of repeat bloom it doesn't have too much longer a blooming season than most others. There are so many inter-esting varieties to choose from that we really don't need to see Stella in *every* commercial landscape in northern BC.

Back to the favourites. Almost all of the 'Chicago' series are worth growing, and I have also been impressed by some new introductions out of Canyon Ridge Daylily Farm in Kelowna. It's nice to be able to support a local (BC) grower and plant breeder; their website has a good basic introduction to the world and vocabulary of daylilies, in addition to "how-to" content.

'Prairie Blue Eyes' is a sturdy and reliable lavender (not blue, sorry), and 'James Marsh' is one of the older but still the top almost-true reds. 'Brass Cup' was my new favourite last year,

indeed a rich and brassy yellow gold with green throat, and the rose-pink 'Miss Quinn's World' a close second. So many plants, so little time.

It may need to be pointed out that while the common name "daylily" does indeed mean that each flower lasts only one day, the overall show is much better than that. Each stem can have half a dozen or ten blooms on it, opening one after another, and a mature clump produces upwards of fifty stems—adding up to a lot of flowers and a huge impact in the garden.

Hesperis – Dame's Rocket, Sweet Rocket

Meadow | *Brassicaceae*

Hesperis matronalis is a biennial, self-seeding happily in most sunny locations, in most types of soils. It is not invasive, but

Hesperis matronalis.

definitely belongs in the natural border or English cottage garden where strict order isn't being maintained. It is fragrant, hence the "sweet," with upright panicles of flowers on long stalks, some years over 36 in. (90 cm) tall. It blooms from early summer through midsummer. Hardy to at least zone 3.

There are several seed strains. My plants, from an original seeding 10 or more years ago, pop up in shades of lavender, with occasional pale lilac and white. I have seen other stands in a consistent dark lavender purple. There is also a pure-white strain ('Alba') that would be outstanding in a white garden or to tie together an overly bright multi-colour scheme. These are also good cut flowers, so the white would be a nice neutral choice for that objective.

Heuchera – Coral Bells, Alumroot

Meadow or Woodland | *Saxifragaceae*

Heuchera are compact mounding plants that will grow at the front of the shady or sunny border, or in the partial shade of the woodland, as long as the soil is moist. They benefit from being mulched every few years to keep the crown (where the roots and the leaves meet) from becoming too exposed: the crown builds up as the plant grows and ages. Tidy gardeners tend to make this problem worse by cleaning up all the old foliage that would have composted down and become the mulch.

A craze for *Heuchera* of all different colours has led to a multitude of strange lime and marmalade and puce plants, which I am not fond of. Maybe I am getting old, but many seem to be different for the sake of being different, and don't really add anything to the garden (except, as one wit has pointed out, the organic matter when they die). Considering that many of them are questionably hardy and rather expensive, maybe it's just as well I haven't become hooked on them.

I am not against different-coloured foliage. A number of the dark-leaf *Heuchera* have found homes in my garden since the early days when 'Palace Purple' was the only game in town and considered quite a novelty. The real winners in the long run, though, have been the sturdy green-leaf species that emerge from the snow looking healthy and vibrant, and carry on right through the season, leaving tall stalks of eye-catching seed heads still standing as the snows fall again.

Heuchera sanguinea 'Fireworks.'

Heuchera cylindrica 'Green-finch.'

The parentage of many of the hybrids and cultivars is confused and confusing, so I have taken the easy way out and lumped the many hybrids by appearance, which, in this case, is also a good indicator of performance. The few actual true species are dealt with separately below.

These all grow to between 12–18 in. (30–45 cm) tall, and usually slightly wider. They are zone 3 or 4, as noted.

VARIETIES

Hybrid **Heuchera.** Green-leaf cultivars. There are hundreds of these, as this has been a popular genus for many years, and a lot of breeding work has been done. The green-leaf forms have white, pink or red flowers, and most seem to be reliably hardy in zone 3. Some of the Canadian-bred cultivars coming out of the prairies are beautiful. Zone 3.

Purple-leaf cultivars. The most reliably hardy of the dark-leaf cultivars here has been 'Palace Purple' (Perennial of the Year in 1991), the foliage of which burns in full sun but can be spectacular in shade. 'Stormy Seas' and 'Pewter Veil' have also proven themselves.

Solid-coloured cultivars other than purple. The many new light-foliage colours, ranging from lime to orange, to some hard to describe, don't seem as hardy, with some reportedly not vigorous even in milder climates. A few are known to have overwintered in sheltered locations in and around Prince George, but there are so many of them that it is a bit of a risky investment for anyone but the enthusiast. The plants seem to be hardy to zone 4, some maybe zone 5.

Variegated-leaf cultivars. These are beautiful and hardy, although not quite as vigorous as the solid-green forms. The clear-white and green mottling suggests snowflakes, which explains the names of 'Snow Angel' and 'Snow Storm.' The flowers are bright rose pink or red, and they are definitely worth a place in the woodland garden. Zone 3.

Heuchera cylindrica. 'Green-finch.' Alumroot. One of my favourites, with evergreen foliage that looks good early in the spring, tall stiff flower stems with tiny flowers and wheat-like seed heads that persist into the winter. Stems top out at 36 in. (90 cm). Zone 3.

H. hispida var. *richardsonii.* Alumroot. Another excellent plant in my garden. Tidy and mound-forming with tall stems bearing panicles of greenish flowers. Up to 30 in. (75 cm). Zone 3.

H. sanguinea. Coral bells. This is the parent of many of the old-fashioned reliable coral bells, with green foliage and flowers in shades of pink, coral and red. Easy from seed, reliable in the garden. To 24 in. (60 cm). Zone 3.

Heucherella – Foamy Bells

Woodland | *Saxifragaceae*

Heucherella are man-made inter-generic hybrids of the closely related *Heuchera* and *Tiarella*. The results, not unexpectedly, are lovely plants halfway between the two in characteristics. Hardiness will vary according to which particular *Heuchera* and *Tiarella* are the parents, of course, and those facts are not always available at point of purchase or anywhere else (trade secrets). The flowers are showier than the wild *Tiarella* (beauties in their own right) and the foliage sometimes has interesting, but not overpowering, dark markings.

The oldest cultivar is 'Bridget Bloom,' which didn't do well here so is probably zone 4. The newer 'Snow White' and 'Pink Frost' also seem to be zone 4, although I can't claim to have done systematic trials.

'Viking Ship,' on the other hand, is a winner in my garden, and has done well for many years, spreading slowly and quietly in a moist lightly shaded corner. It has mid-pink flowers and attractively marked foliage, growing to only about 8 in. (20 cm), twice that if you count the flower stems. Like all these hybrids, it is sterile and doesn't set seed, so this is one plant I don't have to worry about taking over the garden.

Heucherella 'Viking Ship.'

Hosta – Hosta, Plantain Lily

Woodland or Meadow | *Asparagaceae*

There are probably thousands of *Hosta* species, hybrids and named selections by now, and good reason for their popularity. The mounding plants range from tiny miniatures that would barely shelter a mouse to humongous specimens a smallish dinosaur wouldn't look out of place underneath. Their foliage comes in bright to dark greens, powder and silvery blues, chartreuse and even a ghostly white, and can be stiletto narrow or as broad as a platter. The variegations for which they are prized can be dark in the leaf centre with lighter edges (white or gold, or both), or reversed. They can be streaked or striped or picotee edged. The lily-like flowers come in shades from white to lavender to purple, and on many varieties are fragrant. They can also get repetitive after a while. How many variations on green and white striped does the world need?

That said I apparently need about 50 just to fill in the shady spots with these lush easy plants. A large expanse of solid green would be boring, and a collection of different variegated specimens dizzying, but somewhere in between those two extremes, and interspersed with ferns, snakeroot (*Actaea* that was *Cimicifuga*, especially the dark ones) and meadowsweets (*Filipendula*) for texture and interest, they are extremely versatile and useful plants.

Hostas are happiest growing in partial shade in moist humus-rich well-drained soil. Some varieties are sun-tolerant, especially when planted in heavy moist soils, and I have seen glorious specimens growing in full sun at Minter Gardens—but the humidity there is much higher than here in the interior of the province. The thinner-leaf varieties tend to sunburn more easily, and are also more susceptible to slug predation. Named selections such as 'Sun Power' correctly suggest a higher tolerance to light, but will still need to be kept well watered to look good—and once a hosta's leaves are damaged it will be a blight on the landscape for the rest of that growing season.

Mixed *Hosta*(s) and flower.

Hosta Virus X

There is a new virus, dubbed "Virus X," attacking hostas and causing strange colourations and/or texture to the foliage. There is no reason to believe that we are immune to it in the north, as our nursery stock comes from the south. Bringing one infected plant into a backyard can infect the whole garden—and then every hosta would have to be ripped out. Heartbreaking and expensive.

The symptoms vary from cultivar to cultivar, so before panicking and destroying any plants that have what seems to be an unusual texture, confirm with experts at your local garden centre that it really is this disease and not a natural puckering that is a highly valued attribute of some cultivars. Stories abound of gardeners who overreacted and ripped out healthy plants before checking that the apparent damage was indeed due to this virus. It is not so fast-moving that you can't take the time to get the facts.

Humulus lupulus 'Nugget.' Photo Darwin Paton

Humulus – Hops

Meadow | *Cannabaceae*

Hops is a rapidly growing herbaceous perennial vine. It is also, of course, a familiar ingredient in beer-making, so the ease with which it can be grown will delight those who believe in self-sufficiency and/or homemade brews.

The common form of *Humulus lupulus* has bright-green foliage and a growth rate that can be almost unbelievable—the one at the Compost Demonstration Garden in Prince George (*www.reaps.org*) is constantly threatening to take over the parking lot outside the garden. It is happy there, growing deep into sandy loam soil, and nourished with compost every year or two. Mine lives in poorer soil and with lower light levels, but still grows up and over a small outbuilding every year.

Young plants will need a year or two to establish good root systems before they can push that kind of annual growth, but it's something to plan for when placing them. Hops do not support themselves with tendrils or suckers the way some vines do, so

need some support or guidance to keep them from just being groundcovers.

The other important point to take into account before planting hops is that some people have a strong allergic response, similar to a poison-ivy reaction, from contact with the bristly stems. It shouldn't be planted around gates, next to paths or on playgrounds.

Several golden-leaf varieties are available, including 'Aurea' and 'Nugget.' They both seem to be less vigorous but just as hardy as the species, which is good to at least zone 3. I have the rough-leaved golden 'Nugget' twining up a wire fence and intermingled with a *Celastrus scandens* vine, which has glossy grass-green foliage. The contrast in colour and texture is stunning.

Hylotelephium – Border Stonecrop

Prairie, Meadow or Rockery | *Crassulaceae*

The border stonecrops used to be included along with all the other types of stonecrops in *Sedum*, and are very similar in appearance. They can still be found under either name in catalogues and references; fortunately the species epithet (the second name) remains the same. *Sedum sieboldii* is now *Hylotelephium sieboldii*. I always feel like I should apologize for this one, or at least request that you don't shoot the messenger. *Sedum* was much easier to say and spell, and there's no fast and easy way to tell the difference between the two genera.

Nonetheless, we gardeners are a tough and adaptable lot, so we will cope. Like the closely related *Sedum*, *Hylotelephium* do best in full sun and deep, well-drained soil. The tall species fit into a prairie-style late-summer border very well, looking at home with ornamental grasses and the whole range of late-summer flowers. They look great planted with daylilies (*Hemerocallis*); soft pinks and dark reds can be used to great advantage to echo the pink to red tones of the stonecrop in bloom. The more compact species do well in rockeries or at the front of dry sunny borders.

Quite apart from the change in the genus name, there has been a good deal of cross-breeding, hybridizing and general

Hylotelephium spectabile 'Matrona.'

Hylotelephium spectabile 'Autumn Joy.'

confusion over the parentage of many of the named cultivars. I have placed them as best I can, and in the end it may not really matter as long as they do well in our gardens. The following are all zone 3 unless otherwise noted.

VARIETIES

Hylotelephium anacampseros. Purple flowers, to 4 in. (10 cm) tall and twice as wide.

H. cauticola. Pink, purple or red flowers, succulent foliage varies in colour from green to dark purple green. 'Ruby Glow' is one of the best dark-leaf forms of this, 6 in. (15 cm) tall and twice as wide.

H. sieboldii. Pink flowers, 4 in. (10 cm), by twice as wide.

H. spectabile. These are the tall upright border stonecrops, of which 'Autumn Joy' is probably the most known and still the best in my garden. Some of the newer and highly touted cultivars have been pretty but not as vigorous, often not lasting. I haven't tried all of them, of course, and the heavy clay soil here doesn't help. They will do better in sandy well-drained soil. The broccoli-like flower heads form in midsummer in pale green, and gradually turn light pink, then red, and finally a dark burgundy as fall progresses. Reaching 24 in. (60 cm), they form large clumps over time. Zone 2–4 (variable by cultivar; 'Autumn Joy' is zone 2, the variegated forms zone 4, the others probably in between).

H. telephium. These are mid-sized mounding plants, and excellent in the rockery or as a border in the herb garden. Both green- and purple-leaf forms are available, all with purple-pink flowers. 'Vera Jameson' is a good dark form, and 'Matrona' has striking grey-green foliage tinged with purple. 'Hab Grey' has

pinkish grey-green foliage (sounds stranger than it is) and creamy-white flowers. These all grow to 12–18 in. (30–45 cm) tall and usually somewhat wider over time.

Iberis – Candytuft

Rockery | *Brassicaceae*

Iberis sempervirens is the only hardy perennial in this genus, although the annuals are also popular. As the name suggests, it is an evergreen (*semper* = always, *virens* = living), which does well in a variety of soil types and conditions. The masses of pure-white flowers in early spring are a perfect foil for the splashes of yellow created by blooming daffodils.

Iberis sempervirens 'Little Gem.'

Although *I. sempervirens* does best in well-drained soil, it is also thriving and spreading in the heavy clay soil here. It does self-seed a bit, and the small clumps of volunteer plants are easy enough to transplant if they don't happen to be in an appropriate place. The taller varieties are better for groundcovers because their height helps suppress weed seedlings; they are all shallow-rooted enough to be spreading quite companionably under roses and a weeping crabapple in my garden.

Candytuft looks good year round with little or no care or maintenance, and doesn't even need a trim in the spring to keep it tidy, although some books suggest it. Cutting it back in early spring would be counterproductive, as that would eliminate the thousands of flower buds formed the year before. By the time it has finished blooming the new foliage is starting to grow, making it look lush and fresh for the rest of the summer. Zone 3.

Inula – Elecampane

Meadow | *Compositae*

The flowers of the *Inula* species are finely feathered yellow daisies, with some species and varieties producing larger and more delicately cut blooms than others. They will grow in sun or light shade, and need relatively moist well-drained soils to do well. They don't like heavy clay, and are all borderline hardy at zone 4. (They do fairly well in the well-drained soils in the sheltered river valley of Prince George itself, but don't survive the clay/climate combination a couple of miles away where I live.) They bloom in midsummer, after the smaller *Arnica* and *Doronicum*, but before the various late-blooming prairie sunflower species.

Inula orientalis.

Iris – Iris

Prairie, Meadow, Rockery, Bog Garden, Rain Garden or Pond & Water Garden | *Iridaceae*

The genus *Iris* consists of a great many species and hybrids, about which whole books can (and have) been written. Irises are generally broken down into classes for descriptive purposes, which does not help northern gardeners, as each class seems to include both hardy and non-hardy members. *Iris* classifications and groupings are further confused by the hundreds of years of hybridizing and selecting that have been carried out on this popular genus.

The preferred growing conditions differ by species; it is said that there is an iris for every place on the continuum from ground that is very high and dry (Rockery Habitat) to standing water (Pond and Water Habitat). The only thing they share is a preference for full sun (but I have seen several different kinds growing fairly happily, if not flowering overly much, in almost full shade).

The wide range of species also provides for a very long bloom season, from the very early species that bloom as the snow comes off to the last late bearded cultivars. Most irises, except for the very dwarf forms, make good cut flowers, and indeed some are grown commercially for just that purpose.

The BC Iris Society has a website with excellent information, and they also have sales at which rare and unusual forms can be purchased.

VARIETIES

Iris chrysographes. Goldvein iris. Dark purple to almost black flowers, some with gold veining on the standards. Fine-textured foliage. Average garden soil and moisture. Early-summer bloom. Grows to 16 in. (40 cm). Zone 3.

I. clarkei. Himalayan iris. Lavender-blue flowers with fine-textured foliage. Drought tolerant. Early-summer bloom. To 20 in. (50 cm). Zone 3.

I. danfordiae. Yellow netted iris. Yellow. One of the very early dwarf species, generally planted in fall as a bulb. Prefers well-drained soil. To 15 cm. Zone 3.

I. ensata (I. kaempferi). Japanese iris. Beautiful, but temperamental in northern gardens. A wide array of colours is available and they are all exquisite. They need moist soil conditions, but do not actually require planting in standing water, even though they are frequently pictured that way. Pots of Japanese iris in bloom are traditionally placed in ponds so that the mirrored image of the flower can be fully appreciated. Summer blooming, 24–36 in. (60–90 cm). Zone 4.

I. × germanica. Bearded iris. Thousands of cultivars in a veritable rainbow of colours, these grow from a distinctive fat rhizome that should be planted at the surface so that it gets heat and

Clockwise from top left: A Miniature Dwarf Bearded *Iris* x *germanica* cv., *Iris reticulata* cv., *Iris sibirica* 'Turquoise Cup,' and *Iris setosa* 'Alba.'

light. They are also subdivided by size of plant and of blossom into Miniature Dwarf Bearded (MDB) up to 8 in. (20 cm). Standard Dwarf Bearded (SDB) up to 15 in. (35 cm); Intermediate Bearded (IB) to 28 in. (70 cm); up to the Tall Bearded (TB) that can be up to 42 in. (105 cm). They prefer well-drained soil in full sun and are drought tolerant, but bloom best in rich moist soil. Zone 3.

I. laevigata. Water iris. Flowers range from pale lavender to purple-blue. Moisture loving. 20 in. (50 cm). Zone 3.

I. pallida. Dalmatian iris. Lilac-blue flowers with yellow falls. This is usually grown for its variegated leaf forms: yellow ('Aureo-Variegata') or white ('Argentea-Variegata'). To 36 in. (90 cm). Zone 3.

I. prismatica. Cubeseed iris. Variable pale- to dark-lavender (rarely white) flowers in late spring. The common name derives from the large square seed head, which is quite decorative and can be used in dried flower arrangements. Moist to wet soil, tolerates clay. 36 in. (90 cm). Zone 3.

I. pseudacorus. Yellow flag. Bright-yellow flowers in summer. This is pretty, but considered invasive in warmer climates, pushing out native wetland plants. I waffle on this, as it doesn't seem to be a problem in the north, and it isn't fair that we should be prevented from growing perfectly good plants just because they are invasive somewhere else. (Everything is probably invasive somewhere.) Individual gardeners will have to contemplate this ethical dilemma for themselves. The variegated leaf forms (green with either gold or white vertical markings) are slightly less vigorous, as are some solid green-leaved named varieties. 36 in. (90 cm). Zone 3.

I. pumila. Dwarf bearded iris. There are many named cultivars of this, which to anyone but a specialist are pretty much the same as an Iris × germanica dwarf bearded iris. They are early-blooming hybrids in a range of colours. The wild form is blue. They do well in average garden soil and moisture. Late spring. 12 in. (30 cm). Zone 3 or possibly zone 2.

I. reticulata. Netted iris. There are several cultivars of this, ranging from the light sky-blue 'Cantab' to the dark-purple 'J.S. Dyt.' Unnamed ones tend to be a bit variable but mostly dark blue with yellow beards. These are extremely tough, thriving in the most exposed and windswept locations as long as they have good drainage. Planted in the fall as bulbs. 8 in. (20 cm). Zone 3.

I. sanguinea. Snow iris. Very similar to the species form of I. sibirica, but slightly smaller and with a more arching (rather than upright) foliage habit. Variable according to the original seed source—also fun and easy to grow from seed. Lavender blue to purple blue, occasionally a white. 24 in. (60 cm). Zone 2.

I. setosa. Arctic iris. Variable species, ranging from pale to dark purple, and including an occasional very classy white form ('Alba'). The height also varies; one of the most popular is a dwarf ('Nana') form 6 in. (15 cm) high. 6–20 in. (15–50 cm). Zone 2.

I. sibirica. Siberian iris. This is deservedly one of the most popular iris species in northern gardens. It is highly variable, and many named cultivars have been released over the years. Most are in shades of purple or blue, with some yellows and whites, and a few lavender pinks. Heights and bloom times also vary, making it possible to extend their season with careful choice of cultivars. Very tough, prospering in moist soil. 'Perry's Blue' is one of the oldest, and still good—very tall, and very early blooming. If I could only have one, it would be the two-tone blue 'Super Ego.' This should not be confused with the pretty but not quite as outstanding 'Ego.' I keep looking for 'Id,' which also must be out there somewhere. The varieties range from 20–40 in. (50–100 cm). Zone 2.

I. spuria. Spuria iris. Violet with yellow falls. 24 in. (60 cm). Zone 4.

I. versicolor. Blue flag. Relatively small flowers in purple blue or occasionally wine red. A moisture-loving species, happy at water's edge or in a bog. 36 in. (90 cm). Zone 3.

Jasione – Sheep's Bit, Shepherd's Scabious, Blue Button

Meadow | *Campanulaceae*

Jasione are an uncommon but attractive group of small plants, with rounded violet-blue flowers from late spring through

Jasione laevis. Photo Georg Ubelhart, Jelitto Perennial Seeds

midsummer. They have a vague resemblance to fuzzy scabious flowers, hence the one common name. Short-lived, especially in heavy soil, they have a tendency to behave like biennials, but will self-seed in loose well-drained soil. Although they look like an alpine plant, their natural habitat is heath meadows and moors, and they do not survive alkaline soils. They require an acidic environment and will even grow in peat soils as long as they are not waterlogged. The species are all fairly similar to each other and hardy to zone 4.

Knautia – Scabious, Field Scabious

Meadow | *Caprifoliaceae*

Knautia macedonica, with dark-red flowers, is an attractive and useful garden plant. *Knautia arvensis,* with violet-blue flowers, is an official BC noxious weed that is still sometimes sold in seed catalogues. (It isn't a weed, or considered one, everywhere—just in many places.) Make sure you get the right species.

This is one of several plants that go by the common name of scabious. *Knautia macedonica* is made unique among them by the dark—almost burgundy—red colour of the multitudes of small domed blossoms. Several new cultivars are available that widen the range of colour and size; the original grows to 32 in. (80 cm), 'Mars Midget' is a brighter red, with looser and more open blossoms, growing to only 16 in. (40 cm). 'Melton Pastels' is a mix in a variety of shades, from lavender pink and lavender blue to salmon and wine red. (The lighter colours in this make me wonder if it isn't crossed with *K. arvensis.* Having had no particular luck with

the species in my heavy clay, I didn't try the more expensive cultivars, but would keep an eye on whether they self-seeded if I did.)

The taller varieties make excellent cut flowers, although like all in this family the blossoms fall apart if left too long on the plant and are best cut before fully open. The dwarf form is mounding and good in rockeries; the others blend well into mixed beds. They thrive and self-seed in a well-drained location, and are short-lived in heavy soil. Hardy to zone 4.

Lamiastrum galeobdolon ssp. 'Argentatum.'

Lamiastrum – Yellow Archangel, Golden Nettle

Woodland or Meadow | *Lamiaceae*

Lamiastrum galeobdolon is one of the plants that people either love or hate. Usually seen in the variegated form (*L. galeobdolon* ssp. 'Argentatum,' also improperly called 'Variegata'), it has heart-shaped green leaves overlaid with silver markings, and upright sprays of small yellow flowers in early summer. It is a sprawling long-stemmed groundcover sometimes used as a trailer in hanging baskets. It will root anywhere it touches down in its travels, hence the problem.

The exception is a beautiful mounding cultivar named 'Herman's Pride.' Herman has every reason to be proud, even if he just had a good enough eye to spot this natural sport or mutant wherever he found it. It grows to 12 in. (30 cm) tall in good soil, and a little bit wider, and does not send out runners at all. It has tidy small silver- and green-veined foliage, and is a beautiful accent plant for almost any shaded area.

The species form is not so polite. In warmer climates it has become a weed, with urban greenbelts infested as a result of people dumping the remains of their annual hanging baskets over the back fence (out of sight, out of mind). If they are thinking at all, it is that they are just adding a bit of compost to the edge of the

Knautia macedonica.

green space, but what they are really adding is a well-nourished and aggressive weed.

For those of us in colder climates, though, *Lamiastrum* is one of the tougher and more maintenance-free of the groundcovers for shade, and a useful cold-tolerant addition to hanging baskets. It can still be a weed in the garden, and is clearly not a good choice for a mixed bed, but nonetheless has its place. That includes those troublesome shady strips between a house and a sidewalk, or as a living mulch in a broad circle under an established tree, patrolled around the perimeter by a lawnmower. In moist soil it can be quite beautiful. About 12 in. (30 cm) tall, it can have an infinite spread. Hardy to at least zone 3.

Lamium – Creeping Lamium, Dead Nettle

Meadow, Woodland, Forest Floor or Rockery | *Lamiaceae*

Lamium is another one of those plants considered either a nasty weed or useful groundcover depending on who you talk to (and where they are from). Cousins of the faster growing and more aggressive *Lamiastrum,* the numerous *Lamium maculatum* cultivars are also spreaders, colonizing by rooting down wherever they touch. The spreading habit makes them a nuisance in a mixed perennial border, although they are good under well-established shrubs, or in those dark narrow beds between house and sidewalk.

Although it does grow in dry shade, *Lamium* can also be grown in more exposed conditions, as long as an increase in moisture accompanies more sunlight. The varieties with yellow or chartreuse markings on the foliage are not as sun-tolerant—the foliage tends to burn and get brown blotches in too much direct light.

Most varieties have silver or white shading on the heart-shaped leaves, although there are also a few gold-leafed and gold variegated forms. They all tend to be 4–8 in. (10–20 cm) tall, depending on not only the soil and light but also the available heat. (This is why greenhouse-grown plants for sale in the spring are quite a bit taller and lusher than they will ever be again in our gardens; literally a hothouse environment.) They are hardy to zone 3.

Lamprocapnos – Bleeding Heart

Meadow | *Papaveraceae*

Lamprocapnos spectabilis is the proper name for the tall bleeding heart, which has been *Dicentra spectabilis* for so long that some of us may never be able to call it by any other name. It will always be in reference books and on many websites as the latter. The smaller western bleeding heart (*D. formosa*) and fringed bleeding heart (*D. eximia*) species are still in *Dicentra*.

The large bleeding heart requires different growing conditions

Lamium maculatum 'Anne Greenaway.'

Lamprocapnos spectabilis.

Niki and *Lathyrus vernus.*

than the small ones, so this change is not a bad thing. It flowers in mid to late spring, with bright rose-pink or pure-white heart-shaped flowers that hang from gracefully arching stems over ferny foliage. While usually less than 36 in. (90 cm) in height, and slightly wider, it can reach twice that and become quite sprawly if grown in rich moist soil. Thriving in full sun and quite tolerant of dry soils, it likes to go dormant after blooming as a natural strategy to conserve water in a dry summer, but will stay green if watered. Although seldom used as a cut flower it can be beautiful in arrangements and lasts quite well. Hardy to zone 3.

Lathyrus – Perennial Sweet Pea

Woodland or Meadow | *Leguminosae*

There are two species of hardy perennial sweet peas, with very different habits. One is a trailing vine, the other has a mounding habit. Both are legumes and therefore fix nitrogen in the soil, and will grow even in poor soil.

VARIETIES

Lathyrus latifolius. Similar in habit to the familiar annual sweet pea, this perennial grows into a small (to 36 in./90 cm) scrambling vine decorated with petite sweet-pea flowers in pastel shades of lilac and pink in late spring and early summer. Seed-grown varieties in single colours are sometimes available, but the mix is pretty and variations subtle rather than contrasting. Easy to grow from seed, and short-lived.

L. vernus. Early-spring blooming, this species produces dark-violet flowers on a tidy mound of dark-green foliage. The flowers turn into 2-in. (5-cm) purple-brown pea pods that

Lathyrus vernus. Photo Darwin Paton

curl as they dry and expel their seeds, then persist on the long-lived plant to add summer interest. Despite this prolific seed production, I have never seen any seedlings around my parent plant, which is actually a pity—it is a pretty thing and I wouldn't mind if it spread in that corner of the garden.

Lavandula angustifolia 'Hidcote.' Photo Georg Ubelhart, Jelitto Perennial Seeds

Lavandula – Lavender

Rockery or Herb Garden | *Lamiaceae*

Lavender originated in the Mediterranean, and thrives in hot, dry climates and well-drained soils. In North America, I have seen it doing well in California and on Salt Spring Island. Northern BC has all kinds of weather but very little of it is hot and dry, and our soils have a tendency towards heavy clay or dense silty loams. For some reason, this makes lavender a very popular plant here.

I had one gardener complain to me that her lavender had up and died one winter, after only 12 years in her garden, but in truth this is probably a record for longevity in a northern garden. Mine usually struggle through a winter or two before giving up; 'Munstead' has been the strongest-growing cultivar of the ones I've tried. The various cultivars are usually rated zone 5, but probably closer to a zone 4.

The (almost) hardy perennial lavender that is so popular for herbal uses is *Lavandula angustifolia*. There are also a number of tender perennial species, including the French lavender, *L. dentate* and highly ornamental *L. stoechas*, that are an unattainable zone 7 or 8.

Lavender, hardy or tender, is well suited to container growing, and can be put outside for the summer and brought in for the

winter. I have a small seed-grown specimen of 'Hidcote Blue' that I made into a bonsai, and it is doing well after one year (a very young bonsai). The fine-textured foliage looks appropriate to the scale, and the plant seems happy. Less extreme dwarfed versions could live on a sunny windowsill for the winter.

Leucanthemum – Ox-eye Daisy, Shasta Daisy

Meadow or Prairie | *Compositae*

The Shasta daisies bloom in midsummer, when the clear white of their large flowers is a welcome addition in the garden. There are varieties with single, double, quilled, frilled and fringed flowers, almost all with egg-yolk yellow centres. At least one pale-yellow variety has recently been introduced, but that kind of misses the point of the pure cool white that plays off the bright colours of summer.

Shasta daisies do best in deep fairly well-drained soils in full sun; they survive but are short-lived and straggly in heavy clay. Ranging from fairly compact plants at 24 in. (60 cm) to long-stemmed varieties 48 in. (120 cm) tall, they all make good cut flowers.

There is one noxious weed in the family, the indigestible (to livestock and wildlife) *Leucanthemum vulgare* or ox-eye daisy. This is a plain white single daisy that is popping up everywhere—it should not be encouraged just for the sake of saving a few dollars on one of the better and non-invasive forms.

Leucanthemum x *superbum* 'Snowdrift.'

Left to right: *Lewisia pygmaea, Lewisia cotyledon.*

Lewisia – Bitterroot

Rockery | *Montiaceae*

The bitterroots are Rocky Mountain alpines perfectly hardy as far as low temperatures go but only overwintering in conditions of absolutely perfect drainage. Any standing water around the crown will be the death of the plant. The necessary growing conditions entail soil that is almost pure sand, or a very sandy loam, packed loosely into crevices in rocks. This must be arranged and graded in such a way that pools of water will not be formed in the spring when the soil is still frozen solid but surface snow begins to melt. I have to confess to killing a lot of plants before arriving at this recipe; now I find them easy to grow.

Lewisia are worth any trouble you have to take. The relatively large flowers—loonie sized, on plants 4 in. (10 cm) across—are produced in clusters in brilliant shades of pink, peach, coral, lavender, lilac and plum. They are stunning floral jewels in full bloom, and attractive small rosettes of succulent foliage when they are not, and a good excuse to build a rockery—or, in my case, extend an existing one with another dump-truck load of good-sized limestone chunks. My back may regret this for a few days, but the reward in the spring when they bloom makes it worth it.

VARIETIES

Lewisia cotyledon. Relatively large blooms in gorgeous shades of peach, pink, lavender and lilac. Several seed strains in specific colours and colour ranges are available. At least one ('Bridal Bouquet') is dwarf at 4 in. (10 cm), the others tend towards 10 in. (25 cm). Zone 4.

L. longipetala. These have a similar range of colours as above, on compact plants to 6 in. (15 cm). Probably a little bit hardier, to zone 3.

L. pygmaea. Lilac-pink flowers, tiny plants to 4 in. (10 cm), and surprisingly tough. Zone 3.

Liatris – Blazing Star, Prairie Blazing Star, Gay Feather, Button Snakeroot

Prairie or Meadow | *Compositae*

Blazing stars are North American prairie natives, blooming in summer with tall fuzzy spikes in purple, lavender purple or white. Their habit makes them useful in many garden settings, upright enough to be an accent but not towering over other plants or shading them out. *Liatris* are adaptable to many soil types, most of the species being both drought and clay tolerant. They self-seed a bit, but not excessively. The florets open first at the top of the spikes and work their way down over a week or so for an interesting colour effect. They all make good cut flowers.

VARIETIES

Liatris aspera. Blazing star. Purple-pink flower spikes in summer, to 36 in. (90 cm). This one prefers wet, even boggy, conditions, so would also be a candidate for the edge of the bog garden or the bottom level of the rain garden.

L. ligulistylis. Meadow blazing star. Similar to the species above, but more drought tolerant, and very clay tolerant. 36 in. (90 cm).

L. punctata. Spotted blazing star. Dense purple flower spikes to 20 in. (50 cm); needs better drainage than most of this species, and will even do well in a rockery. Zone 3.

Liatris spicata. Photo Darwin Paton

L. pycnostachya. Button snakeroot. Masses of violet-purple flowers (the "buttons") are crowded onto tall spikes of flowers. At 5 ft. (150 cm) or more under ideal conditions, this can be the tallest of the cultivated *Liatris*.

L. scariosa. Blazing star. Large white or purple flowers, up to 36 in. (90 cm). Zone 3.

L. spicata. Blazing star. In white or purple, this is the most commonly found garden species of *Liatris*. The compact purple form 'Kobold' grows up to 16 in. (40 cm), while the duet of 'Floristan White' and 'Floristan Purple' can reach 36 in. (90 cm).

Ligularia – Ray Flower, Leopard Plant

Meadow or Bog Garden | *Compositae*

The *Ligularia* are large exuberant plants that thrive in semi-shade or filtered light and moist or wet soils. The more moisture and nutrients they receive, the bigger they get. *Ligularia* can be spectacular grown in an ideal condition, which would probably be a low corner of the garden or a bog edge. They can easily get to be 6 ft. (180 cm) across, so feed them well and give them room.

The flowers seem to come in one of two different formats, although they are all in shades of dark yellow to gold and consist of multiple florets. The look of each is quite different, as the "spike" types add quite a bit of height and draw the eye upward, whereas the flatter "corymb" types anchor the bulk of the plant and draw the eye into it. Both are striking.

The common name leopard plant comes from one non-hardy species that has leopard-spotted foliage—I have always wondered what would happen if I planted leopard plant and leopard's bane together. Oddly enough, they do well in similar habitats.

VARIETIES

Ligularia dentata (L. clivorum). Loose corymbs of orange-yellow flowers. The dark-leaf forms are popular, for good reason—although too much dark foliage in a dark corner of the garden isn't always a good thing. Excellent paired with large ferns, or large gold-leaf hostas, a number of cultivars are available, varying in foliage colour and size. To 48 in. (120 cm) high by 5 ft. (150 cm) wide. Zone 3.

L. przewalskii. Tall spikes of bright yellow-gold flowers, deeply toothed palmate leaves, dark-purple stems. 6 ft. (180 cm) tall, 5 ft. (150 cm) wide. Zone 3.

L. sibirica. Rounded corymbs of yellow-gold flowers, leathery rounded leaves. 4 by 5 ft. (120 by 150 cm). The hardiest of the lot. Zone 2.

L. stenocephala. 'The Rocket' is the cultivar most often seen offered for sale; it doesn't seem to differ that much from its parent. Striking heavily serrated leaves, and tall spikes of golden-yellow flowers. 4 by 5 ft. (120 by 150 cm). Zone 3.

L. tangutica (Sinacalia tangutica). Pyramidal corymbs of bright-yellow flowers, 36 in. (90 cm) high and wide. Zone 5.

L. veitchiana. Yellow-gold flowers in tall spikes; deeply serrated, almost triangular, foliage. 5 by 4 ft. (150 by 120 cm). Zone 3.

Ligularia dentata 'Dark Beauty.' Photo Darwin Paton

Above: photo Darwin Paton

Clockwise from top left: a variety of *Lilium* x *asiaticum* cultivars.
Left: *Lilium dauricum.*

Lilium – Lily

Meadow or Prairie | Asparagaceae

Lilies really should need no introduction. There are a number of species and groups that do well in northern climates, and indeed there is a major retail (online) lily grower in Fort St. John (Alyssa's Garden), with a somewhat overwhelming selection of hardy varieties. May they live long and prosper.

This is one of those genera of which whole books can and have been written. For more information on lilies, see the website of the Pacific Bulb Society. The nice thing about most plant enthusiasts is that they enjoy sharing information, and this site excels at that.

Lilies all prefer deep well-drained soils. Most need full sun, but a few (as noted) are shade tolerant. There are many more obscure species from the northern parts of Eurasia that could easily turn out to be hardy—they would most likely have to be grown from seed. It would be a small investment.

Lilies are easy from seed, although this is not a fast way to enjoy the flowers. The first year after sowing, only a root is generated, the second year offers a single leaf. Lilies don't rush into things. It can take four or five years to get a bloom, but it is worth it. All lilies seem to be popular used as cut flowers, and some are fragrant. They tend to bloom in midsummer, between the big poppies and the daylilies.

The nomenclature is a mess, due to centuries of breeding and cross-breeding—I haven't even tried to sort it out. The most common hardy groups offered for sale are Asiatic hybrids, Oriental hybrids and tiger lilies, along with the less-hardy trumpet (Easter) lilies. There is an increasing number of artificial groups ("giant tree lilies!") being created, seemingly at the whim of catalogue companies.

VARIETIES

Lilium × asiaticum. Asiatic lily. One of the most popular and probably the hardiest of the lily groups, growing into mature clumps that can be breathtaking. Flowers are mostly upwards facing and come in a wide range of single, spotted, flecked and bi-colours; plants range from dwarf to large, up to 36 in. (90 cm). Zone 2.

L. columbianum. Columbia tiger lily. Downward-facing blooms in dark yellow to orange. Native in southern parts of the BC interior, 36 in. (90 cm). Zone 4.

L. dauricum (L. pensylvanicum). Dahurican lily. If this has been found in both Pennsylvania and China, it has a very wide natural distribution, and therefore undoubtedly a great deal of genetic variability. My strain originated with seed from China, the flowers in soft shades of apricot orange, some speckled and

some clear. A very pretty small lily, 24 in. (60 cm). Zone 3 or maybe even zone 2.

L. martagon. Martagon lily. Tall clusters of downward-facing ('Turk's Cap') flowers, usually deep rosy-red (almost maroon), occasionally white. There is a seed strain, probably a hybrid of this and some other lily, in brilliant and most un-Martagon shades of yellow, apricot, pink, wine red, orange and white, "mostly purple spotted." I keep trying this from seed, but haven't had any luck so far. The lack of success and the suggestiveness of the name ('Painted Ladies') are making me stubborn. I'll get it one of these years; there is always room in the garden for one or fifty more lilies. Shade tolerant. Grows to 36 in. (90 cm). Zone 3.

L. × orientale. Oriental lily. A wide range of heights and colours. Popular because of their beauty and fragrance, but not quite as tough or hardy as the Asiatics, and in need of better drainage. Grows to 48 in. (120 cm). Zone 4.

L. philadelphicum. Wood lily. Native to the southern parts of the interior, this one will sometimes survive in the Prince George area (although it does not thrive). Very pretty small dark-orange flowers, to 36 in. (90 cm). Zone 4.

L. × tigrinum (L. × lancifolium) Tiger lily. The nomenclature is dubious, but the lilies are pretty things, leopard spotted (rather than tiger striped) and somewhat shade tolerant. Usually orange, sometimes white, yellow or pink, 48 in. (120 cm). Zone 3.

Limonium – Sea Lavender, Hungarian Statice, German Statice

Prairie or Rockery | Plumbaginaceae

Sea lavender produces airy sprays of pale-lavender flowers over a basal rosette of broad foliage that is almost succulent. These plants are extremely drought tolerant, and require well-drained alkaline soils and full sun to do well. They are taprooted, and should not be transplanted once established. Sea lavender is popular as a dried flower as well as in the garden.

The best planting of this I have seen was at Hill's Health Ranch down by 108 Mile, mixed in with the subtle shades of yarrow 'Summer Pastels' (*Achillea millefolium)*. The similar tones blended harmoniously, while the textures of the two plants offered contrast. Both species loved the hot dry conditions.

VARIETIES

Limonium gmelinii. Hungarian statice. Bright lilac-blue flowers, good cut flower and everlasting dried flower. To 20 in. (50 cm). Zone 4.

L. latifolium (L. platyphyllum). Sea lavender. Lavender-grey blooms in summer over a long period. It will grow in the

Limonium latifolium.

Lupinus x polyphyllus 'Russell Hybrids.'

heavier soils found in some places around Prince George, but sulks and is short-lived and much smaller. Grows to 24 in. (60 cm), zone 4, borderline in zone 3.

L. tataricum. German statice. Pale lavender-blue flowers, to 18 in. (45 cm). This may be the same as *Goniolimon tataricum*; confusion reigns in the nomenclature between these two genera. Hardy to zone 4, borderline in zone 3.

Lupinus – Lupine

Meadow | *Leguminosae*

Today's garden lupines are complex hybrids, first developed over a hundred years ago from crosses made with, among other things, the western North American wild lupine, our own *Lupinus polyphyllus*. The first Russell lupines were introduced before World War II by George Russell, who spent most of his life perfecting tall straight full-flowered lupine spikes in a wide range of colours. (Gardeners have always tended towards obsessiveness.)

Lupines bloom in late spring and early summer, and are beloved by aphids as well as gardeners. A good population of insect predators, as found in a healthy mixed plant community, will help keep the aphids under control. Lupines can cause a problem in more temperate climates with their tendency to self-seed, but that isn't an issue in northern gardens and ditches, where seedlings are fewer and less aggressive.

The seedlings will tend to revert to the purple blue of the wild stock after a few generations, and indeed many of the seed strains available today are drifting away from Russell's ideal. Plants in the relatively new 'Woodfield' strain are the exception—they are strong-stemmed and beautifully coloured, in solids and bi-colours. The Woodfields are so much better than many of the other strains that they are worth a premium; even their volunteer seedlings will be superior.

VARIETIES

Lupinus × polyphyllus. Hybrid lupine. Many named cultivars and seed strains are available, most of them descendants of the original 'Russell' hybrids (of *L. polyphyllus* origin). Volunteer seedlings do not come true to colour. They grow from 16–36 in. (40–90 cm). Zone 2.

L. nootkatensis. Nootka lupine. Purple-blue and white flowers; compact dwarf plants. Short-lived, especially in heavy clay. 16 in. (40 cm). Zone 3.

L. perennis. Lupine. Eastern North American native, usually purple blue, occasionally pink or white. To 36 in. (90 cm). Zone 3.

L. polyphyllus. Wild lupine. Western North American native. This is the parent of the hybrid garden lupines. The original form is a purple blue; occasional white flowers are seen in wild populations. Blooms at the same time as wild roses for a very pretty effect that we might do well to duplicate in our gardens. 36 in. (90 cm). Zone 2.

Luzula nivea. Photo Georg Ubelhart, Jelitto Perennial Seeds

Luzula – Wood Rush

Woodland | *Juncaceae*

This small member of the rush family does well in light shade or filtered sunlight as long as the soil is moist. The two varieties commonly available (usually from seed) are *Luzula nivea* and *Luzula sylvatica*, which translate literally to snow rush and forest rush, respectively. They both have tufts of cottony-white or off-white flowers at the top of round stems, rising just above the fine-textured foliage, and are very similar, with the snow rush being whiter of flower, lighter green of foliage, and slightly taller at 14 in. (35 cm). Either is a useful small accent plant in semi-shady conditions where grasses won't grow, with some tendency to self-seed.

Lychnis – Campion, German Catchfly, Maltese Cross, Ragged Robin

Meadow or Rockery | *Caryophyllaceae*

Lychnis comprises a varied group of plants, most of which do well in ordinary garden conditions, preferring well-drained soil and full sun. Some of this genus have a tendency to self-seed to the point of weediness—*L. chalcedonica* (Maltese cross), for example, is a vicious thug that I regret planting in my garden. *Lychnis* is closely related to *Silene*, and they may actually all be members of *Silene* rather than *Lychnis*, but I am going to leave them here for now.

Varieties

***Lychnis alpina* (*Silene suecica*).** Alpine campion. Rose-pink flowers in late spring. Short-lived in heavy soil. Compact plant, growing to only 4 in. (10 cm) high and wide. Zone 3.

L. × arkwrightii. Campion. Dark purple-green foliage, bright orange-red flowers (a clearer orange than the familiar Maltese cross). Several different cultivars of different heights are available. Mine have been struggling along for years in heavy clay and a shady location; this suggests to me that, while hardy, they would do better in well-drained soil and more light. They are a striking colour, and worth finding the right home for—I am going to try for a larger grouping in amongst the blues and purples of the campanulas. 12 in. (30 cm). Zone 3.

L. chalcedonica (*Silene chalcedonica*). Maltese cross. The most common colour is a fiery red, but pink, apricot and white forms also exist. They all self-seed aggressively and pop up everywhere. Great in the cottage or "wild" garden, but a thug in a mixed flower bed. I am sorry I ever planted this one, and am working at deadheading it every year in the hopes I can outlive it. Clay tolerant. 48 in. (120 cm). Zone 3, maybe zone 2.

Lychnis × arkwrightii 'Vesuvius.'

L. coronaria (*Silene coronaria*). Rose campion. Silver-grey felt-like foliage provides a perfect contrast to the striking magenta-pink flowers. White forms also exist (pretty but not outstanding), along with a white with a bright-pink eye that mixes beautifully with pastel colours. All do best in long hot summers and dry loose soils, where they will self-seed, but they will not grow in heavy clay. To 28 in. (70 cm). Zone 4.

L. flos-cuculi (*Silene flos-cuculi*). Ragged robin. Flowers in shades of pink, sometimes white, with very narrow petals that look like ragged feathers. They self-seed enthusiastically, which can be a bit of a problem—or a bonus, depending on your attitude and how wild a garden you have. Selections range from 4 in. (10 cm) to 16 in. (40 cm). Zone 3.

L. viscaria (*Silene viscaria*). German catchfly. Flowers in late spring and early summer in shades of magenta purple or pink, sometimes white. A number of cultivars are available, varying in height and colour. These self-seed, but not aggressively; they add to the wild meadow look of that part of my garden. 20 in. (50 cm). Zone 3.

Lysimachia – Creeping Jenny, Golden Alexander, Gooseneck Loosestrife, Loosestrife

Meadow or Woodland | *Primulaceae*

The hardy species of *Lysimachia* are a diverse group, from very low ground-hugging crawlers to tall arching spires, and should not be confused with the invasive purple loosestrife (*Lythrum salicaria*), an entirely different genus. They do best in moist well-drained soils, in filtered light or half-day sun.

VARIETIES

Lysimachia atropurpurea. Beaujolais. I keep wanting this one to be hardy, because of the dark purple-red flower spikes. It is not—zone 5 at best.

L. ciliata. Yellow loosestrife. The species form is unassuming, growing to 24 in. (60 cm) with light-yellow flowers. The real winner is *L. ciliata* 'Firecracker,' with dark-purple foliage and small bright-yellow flowers nestled in the leaves. Quite hardy and clay tolerant, it spreads by rhizome, but not excessively, and would be best paired with chartreuse-leaved plants or bright-blue flowers for contrast. Zone 3.

L. clethroides. Gooseneck loosestrife. Valued for its arching and densely packed white "gooseneck" flower stalks, but refusing to grow in heavy clay soil, this one needs moisture as well as loose open soil. It would do well at the back of a pond or other wet area. An ideal companion for any of the ray flowers (*Ligularia*). 24 in. (60 cm). Zone 3 or 4.

L. nummularia. Creeping Jenny. Ground-hugging plant with bright-green leaves and golden-yellow flowers in late spring. The cultivar 'Aurea' has chartreuse foliage, against which the flowers are lost. The foliage burns in too much sun, but will

Above: *Lysimachia nummularia* beneath a contorted hazelnut, photo Darwin Paton; right: *Lysimachia punctata* 'Alexander.'

brighten up moist shady areas. Good groundcover under small shrubs, for hanging over retaining walls and in partially shaded rockeries. Suitable for growing in containers, and will drape gracefully over the edges. Barely 2 in. (5 cm) tall, spreading to up to 18 in. (45 cm). Zone 3.

L. punctata. Yellow loosestrife or spotted loosestrife. Golden-yellow flowers appear up the stalks of this sturdy plant from early summer on. It forms a good-sized clump over time, spreading slowly, and does best in moist soil but is clay tolerant. The cultivar 'Alexander' has variegated foliage, each leaf trimmed in white, and from a distance looks like the plant is washed in sunlight, a very nice effect. Like its parent this spreads slowly to form a clump, but it is not at all aggressive. Both the green-leaf and variegated forms grow to 24 in. (60 cm), and are hardy to zone 3.

Macleaya cordata. Photo Georg Ubelhart, Jelitto Perennial Seeds

Macleaya – Plume Poppy

Meadow | *Papaveraceae*

This unlikely giant is indeed a member of the poppy family, as well as being a spectacular thug. It grows to well over 6 ft. (180 cm) high when happy, and has huge grey-green leaves up to 12 in. (30 cm) across. The feathery and fragrant plumes, in off-white or pale coral, are quite un-poppy like, as is its habit of spreading by rhizome. *Macleaya cordata* can be spectacular in a bed by itself, perhaps behind a small pond in the backyard, but will try to take over a mixed flower bed. Very hardy, to at least zone 2, and also quite drought tolerant.

Malva moschata 'Alba.'

Malva – Mallow

Meadow | *Malvaceae*

The mallows are closely related to the hollyhocks (*Alcea*) and the Prairie mallows (*Sidalcea*), but generally speaking are lower, bushier and more tolerant of less than perfect conditions. They are a pleasant addition to the natural garden, blooming through the summer into fall, and make good cut flowers.

VARIETIES

Malva alcea. Masses of good-sized mid-pink flowers on bushy plants to 28 in. (70 cm). Zone 4.

M. moschata. Flowers are clear mid-pink, light pink, or white touched with pink in the centre, on vigorous plants with rich-green foliage. These can get knocked right down by a late hard frost and regrow as though nothing had happened. Any or all of the colours play well with the lavender-blue flowers and grey-green foliage of catnip (*Nepeta racemosa*). 20 in. (50 cm). Zone 3.

M. sylvestris. Violet flowers, solid or veined, on tall plants to 36 in. (90 cm). The cultivar 'Zebrina' is white streaked with rose pink and violet, and can reach 48 in. (120 cm). A striking specimen, but borderline hardy north of Quesnel. Zone 4.

Meconopsis grandis.

Meconopsis – Himalayan Poppy, Blue Poppy

Woodland or Meadow | *Papaveraceae*

Back in the days when the nursery was open for retail sales, I could tell when my patch of Himalayan poppies was in bloom by the screams of delight when people first saw them. These poppies are the most incredible shade of clear light sky-blue in the world—they put a summer prairie sky to shame. They were probably the most photographed flower here. A single blue poppy in bloom is breathtaking, a grouping of them is unforgettable.

Meconopsis are fussy about the soil and moisture conditions, but worth every bit of care needed in finding exactly the right site. They do best in conditions opposite to that of every other poppy you have grown; they need moist, humus-rich soil and light shade. There is a huge group of them growing at Butchart Gardens, near Victoria, in full sun, but they are at a low elevation there and close to the ocean, in what is known as a maritime climate, where the humidity in the air is very high. In the higher and drier continental climate of the BC interior, the humidity is much lower, and these poppies and other Himalayan native plants (including rhododendrons) need regular watering to keep the mulch moist and the plants happy. If the conditions are right, they are vigorous and easy to grow. If they are not, the plants won't overwinter.

Most of the *Meconopsis* species are monocarpic (literally, once-seeding), which means they need to be deadheaded after the bloom is finished, at least for the first time they flower, otherwise they will set seed and then die. They can become large clumps over time, and can then be divided like any other clump-forming perennial.

VARIETIES

Meconopsis betonicifolia. Blue poppy, Himalayan poppy. Absolutely stunning pure-blue flowers. The occasional white or violet plant will pop up (and a white form is available as a separate seed strain); while these are pretty, they just don't have the same impact. Grows to 24 in. (60 cm). Zone 3.

M. grandis (M. × sheldonii). Blue poppy. Very similar in flower to *M. betonicifolia,* but taller, to 32 in. (80 cm), and with hairy leaves and buds. Zone 3.

Melissa officinalis. Photo I. Kenpei*

Melissa – Lemon Balm

Meadow | *Lamiaceae*

Melissa officinalis is a member of the mint family, with some of the spreading tendencies of its relatives. Like its cousins in the genus *Mentha,* it is best grown alone in a raised bed or turned loose in a naturalized moist meadow where control isn't an issue. Unlike the other mints, it can also self-seed prolifically as well as spreading by rhizome, so it is wise to cut the whole plant back before it goes to seed. Like the other mints, it does best in deep moist soil, and keeping it happy is important if you are growing it to harvest the foliage or if you simply want it to look lush and healthy in the garden.

Lemon balm is a mounding perennial with bright-green foliage and small white flowers, grown more for its herbal uses than any ornamental quality, although it isn't unattractive. There are a number of named cultivars that do not come true from seed, but are easy from cuttings. The gold leaf form, imaginatively named 'Gold Leaf,' sometimes labelled as 'Aurea' (i.e. 'gold'), is similar in habit to the species but needs to be grown in partial shade as the foliage will burn in full sun.

Lemon balm imparts a pleasant lemon flavour to food dishes or tea and isn't known to have any dangerous side effects. The foliage is said to help repel mosquitoes if rubbed on the skin, which would be a good reason to grow it in the garden. It also attracts beneficial insects. Lemon balm can grow to 16 in. (40 cm) high, and is hardy to zone 3.

Mentha – Mint

Meadow or Herb Garden | *Lamiaceae*

Mints evolved in moist meadows, often by stream-sides, and that is where they are happiest, but they are quite capable of taking over terrain far less favourable. New gardeners are sometimes warned to plant these in buckets (with the bottoms cut out) so that the plants don't escape and take over the rest of the garden by rhizome. By the time the gardeners find out that this is only a temporary solution it is too late. Mints are strong and persistent, plastic buckets break down in time, mints grow over the tops or under the bottoms, and are off and running. The safest place to grow them is alone in a raised bed, so they can be cut off at the pass.

It is not always necessary to be safe, of course. Mint plants can be turned loose in a moist wild meadow, or perhaps over a septic field. They will learn to live with other plants in a community, in a natural ecological process of give and take, although it may require a few years for some kind of equilibrium to be reached. Wild mints have existed this way since the beginning of time— it is just humans who have a problem with it weaving through everything else. If mint is allowed to grow wild along the edges of paths it will release a pleasant fragrance when trodden on.

Mints are useful and prolific herbs, and easy to grow, so building a series of small raised beds, or growing them in half barrels or large sections of concrete drainage tile, or whatever comes to mind and hand, can be worth the trouble. They are delightful in tea as well as cooking, either fresh or dried. Hanging up great handfuls of the freshly cut herb to dry in a dark corner is fast and easy, and the dried leaves can be made into refreshing tea all winter.

There are any number of cultivars ('Spearmint,' 'Peppermint,' 'Ginger Mint,' 'Lime Mint,' 'Apple Mint,' etc.), most of which have to be multiplied vegetatively as they do not come true from seed, being hybrids or selections.

Mertensia – Oyster Plant, Virginia Bluebells

Rockery or Woodland | *Boraginaceae*

The two hardy *Mertensia* species have little in common with each other, except for the blue forget-me-not like flowers.

Mertensia maritima ssp. *asiatica*.

Mentha spicata (spearmint).

Mertensia maritima ssp. *asiatica* is called the oyster plant, although truthfully it doesn't look too much like an oyster but more a member of the stonecrop (*Sedum*) family—until it blooms. The foliage consists of succulent blue-green leaves on a sprawling plant that reaches 8 in. (20 cm) high and several times that wide. It looks good draping over rocks, and is happiest in sandy well-drained soil in full sun. The sprays of pink and blue forget-me-not flowers are a pleasant surprise. The oyster plant does self-seed, but is easy to control, and despite a fragile appearance is hardy to zone 3.

Mertensia pulmonaroides (*M. virginica*) is commonly known as Virginia bluebells, and is an upright plant, to 12 in. (30 cm), with dark-green foliage and blue flowers reminiscent of forget-me-nots. It grows best in woodland conditions in partial shade or filtered light, and tends to go dormant in midsummer after blooming. Although it is usually sold in the fall along with spring-blooming bulbs, it is a rhizome rather than bulb. Hardy to zone 3.

Monarda – Bee Balm, Bergamot

Meadow or Prairie | *Lamiaceae*

Bee balm is one of the most ornamental members of the mint family, with much less tendency to spread than some of its relatives. It has showy flowers in a good range of warm colours, blooming through the summer into fall. The bee balms do attract bees, but the common name was given because a salve made from this plant can be used to take the sting out of bee stings.

The leaves are a standard component in herbal teas, adding a pleasant mint flavour. Lemon bergamot (*Monarda citriodora*), the best for tea, is a short-lived tender perennial, but it can be grown as an annual. All of the *Monarda* make good cut flowers, and bring a gentle minty fragrance with them.

VARIETIES

Monarda citriodora. Lemon bergamot, lemon mint. Blooms rose-purple the first year from seed, and grows to 30 in. (75 cm). Hardy to zone 5 but short-lived at the best of times.

M. didyma. Bergamot. There are a number of cultivars of this, including the popular colour blend 'Panorama Mix,' and a growing selection of named single colours. The newer varieties are available in clear bright tones including violet purple, orchid, hot pink and clear red, as well as a few pastels. There are both tall (48 in./120 cm) and dwarf (24 in./60 cm) selections in almost every colour. These varieties all need rich moist soil to do well. They can suffer from powdery mildew if stressed—a greyish mildew on the leaves tells you they need more water and/or better air circulation. If this appears, cut the plants back, fertilize, and keep them well-watered until you can move them. Adding organic matter to the soil can help hold moisture. Some cultivars are more susceptible to powdery mildew than others; while not fatal, it's definitely not attractive.

M. fistulosa. Horsemint. With nice lilac flowers, this one is more drought tolerant than most of the *Monarda* species, and is a good choice for the herb garden. To 30 in. (75 cm). Zone 4 or 5.

M. punctata. Spotted bee balm. The pink bracts (the showy bits that surround the actual small flower part in the middle) are flecked with yellow and purple. This looks better than it sounds. It blooms the first year from seed, and grows to 36 in. (90 cm). Zone 4.

Monarda didyma.

Monarda didyma. Photo Darwin Paton

Moose in the Garden

Although moose can do a lot of damage in gardens, herbaceous perennial plants themselves are not the targets or (usually) the victims. Moose are browsers and fond of willow (*Salix*) and dogwood (*Cornus*) twigs, although they will expand their diets and can get used to eating other types of shrubs and trees. I didn't mind the resident cow and calf munching the willows in the ditch; it's what moose do. She branched out to the dogwoods in the display garden; those are natural moose browse as well so I couldn't really complain. Then she started ripping the mountain ash (*Sorbus*) apart to eat the swelling buds on the ends of the branches. I wasn't happy, but she wasn't afraid of me or my lone dog so there wasn't too much I could do that was consistent with my pacifist tendencies, and at least she wasn't eating my precious maples (*Acer*).

Moose passing through.

The next year she started in on the maples, and it was war. Not the armed kind, I hasten to say—there would be no point. I have moose habitat therefore I have moose; if not this one then another one. I started using a repellent spray on the trees I wanted to protect, and this seemed to help a little bit, and then I fenced the garden and got a second dog. The moose went right through the fence once before she noticed it, but as the young Akita matured and became more protective of territory, and the moose figured out that my trees tasted bad, she just stopped coming around.

Mulch

I am a big fan of surface mulches, which solve a lot of problems in this climate with this soil. They are not the answer everywhere, any more than anything else is, so I cannot and will not say "you must mulch," as some mulch advocates do, to the dismay of bare-earth proponents. (It's amazing the things people can find to argue about!)

In 1997, my property was the remains of a gravel pit, with the gravel scraped off down to the clay below. A number of dead washing machines and dryers and two rusting truck carcasses littered the landscape. Naturally, I thought this was the perfect place to start a nursery.

The heavy clay had no topsoil, but it did have a fine collection of well-established local weeds, noxious and otherwise. By the time the pond (for water collection and storage) and the house foundation were dug, the weeds were gone, and I had an acre of pleasantly rolling moonscape to work on.

As I marked out the planned display garden area with paths and flower and shrub beds, the weeds started to come back. Planting the trees, first to go in, I mulched around them to save myself watering through the summer. It quickly became apparent that the mulched areas had no weeds while the adjacent bare earth was a magnet for them. I starting mulching everything, and never looked back.

As the years went by, the nursery grew and the big issue became water. A large area of nursery stock in containers had to be kept watered, and there was not enough time, water or hose to irrigate an acre of perennial and shrub garden as well. One year, in midsummer, my display garden was converted cold turkey to a xeriscape. Originating in Denver, xeriscaping is a style of garden design that reduces or even eliminates supplemental watering. Water restrictions in the high desert of Colorado made the shift necessary there, but it makes sense everywhere else as well. The concept is simple: garden with the amount of water that falls from the sky, channel and conserve the water you do have, group plants according to their water needs, and keep the thirstiest plants closest to the water source.

In my garden, this meant survival of the fittest in a large landscape with many microclimates. Of the 1,700 different species and varieties of trees, shrubs and perennials growing in the garden, perhaps 10 percent of them died over the next year as a result of drought or natural selection. The rest thrived, and the reason for that was largely the heavy layer of mulch that had been laid down.

Wood Chip as Mulch

Around the plants I use an aged wood-chip mulch, a mix of spruce and pine that has weathered to the golden brown of cedar bark. It comes from an old sawmill site abandoned 30 or more years ago (and there are many such sites through the north). The texture of

The freshly mulched display garden in 1998.

Aged wood chip makes the perfect mulch.

the chips is rather like that of coarse coffee grounds; not flat flaky chips that would pack together. As mulch they look beautiful, hold water in the ground and suppress weeds. I originally spread the wood chips 4–6 in. (10–15 cm) deep, and have topped up here and there since. They break down slowly, but fast enough to enrich the soil as they do; my garden now has earthworms wherever I dig, always a good sign. The mulch has contributed to the health of my soil and therefore my plants and garden, and in the process saved me a lot of work—I don't honestly think I could have built or maintained this garden without it.

Fertilizing when Organic Mulches are Used

Permanent organic mulches have many benefits for the soil, including preventing compaction and surface caking, significantly reducing moisture loss, suppressing weed growth and preventing soil erosion. Any organic material used for mulch breaks down over time and is incorporated into the soil by worms, so it has to be renewed periodically. Some garden references warn that organic mulches will remove nitrogen from the soil. The decomposition process can indeed temporarily tie up nitrogen in the soil, but this element is something we should be adding with fertilizer anyway. Nitrogen is the first number in the three on the fertilizer box or bottle. Fish fertilizer may be 6-1-0, for instance, indicating the percentage by volume of nitrogen and phosphorus, but no potassium. Either fish fertilizer or a kelp-based fertilizer with a similar formula would be a choice if you don't have soil test results to give more specific guidance. A chemical fertilizer with a formula of something in the range of 10-10-10 or 14-14-14 is the equivalent of a supersized fast-food meal—it may promote fast growth but won't do anything for long-term soil or plant health.

Mulch Tips

Adding too much mulch can smother tree roots just beneath the surface—4 in. (10 cm) is generally sufficient. Do not push soil or mulch up against existing tree trunks or shrub stems, as this can cause them to rot. Hold the soil or mulch back a good hand-span of 4 in. (10 cm) so that the bark can breathe. Arborists advise "think bagel, not volcano."

Only mulch where needed—most alpine and rockery plants grow best in very well-drained soil low in organic matter. Many of these otherwise perfectly hardy plants will rot in the cool wet northern springs and falls if they have organic mulch around their crowns.

A permanent surface mulch of wood chips, hog fuel, shredded straw or any other organic material provides an insulating blanket that can keep the ground from heating up as quickly in the spring as would bare soil. The ground will stay frozen a week or 10 days longer under a light-coloured oat-straw mulch than under an aged (dark-brown) wood-chip mulch, which thaws within a day or two of bare soil. If you mulched your vegetable beds for the summer, which can be a good idea, remove any light-coloured mulches to the compost pile in the fall for earlier thaw and planting dates the next spring. Delayed soil warming, on the other hand, can be good for perennials and woody plants, preventing early growth that can be damaged by the inevitable late frosts.

Mulch Materials

There are a number of choices for mulch, none of them perfect. The ideal mulch may simply be the one that is locally available and affordable.

Partially composted aged wood chips from spruce, pine or fir are excellent mulch material. These should not be confused with sawdust, which is very fine and packs down too easily, or freshly milled wood chips, too raw and likely to damage plants with leachates (but good for paths, as they pack well).

Leaves of poplar, birch and maple are safe to use, and best if they are shredded so that they break down more rapidly. An annual application of these to gardens in the fall is one of the best ways of building up soil, as well as providing all the other benefits of mulch. The leaves and bark of some trees, including oaks and walnuts, contain tannins that may be toxic to some plants if used in large quantities. Fortunately these species are not abundant in our region.

The Fraser Fort George Regional District Landfill in Prince George has a composting facility that turns out a uniform and closely monitored compost free of weed seeds. Although the pH can be a bit high (usually over 7), it makes a good mulch; the City of Prince George uses it on their flower beds and it suppresses weeds well. I would advise soil testing on a regular basis if using this every year, as it may contain high (but not toxic) levels of such elements as calcium and magnesium, fine in small quantities but you don't want to add excessive quantities.

Mushroom manure is best used as a soil amendment rather than a mulch, due to its richness and variable nutrient content.

While texture and source vary widely, the bark mulch or nuggets available at most landscape-supply stores and garden centres work well if used properly. Putting them down over landscape fabric, as has become standard practice in many places, turns out to be not such a good idea. Studies are showing that although landscape fabric is permeable and does breathe, it doesn't do either well enough, essentially killing the soil over time by preventing organisms from moving organic material between the soil's layers. If that weren't bad enough, weeds will grow in the mulch on top of the fabric, embedding roots into it and making removal almost impossible. In five to ten years, the fabric will have to be ripped out anyway, not an enjoyable process. The healthy solution for the garden and environment is to put the mulch material directly onto the soil—this replicates the natural duff layer in the woods. Occasional weeding or a brisk raking to uproot small weed seedlings until the landscape plants get big enough to shade the ground and choke out weeds is all that is needed. The mulch may require replenishing every few years as it breaks down—a good thing, as this means it is building up the soil below.

Putting crushed rock or gravel down over landscape fabric creates all the problems mentioned above, and makes it even harder to hand-weed, as the gravel is tough on hands.

The hulls of coffee beans are packaged and sold as mulch, but these are extremely toxic to dogs, and unfortunately also very attractive to some of them.

Peat tends to cake and form a hard surface, and sheds water when it is dry. Use it, if you must, only as a soil amendment, not a surface mulch. The coir (coconut-husk) products that have been appearing on the market in recent years are also better used as soil amendments, mixed into the soil rather than spread on top of it.

Straw makes a great temporary mulch around vegetables or berries, but is dangerous as a winter mulch as it provides a safe home for hungry voles who will eat your plants while being protected from predators.

Hay has the same problems as straw, with the addition of millions of grass seeds.

In the end what I always come back to is a solution that mimics as closely as possible what nature provides. In our northern forests, the naturally occurring duff layer on the forest floor, which nature seems to think is the perfect mulch for this climate, is a mix of assorted tree needles and leaves, pine and spruce cones, decaying wood, and the other debris left behind by the cycle of life and death in the forest. The best mulch in the northern garden is a mix of aged wood chips and chopped leaves to start, and then the accumulation of leaves, twigs, spent flower heads, dead beetles, moose droppings, old pine cones and dead plant material that the garden produces. Leave it to compost where it lies, rake it around a bit early in the spring to even it up and speed the process, but don't haul it out of the garden. Today's leaf litter is tomorrow's soil and the future of your healthy low-maintenance garden.

Myosotis sylvatica. Photo Georges Jansoone*

Nepeta racemosa.

Myosotis – Forget-Me-Not

Meadow or Woodland | *Boraginaceae*

Forget-me-nots are spring-blooming biennials, annuals or short-lived perennials, all with a non-invasive tendency to self-seed. They are old-fashioned plants that no one has bothered to try and improve much, and they trigger fond memories in many people, with their sprays of cheery little yellow-eyed blue flowers.

Ripping or raking out (depending on the surrounding plants) handfuls of the spent plants after they finish blooming can prevent some of the self-seeding and much of the straggly appearance. Interplanting with later-blooming perennials such as Oriental poppies and daylilies will also help, as their strong-growing foliage soon hides the remains.

Nepeta – Catnip, Catmint

Meadow | *Lamiaceae*

Nepeta is more than just the favourite recreational herb of Miss Josephine Lightfoot, the cat who owns me. It includes some very useful garden plants.

Some cats will enjoy any of these species, with varying degrees of intoxication, others are not interested at all, and still others are quite selective and will only target the genuine catnip species. Miss Josie nibbles, but does not destroy, her favoured plants in the garden.

Nepeta is becoming increasingly popular in low-maintenance gardens due to the extended bloom time, drought tolerance, and pest and disease resistance. It also attracts beneficial insects, and looks good through the growing seasons.

Psychological warfare, with the weapon of catnip plants, can be used to keep the neighbourhood cats from using your flower and vegetable beds as litter boxes. A plant of catnip here and there throughout the garden will be enjoyed by the cats, who are (usually) too clean to use their recreational area as a toilet. It's a win-win situation.

Varieties

Nepeta cataria. Catnip. Pale-lavender flowers, to 36 in. (90 cm) tall, forms a large clump. Zone 3.

N. grandiflora. Clusters of soft-blue flowers on tall spikes to 32 in. (80 cm). Zone 3.

N. nervosa. Cultivars in pink ('Pink Cat') and blue ('Blue Moon') make a nice addition to the front of the border, coming in at 16 in. (40 cm). The showiest flowers of all these species, but slightly less hardy at zone 4. The species form grows to 24 in. (60 cm).

N. racemosa **(formerly *N.* × *faassenii*).** Catmint. Varieties range from the dwarf 'Little Titch' to 'Six Hills Giant.' Most are in the mid-range, and can start to look alike after a while. 'Walker's Low' was the 2007 Perennial Plant of the Year, and for good reason with its continuously blooming spikes of rich lavender-blue flowers through the summer. There is also a white form, 'Alba.' Heights vary from 6 in. (15 cm) to 36 in. (90 cm). Zone 3.

N. sibirica. Blue or lavender flowers, to 36 in. (90 cm). The recently introduced French cultivar 'Souvenir d'André Chaudon,' apart from the fancy name, is supposed to be superior in every way to every other catnip ever grown, including having strong stalks which help to keep this from flopping around in late summer, as some of the others can be inclined to do (especially if a cat has been rolling in them). I shall have to try it if

I ever come across it—I'm as much a sucker as anyone else for "new and improved." The species and the cultivars are variously zone 3 or 4; the ones I have tried don't seem quite as vigorous as *N. racemosa.*

N. subsessilis. One of the larger species, both in florets and overall size. The flowers tend to blue, with occasional pinks. Seed strains in a bright blue ('Blue Dreams') and clear pink ('Pink Dreams') grow to only 24 in. (60 cm), and bloom the first year from seed. Unfortunately they re-bloom only if they are deadheaded; the requirement for maintenance may get these kicked off my island. Zone 3.

'Herb' the nomenclature gnome.

Nomenclature

Classification levels (example)
Family: Campanulaceae
Genus: *Campanula*
Species: *Campanula carpatica*
Cultivar/variety: *Campanula carpatica* 'Deep Blue Clips'

Relationships between plants are important to the extent that within plant families, like human families, there can be similarities in habit as well as appearance. In Ericaceae, for example, we find a lot of moisture-loving plants adapted to cold climates and acidic soils, and many of them are evergreen. If we look at where *Ledum* grows in the wild we have an idea of where to grow *Andromeda.* There are also, of course, black sheep and exceptions to every rule.

In the rapidly changing world of plant nomenclature, I have used the universally accepted authority of "The Plant List" (*www. theplantlist.org*). The Plant List is, as they say, "a working list of all known plant species. Collaboration between the Royal Botanic Gardens, Kew and Missouri Botanical Garden enabled the creation of The Plant List by combining multiple checklist data sets held by these institutions and other collaborators."

Paeonia – Peony

Meadow | *Paeoniaceae*

The genus *Paeonia* consists of a great many species, groups and cultivars. Peonies have been cultivated, collected and bred for hundreds of years, most notably by the Japanese, who do a splendid job of these things. There are hundreds of cultivars of peonies that will do well in northern gardens, and it is a pity that most garden centres only offer a red, a pink and a white, with one or two other fancy ones thrown in for good measure. The world of peonies is far more interesting—and exciting—than that.

The Canadian Peony Society's website (at *www.peony.ca* in French or English) is loaded with information, as are those of some of the specialty growers—checking them out is not a bad way to spend a winter evening.

I once had the opportunity to look at an old (1920-era) peony catalogue that offered and described in loving detail more than 250 different named varieties of *Paeonia lactiflora,* the common garden peony. They varied in height and season of bloom, of course, and consisted of single forms, doubles, semi-doubles, and that exquisite peony invention, the "bomb." Many were fragrant, and the type and degree of fragrance varied. Colours ranged from clear pure white to deepest burgundy, some had yellow stamen clusters while others had red. Please do not settle for generic red peonies or generic red anything. Northern gardeners and gardens deserve better.

Peonies are one of those plant families that do well in the north, coping valiantly with the frozen winters and growing happily free of many of the pests and diseases they are afflicted with in warmer climates. Peonies need decent soil and some degree of drainage, yet still manage to survive in my heavy clay. They would prefer that mythical rich moist but well-drained soil none of us have, and the full sun most of us have in at least one corner somewhere—give them the best and most visible location possible, because peonies are spectacular when in bloom. As they can live 50 or more years in the same location, it wouldn't be a bad thing to improve the soil and drainage before planting them. (This is the "do as I say, not as I do" school of gardening: I am embarrassed to admit that, with the exception of two new 'Itoh' peonies that went in last year, mine were all jammed into the clay and left to fend for themselves. The old peony bed is getting a complete overhaul next year, with the plants finally receiving the care they deserve. Then I can sit on the new bench and admire them instead of feeling guilty.)

Division, if necessary, should be done early in the fall. Peonies

Clockwise from top: *Paeonia* 'Dancing Butterfly,' *Paeonia* 'Mons. Jules Elie' and *Paeonia*, an unknown beauty.

Above photo Darwin Paton

resent being disturbed, so leave them where they are unless it is really crucial. Sharing an old and unusual variety with a good friend would qualify as crucial.

Peonies need to be planted shallowly, as they don't flower well if the crown is buried deep in the soil away from the light and heat. As much as I refuse to stake or do any other unnecessary maintenance on garden plants, I do put cages around the peonies (when I remember in time), otherwise the huge flowers will fall over into the mud with the first good rainstorm. They never look right again if they are propped up after having fallen over. Simply place a peony ring or large tomato cage or some kind of support around each plant early in the spring as soon as they begin to grow. This also prevents dogs from running over emerging sprouts.

VARIETIES

Paeonia lactiflora (P. albiflora, P. japonica). Peony, Japanese peony. These are the common garden peonies that do so well in the north. At one time there were hundreds of named cultivars available, each one different and beautiful. Specialty nurseries are worth seeking out through catalogues and the Internet; the many colours (including a few yellows) and flower shapes (singles, doubles, bombs) and range of flowering season (relative to other peonies) can become addictive. Peony roots ship well in the fall, and of course you will have the planting location all ready for when they arrive. Planting container-grown peonies in the spring is not as good, but we do what we have to do. While heartbreaking, it's necessary to cut off the stunning blooms of a newly planted peony to enable it to put its energy into rooting, not the flower. Varieties range from dwarfs at around 24 in. (60 cm) to taller forms well over 36 in. (90 cm). Time of bloom also varies, making it possible to extend the season by growing early, mid-season and late selections. They are all hardy to zone 3; many to zone 2.

P. × 'Itoh.' The 'Itoh' hybrids have been in development for half a century and just now are starting to become available to North American gardeners at somewhat reasonable prices. (They have gone from $300 a plant to $30 in the last 10 years.) Complex hybrids of *P. lactiflora* and the tree peonies, with the best characteristics of each and hardiness of the former, they come in stunning yellow, peach, lilac and bi-tone varieties. The flowers are of good substance, the stems strong, and the foliage remains healthy through the summer. I am trying not to "need" all of them, as my avowed goal these days is to downsize the garden, not add to it.

P. officinalis. Common peony. These can be distinguished from the Japanese peonies by the sheen on the flowers, which come in a more limited range of colours—usually dark red or deep pink. 'Rubra Plena' is a very good double dark red. They grow to 32 in. (80 cm) and form large clumps over time. Zone 3.

P. suffruticosa. Tree peony. Some gardeners like the challenge of these, but they are only hardy to zone 5, and although a tree peony may struggle along, it will never come into its full glory in zone 3. They will sometimes overwinter in the Prince George area, ever so occasionally producing a bloom.

P. tenuifolia. Fern-leaf peony. Difficult to grow, but made more beautiful by the challenge. The species form is single deep red with prominent yellow stamens; 'Plena' is a deep-red double. Zone 5.

Papaver – Poppy

Meadow, Prairie or Rockery | *Papaveraceae*

Papaver includes many hardy perennial species in addition to the popular annuals. The huge and showy poppy famed for seeds and opium is an annual, *Papaver somniferum*, which has naturalized in gardens on southern Vancouver Island and the Gulf Islands. It grows fairly well in northern BC as well, with some people having trouble believing it is an annual due to its size and stature. It is distinguished from the somewhat similar Oriental poppy by smooth, almost lettuce-like pale-green leaves. Oriental poppies have rough prickly dark-green leaves that look more like thistle in foliage.

Poppies thrive in hot dry locations with relatively poor well-drained soil. Some species are short-lived but will reseed in the right location. They start blooming in early spring with the small Icelandic poppy (*P. nudicaule*), also the last to finish off the season in the fall. The bulk of the species bloom in the heat of summer. All of the poppies with long enough stems make good cut flowers, and they will last quite a period of time if the cut stem ends are seared and sealed with a lighter or match.

VARIETIES

Papaver alpinum (P. rhaeticum). Alpine poppy. Delicate-looking small poppy, which is surprisingly tough when grown in nutrient-poor well-drained soil, which is where it wants to be. Range of white, yellow, orange and pink colours, including both brilliant and pastel tones. Blooms first year from seed. Grows to 8 in. (20 cm). Zone 3.

P. atlanticum. Atlas poppy. The flowers are the colour of an orange Creamsicle, perfect with the grey-green foliage. Flowers are sometimes single, sometimes double; this trait doesn't appear to come reliably true from seed. Pretty either way. To 12 in. (30 cm). Zone 3.

P. orientale. Oriental poppy. This is the Mae West of poppies—large, loud and proud of it. The species form is a brilliant scarlet red, but cultivars range from pale watermelon pink

Clockwise from top left: *Papaver atlanticum, Papaver orientale,* the heart of an Oriental poppy, photo Darwin Paton, and *Papaver radicum.*

to deep orange (some with darker eyes, some fringed, some picotee edged). Dwarf forms are also becoming popular for smaller gardens. The plants tend to fall apart in midsummer after the bloom is finished and all their energy is directed to seed production, so these are best interplanted with something like daylilies (*Hemerocallis*), that come on strong and take up a lot of space at that time. To 36 in. (90 cm). Zone 3.

***P. nudicaule* (*P. croceum*).** Icelandic poppy. Usually available as one of several seed strains or in single colours selected out from those, in shades from white and yellow through to deep orange and pink. Flowering the first year from seed, they have a very long bloom time, from early spring to late fall. A tendency to self-seed in my driveway suggests they prefer a dry gravel habitat to what passes for good soil. To 12 in. (30 cm). Zone 2 or 3.

Penstemon – Beardtongue

Rockery, Meadow or Prairie | *Plantaginaceae* (recently moved from Scrophulaceae Family)

Penstemon is the quintessential North American plant—it is said there is at least one species native to every state or province on the continent. Found from the tundra to the desert, from moist meadows to high alpine, there are probably several dozen more species than those listed here that are rated zone 3 or 4 and capable of thriving in northern gardens.

Most have upright stems covered with tubular flowers in various shades of blue, lavender, violet, cream or yellow, but there are also white-, red- and orange-flowering species. Some are tall, others ground-hugging, depending on their original habitats and pollinators. All are attractive to hummingbirds.

Most prefer dry well-drained soil, but a number of species have proven adaptable to heavy clay. Some of the tender perennials and short-lived perennials bloom their first year from seed, so could be grown as annuals. Most are true herbaceous perennials, but a few alpines are woody based, and as such need good snow cover to keep that crown alive over winter. (This is not a bad strategy for alpine plants, if you think about it. Wherever there is a reliably heavy snow cover, the ability to burst into bloom immediately from established wood, still tucked against the ground for shelter, improves the chances of setting seed during a short growing season.) The following have proven to be hardy in my zone-3 garden outside of Prince George.

Varieties

Penstemon barbatus. The species and the selection 'Coccineus' are both tall (48 in./120 cm) and display tubular orange-red flowers; they can be mistaken for *Lobelia cardinalis* from a distance. While there are a number of named selections and

Penstemon confertus.

Penstemon fruticosus 'Prairie Dusk.'

seed strains, I have my doubts about the alleged parentage of some—the seed strains that are commonly available ('Rondo,' 'Elfin Pink') are short (8–12 in./20–30 cm) and bloom in shades of pink, lilac and blue.

***P. fruticosus* (*P. scouleri*).** With violet-purple flowers, the sprawling woody-based 'Purple Haze' is a UBC selection, and royalties from the purchase of it go towards supporting UBC's Botanical Garden. To 12 in. (30 cm).

P. grandiflorus. With lavender blossoms, this one is grown commercially for cut flowers. To 36 in. (90 cm).

P. hirsutus. Violet flowers, to 24 in. (60 cm). A commonly available selection is the dwarf 'Pygmeaus.' To 8 in. (20 cm) and short-lived.

P. laevigatus ssp. digitalis. Pink or white flowers, one of the few hardy varieties to be successfully commercialized. 'Husker's Red,' the 1996 Plant of the Year, has striking purple-red foliage and mauve-tinged white flowers.

P. ovatus. Deep-blue to violet-blue flowers. This one has naturalized in the heavy clay soil in my garden, but shows no sign of moving out of the bed it is in. At nearly 36 in. (90 cm), it makes a good cut flower.

P. strictus. Violet-blue flowers. To 18 in. (45 cm).

Perovskia – **Russian Sage**

Prairie or Rockery | *Lamiaceae*

This may be in the mint family but does not like the cool, moist growing conditions typical of that; just the opposite. Easy to grow south of Quesnel in the hotter drier regions of the interior or the summer heat of the prairies, *Perovskia* can be short-lived in the north. It is not the winter cold that kills it, but rather the cold heavy soils and chilly wet spring and fall. It could be happier in a limestone rockery with a higher (more alkaline) pH as well as better drainage.

Perovskia atriplicifolia, Russian sage, designated Perennial Plant of the Year in 1995, has sprays of tiny lavender-blue flowers

Perovskia atriplicifolia. Photo Georg Ubelhart, Jelitto Perennial Seeds

over silver-grey foliage. The open branching plant habit is reminiscent of the tumbleweed also known as sage, hence the common name. It can grow to 5 ft. (150 cm), and is hardy to zone 4. Several dwarf cultivars, including 'Little Spires' and 'Blue Spires,' differ from the species in size, and possibly in hardiness—they may be a zone less hardy, losing vigour as well as height with the dwarfing.

Pest Control

Northern gardeners have a huge advantage over those down south in Lotus Land, in that there are far fewer kinds of pests in the north. Many of our pests are the large furry ones—bears, moose, deer, rodents, or even our own pets. One of the few bugs that thrive in our gardens is aphids.

Aphids

There are almost as many kinds of aphids as there are plants, and they are good at what they do. The first generations of aphids hatch out in the spring from overwintered eggs, then disperse to their new homes. Later generations don't waste time or energy growing wings—they just eat and multiply on the plants where the first generations ended up. We can take advantage of this lack of mobility when controlling them.

The first line of defence is hitting that early generation with an organic pesticidal soap spray. In my garden I have learned to spray the dogwood (*Cornus*), the high bush cranberry (*Viburnum*) and the shrubby *Prunus* species just as the leaf buds are getting ready to expand. The aphids are there, even if I can't see them at a quick glance, and there are no leaves for them to hide under. If I get this right, I will have little or no problem with aphids for the rest of the year on the shrubs or the perennials. This doesn't mean no aphids—just not enough to be a problem.

The old advice to knock the aphids off leaves with a stream of water is based on this fact that the generation under attack at that point is wingless. The aphids will probably get lost and not return to the plant, seeing as they have to walk. There are a lot of plants and leaves in my garden, so this doesn't work well for me. In a smaller garden or greenhouse this kind of warfare could be effective.

I have also been known to simply rip out any plants that persist in getting massacred by aphids (or anything else) year after year. If the plants, pests and predator bugs can't come to some compromise in the garden without my interference, then the problem gets removed. I do like to leave a small patch of lupines or valerian off to one side to act as an aphid magnet (greenhouse growers call this a trap crop). It is perfectly acceptable to have a few aphids, along with the other several hundred types of bugs in my garden, most of which I can't identify, as long as their damage isn't excessive and staring me in the face all the time.

I try to attract beneficial insects (see Beneficial Insect Attractors) and provide habitat for other things that eat bugs, including toads, frogs and salamanders, which I like, and snakes, which I don't but know they are good for the garden. Habitat includes a diversity of plants and shelter, including rock piles, stumps, old logs and a rich layer of gently decaying plant material on the surface of the soil. In addition, I set out water for birds, frogs and toads. My garden also includes a mud puddle for the butterflies to play in and derive minerals from. In a well-designed garden, this could be at the base of a bird bath, fed with a drip line. In mine it is a leaky hose. The butterflies do not judge.

My pests all have predators. Everything does. The hawks eat mice, so trees for them to hunt from and nest in are useful; the forest houses owls and bats who hunt their respective prey at night. Birds and bats eat flying insects, toads eat slug eggs, magpies eat baby toads, everything eats something else. I try not to interfere any more than I feel I have to because I really don't understand well enough all that happens here in my little corner of the world.

Having espoused this philosophy of "live and let live," I have to admit to an exception to the rule—slugs. I have a large collection of hostas that I am very fond of, so I use a fair amount of diatomaceous earth every year or so around the shade beds (and the vegetable beds). This and a layer of the coarse-grained, aged wood-chip mulch that I am so fond of seem to do the trick. The diatomaceous earth is relatively inexpensive when purchased in large bags (50 lbs/20 kg) from feed stores, or relatively more expensive in small cans from the garden centre if you just need a little.

Above: Every summer a new generation of baby toads overruns the garden, eating every slug and bug in their path.

Left: Spiders are effective predators of many small insects.

Photos Darwin Paton

Pets in the Garden

Pets also require a suitable habitat in the garden, including a supply of fresh water, of course, and a place to lie in the sun, along with another where there is shade. Depending on the breed and activity level, you may wish to supply them with an opportunity to dig, run and to play fetch or keep-away or tug. It is possible to integrate the better part of an agility course into a garden design if this is desirable or necessary.

Our pets (and, unfortunately, sometimes our neighbours' pets) need toilet facilities that don't infringe on human activities. Both cats and dogs, along with almost all domestic animals, can be trained to use a specific area or surface type, given a bit of patience on the part of the trainer. A wood-chip area behind the garage or compost bin might be the solution for your own pets. This has to be kept clean, obviously, or the animals will quit using it.

Even an Akita can learn to respect visible boundaries.

Clearly defined paths can guide traffic away from sensitive plants.

Phlomis – Jerusalem Sage, Sage Leaf Mullein

Meadow | *Lamiaceae*

The *Phlomis* are tall plants that add a strong statement to the garden with their height and bulk. Flowers grow in whorls at intervals around the stems, rather like a bee balm (*Monarda*) on steroids, appearing from early summer on. Hummingbirds and butterflies both gravitate to them.

Although the one common name suggests a relationship to the sage family, it is very remote; they aren't closely related to mullein (*Verbascum*) or from Jerusalem either.

Phlomis do best in moist well-drained soil, in full sun. Give them lots of room to grow at the back of a border or in the middle of a large mixed bed. They are great for adding height and screening while you wait for shrubs or small trees to grow in.

Varieties

***Phlomis russeliana* (*P. samia*).** Yellowish flowers grow at neatly spaced whorls up the stems. Up to 36 in. (90 cm) tall, with decorative seed stalks persisting after the flowers have faded. Zone 5.

P. tuberosa. Tall structural plant, with broad thick leaves and whorls of lavender flowers on spikes. Grows from edible

Phlomis tuberosa.

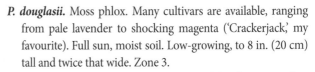

potato-like tubers, and can be easily transplanted as such in early spring. Clay tolerant. This grows to close to 6 ft. (180 cm) in my heavy clay soil in good years (those being the years we actually have more than four hot sunny days during the summer). Zone 3.

Phlox – Phlox

Meadow, Woodland or Rockery | *Polemoniaceae*

Phlox are a diverse group of plants, ranging from tall varieties suitable for the sunny border to ground-hugging ones that prefer a woodland environment. The lower-growing varieties tend to be spring blooming, while the taller, upright varieties wait for summer. They are all fairly clay-tolerant (the tall varieties live much longer and grow higher in deeper and more open soils), and do best in moist soils.

While there are hundreds of cultivars, and new ones all the time, some of the old garden varieties (those that no one knows the names of that get passed around at plant sales) may still be among the best.

VARIETIES

Phlox divaricata. Blue phlox. Lavender-blue flowers. Despite the common name, there is also a white variety, along with several named cultivars in various shades. Full sun, moist soil. Mounding habit, to 18 in. (45 cm). Zone 4.

P. douglasii. Moss phlox. Many cultivars are available, ranging from pale lavender to shocking magenta ('Crackerjack,' my favourite). Full sun, moist soil. Low-growing, to 8 in. (20 cm) tall and twice that wide. Zone 3.

P. maculata. Meadow phlox. A nice mid-height variety, less showy and more natural looking than many of the *P. paniculata* selections. Doesn't seem to be susceptible to powdery mildew; unfortunately also not fragrant. Full sun. Upright habit, to 24 in. (60 cm). Zone 4.

Above photo Darwin Paton

Phlox paniculata 'Black Jack.'

Top and above: *Phlox subulata.*

P. nana. Sante Fe phlox. Mounding habit, with several cultivars in differing shades of lilac. Seems to be fairly hardy in the north, despite the southwest name. To 8 in. (20 cm) tall and slightly wider. Zone 4.

P. paniculata. Garden phlox. This is the common and very popular tall garden phlox, available in a wide range of flower colours and plant sizes, not to mention those with variegated foliage. Some cultivars are quite prone to powdery mildew, but most of the newer ones, including the dwarf varieties of the vigorous 'Flame' series, are mildew resistant. The pure-white tall 'David' was the 2002 Perennial Plant of the Year and is mildew resistant. Heights range from 18 in. (45 cm) to 36 in. (90 cm). Zone 3.

P. × procumbens. Creeping phlox. This group includes a number of low-growing hybrids, with flowers usually in pink or purple pink; a variegated-leaf form is also available. Grows to 8 in. (20 cm) and spreads to twice that width. Zone 4.

P. sibirica* var. *borealis. Northern phlox. Low-growing Alaskan native with lavender or lilac flowers (very occasionally white). Full or partial sun, moist soil. 4 in. (10 cm) tall and several times that wide. Zone 2.

P. stolonifera. Creeping phlox. This is one of the few shade-tolerant phlox species, good in a Woodland Habitat. An excellent low-flowering groundcover around large hostas and astilbes or under shrubs, it travels (although not invasively) by means of stolons, as the name suggests. Flowers in shades of pink to magenta. The species was named Perennial Plant of the Year in 1990. To 8 in. (20 cm) by twice that width. Zone 3.

P. subulata. Moss phlox. Flowers in various shades of pink, many with contrasting eyes. Fine-textured foliage, low mounding habit to 10 in. (25 cm) and twice that wide. Zone 3.

Physostegia – Obedient Plant

Meadow | *Lamiaceae*

Physostegia are at home in moist meadows, and do well (sometimes too well) in most sunny garden locations, tolerating heavy clay soil but not thriving in it.

Physostegia virginiana is a native North American plant, first "discovered" on the eastern seaboard and named after the brave new land of Virginia. (There were a lot of *pensylvanica* and *virginiana* added to the taxonomic record in those days; later it was found that many of these plants had a very broad distribution, but once a plant is named and published it cannot easily be changed.) The species form can be a bit aggressive in good soil, but the named cultivars are all better behaved. Most bloom the first year from seed, and were named "obedient" plants because

Physostegia virginiana 'Crown of Snow.'

the stems stay in the position or shape in which they are placed, not because the plants don't spread.

There are several white varieties, pink ones and at least one white-flowered version with variegated foliage. All naturalize well and while not spectacular are useful in a mixed bed or border, especially with the blues of the taller *Campanula* species. They also make good cut flowers.

Platycodon – Balloon Flower

Meadow | *Campanulaceae*

The balloon flowers are related to and somewhat similar to the familiar bellflowers, except the flowers start out as nearly perfect little balloons of the common name before fully opening. *Platycodon grandiflorus* has showy blue or white flowers in summer, on 24-in. (60-cm) stems. A number of named cultivars and seed strains are available, mostly in different mid-tones of blue (light, mid, sky, lavender, etc.) and different heights, from 8–24 in. (20–60 cm). Semi-double forms of both white and blue are also occasionally available, although they aren't reliably double from seed and tend to revert back to singles (that are really as pretty as any flower needs to be anyway). They will usually bloom first year from seed.

Platycodon grandiflorus 'Fairy Snow.' Photo Georg Ubelhart, Jelitto Perennial Seeds

Balloon flowers make good cut flowers, and indeed there is a strain named 'Florist Blue' and 'Florist White' bred for just that purpose. The very dwarf forms fit well into rockeries, and all of them do well in any well-drained soil in full sun. They do not tolerate clay well. Hardy to zone 3.

Polemonium – Jacob's Ladder

Meadow | *Polemoniaceae*

Polemonium are tough and resilient plants, with ferny foliage that bounces right back from late-spring freezes or summer hailstorms. They prefer cool moist soil, and are somewhat clay tolerant (although the less common yellow- and apricot-flowering species seem happier in well-drained soil, and do well in Rockery Habitat conditions).

All of the Jacob's ladders have a tendency to self-seed, which I don't find a problem but some people do. They could be an issue in a tidy formal garden, I suppose, but here in my garden if there is an empty space and a Jacob's ladder wants to grow there, it is fine with me. The seedlings are shallow-rooted and easy to weed out if necessary. For those gardeners who can't tolerate the extra maintenance, which is fair, there is a sterile hybrid, 'Northern Lights,' that does not set seed.

The variegated foliage varieties, of which there seem to be new introductions every year, self-seed as well, but in a more self-restrained manner, and producing solid-green seedlings. They must be propagated vegetatively and are generally protected by copyright or plant protection laws against unlicensed propagation. Please respect this—no one is getting rich in the plant business and the minor amount of royalty fees we pay helps to support testing and introduction of new plants. In the case of plants introduced by the University of British Columbia, the royalties are essentially an endowment to support their—and our—Botanical Garden. (See *www.copf.org* for more information on plant licensing and protection issues.)

Polemonium pauciflorum.

VARIETIES

Polemonium × **'Northern Lights.'** Compact mound with sterile blue flowers—no self-seeding. Mounding habit, to 36 in. (90 cm) tall and wide. Zone 3.

P. boreale **'Heavenly Habit.'** Northern Jacob's ladder. Compact plants with solid-green foliage, covered with bright-blue flowers in late spring and early summer; very nice. Mounding, to 12 in. (30 cm) tall and wide. Zone 3.

P. caeruleum. The tallest of the species, and most likely to self-seed. A white form (which comes true from seed) is both pretty and fairly common. Upright plants to 36 in. (90 cm). Zone 2. The cultivar 'Brise d'Anjou' is shorter, at 24 in. (60 cm) and has striking green and cream variegated foliage and blue flowers. Zone 3. This was the first of the variegated Jacob's ladders to be released, and although it created quite a stir at the time, we have become blasé now, with numerous choices. 'Brise d'Anjou' plants have a tendency to revert back to solid green.

'Snow and Sapphires' was the next to be released, reaching 30 in. (75 cm) with crisp green and white foliage and blue flowers. So far, this does not show the same tendency to revert to solid green (which variegated cultivars of many plants—not just Jacob's ladder—do).

P. cashmerianum. Similar to the other upright, blue-flowered, green-leafed varieties, but halfway between in size, with a very nice tidy habit. To 24 in. (60 cm). Zone 3.

P. pauciflorum. Sulphur trumpets. Tubular yellow flowers with a hint of apricot. Graceful ferny grey-green foliage, very open habit, an unusual but worthwhile addition to the Rockery Habitat. Best planted where it can be appreciated close up. To 16 in. (40 cm). Zone 3.

P. pulcherrimum. Masses of sky-blue flowers in late spring, spreading by seed to form an airy groundcover. Very pretty native species for sun or light shade. To 8 in. (20 cm). Zone 3.

P. reptans **'Stairway to Heaven.'** Green and creamy-white foliage tinged with red, especially in cooler weather. Mounding habit and blue flowers. It doesn't seem to self-seed. This is my favourite of the variegated cultivars so far. To 12 in. (30 cm). Zone 3.

P. yezoense **'Purple Rain.'** Violet-blue flowers are accentuated by foliage that is purple red with the cool weather of spring, and turns green in summer. This is a seed strain and variable, but they are all pretty. To 18 in. (45 cm). Zone 3.

Polygonatum – Solomon's Seal

Meadow or Woodland | *Asparagaceae*

This European genus is very similar in appearance to our native "false" Solomon's seal, which many of us prefer to call wild Solomon's seal. There are a number of imported species on the market, and some confusion in the trade as to nomenclature and bloodlines, which hardly matters because they are all pretty and fairly similar to each other. If you have the moist, humus-rich soil in the filtered sun or partial shade they like, then any of them should do well. They are not happy if they dry out.

Solomon's seal are grown primarily for their foliage, although the flowers and berries are a nice touch. The flowers are white or whitish, hanging like tiny bells along the stems at the leaf axils, followed by bright-red berries.

These are slow to establish from seed, but not difficult: sow in place or in a nursery bed and wait two years. I didn't realize that it took two years at first, and so my garden is scattered with volunteer seedlings that were in the compost, from seed flats that were dumped after one year with no visible germination. It was a fairly inexpensive lesson, all things considered.

VARIETIES

Polygonatum biflorum (*P. communtatum*). Small greenish-white flowers; gracefully arching foliage to 5 ft. (150 cm).

P. × hybridum (*P. multiflorum × P. odoratum*). There are a number of quite hardy named cultivars of this parentage, some with double flowers, and several with variegated foliage. Those variations seem to occur fairly frequently with this cross, making it an interesting prospect to hybridize, if you have the time and space for such a project. They all tend to grow to 36 in. (90 cm).

P. multiflorum. White flowers in small clusters, to 24 in. (60 cm). Slightly less hardy (or less vigorous) than the others listed— probably zone 4.

P. odoratum (*P. officinale*). Japanese Solomon's seal. White flowers tipped with green, to 36 in. (90 cm), forming a large clump over time. Fragrant and one of the showiest. There is also a variegated leaf version of this one, which is slightly shorter.

Polygonatum odoratum 'Variegatum.' Photo Darwin Paton

Left to right: *Polygonum affine* 'Dimity,' *Polygonum bistorta*.

Polygonum – Fleece Flower, Silver Lace Vine, Snakeweed

Meadow or Woodland | *Polygonaceae*

Polygonum (previously *Persicaria* or *Bistorta*) have low-growing foliage topped with long-stemmed densely packed flower spikes, usually in white, pink or red. They do well in partial shade, filtered light or full sun as long as the soil is kept moist. While not particularly drought tolerant, the smaller species is more so than the larger.

Fleece flowers make good cut flowers, especially nice in combination with large daisy-type blooms or flat-topped umbels, to which their bottle-brush spikes provide a good contrast.

VARIETIES

Polygonum affine. Fleece flower. Pink or red bottle-brush flowers grow on short stems over low-growing semi-evergreen foliage. This is a good low groundcover, and will tolerate occasional foot and paw traffic. Several cultivars, virtually identical except for a difference in shade of pink or pinkish-red flower colour, are available. The foliage will suffer from wind-burn if not protected by snow cover in the winter. Grows to 8 in. (20 cm) and twice that in width. Zone 3.

P. aubertii (*Fallopia aubertii*). Silver lace vine. This is a woody vine, but mentioned here for the sake of keeping the family together. With green foliage and panicles of lacy white or pinkish-white flowers, it can grow 10–12 ft. (3–4 m) a season in warmer climates. At zone 4 silver lace vine is borderline

hardy in the north—and this is a good thing, preventing it from becoming the noxious weed it is in other places.

P. bistorta (*Persicaria bistorta*). Snakeweed. Pale-pink to rose-red bottle-brush flowers stand on long stems over low clumps of strap-like leaves. Named cultivars vary in flower colour. These are a larger version of *P. affine*, with the flower stalks reaching up to 24 in. (60 cm). Very tough plants, easy to grow and clay tolerant, they are clump-forming rather than spreading, and do well in partial shade or full sun with moist soil. Zone 3.

Potentilla nepalensis 'Miss Willmott.'

Potentilla – Cinquefoil

Meadow, Woodland, Forest Floor or Rockery | *Rosaceae*

Potentilla is best known for the ubiquitous yellow-flowering shrubs that are a cliché in northern commercial landscapes, however the genus also includes a number of herbaceous perennial species worthy of a place in any garden. The herbaceous species are useful groundcovers and low plants for the front of the sunny border, some more spreading than others. Most will grow almost anywhere, and there is at least one adapted to dry shade, that most difficult of conditions.

There are more than a dozen species of native cinquefoils, and at least one introduced noxious weed. This is a very diverse and adaptable genus. I am not going to even try to sort out the native species; for a good identification key and reference on these (and many other native plants), see *Plants of Northern British Columbia*, by MacKinnon, Pojar & Coupé.

Potentilla argyrophylla var. atrosanguinea.

VARIETIES

Potentilla argentea. Silver cinquefoil. Yellow flowers, silvery foliage to 16 in. (40 cm). Zone 3.

P. argyrophylla var. **atrosanguinea (P. atrosanguinea).** Cinquefoil. Flowers in red to orange red, 16 in. (40 cm). Zone 3.

P. aurea. Cinquefoil. Golden-yellow flowers. Very similar to *P. neumanniana*, but with more of an open habit and not quite as hardy, 6 in. (15 cm). Zone 4.

P. crantzii. Alpine cinquefoil. Yellow flowers, occasionally tinged red in centre. Very pretty foliage unfurls from silver green to green, 6 in. (15 cm). Zone 3.

P. nepalensis. Cinquefoil. Red flowers. Upright habit, 20 in. (50 cm). Zone 4.

P. neumanniana. Cinquefoil. Tidy compact plant with bright-yellow flowers over a long period, blooming from spring on. 'Nana' is slightly smaller than the species. One of the nicest of the low-growing perennial potentilla, 4 in. (10 cm). Zone 3, maybe zone 2.

P. recta. Cinquefoil. Invasive very similar to the native *P. gracilis*, but flowers are a softer pale yellow that makes me regret this is a weed. Upright habit to 18 in. (45 cm). Zone 3.

P. thurberi. Cinquefoil. Red, some cultivars with dark eyes. Mounding habit, 16 in. (40 cm). Zone 4.

P. tridentata (Sibbaldia tridentata). Cinquefoil. Small starry white flowers, with dark-green foliage that takes on red and orange shades in fall. Hardy circumpolar species, and a useful groundcover adaptable to sun or shade (including dry shade) and most soil types. To 6 in. (15 cm) and spreading slowly by rhizome. Zone 2.

Primula – Primrose, Oxslip, Cowslip

Woodland or Meadow | *Primulaceae*

Many *Primula* species are surprisingly hardy, with a larger number of different types than we might expect doing well in the north if given moist cool soils and partial sun. Sorting out the nomenclature and bloodlines turns out to be more difficult than growing them. Primroses have been bred and hybridized for centuries, and many named cultivars are of complex parentage. This is an excellent genus for collectors and would-be hybridizers to play with, as the possibilities are endless. Many are easy from seed.

As a bonus, many of the unnamed varieties available as flowering potted plants in late winter, in grocery stores and garden outlets, can be planted out in the garden later in the spring and will usually overwinter at least a year or two.

VARIETIES

Primula auricula. Primrose. Many of the plants commonly sold as these are actually hybrids, not that it matters. Grey-green foliage, bright-yellow flowers, 6 in. (15 cm). Zone 3.

P. chionantha. Primrose. Fragrant milky-white flowers, grey-green foliage, 16 in. (40 cm). Zone 3.

P. cortusoides. Primrose. Small bright-pink flowers, very early to bloom, 6 in. (15 cm). Zone 3.

P. denticulata. Drumstick primrose. A wide variety of cultivars are available, in white, pink, lavender and darker shades of magenta and purple, 20 in. (50 cm). Zone 3.

Primula chionantha.

P. japonica. Primrose. A number of cultivars are available, mostly pinks, some with darker eyes, 20 in. (50 cm). Zone 4.

***P.* × *pruhonicensis* (*P. polyantha*).** Polyantha primrose. These are complex hybrids of several hardy species. A wide range of colours and hardiness, 12 in. (30 cm). Zone 4.

P. pubescens. Auricola primrose. A wide variety of colours. Some selections are probably hardier than others, 8 in. (20 cm). Zone 4.

***P. rosea* 'Gigas.'** Bog primrose. Magenta-pink to purple flowers. Will overwinter in zone 3 planted in heavy clay but does not thrive; does better with decent drainage but will not tolerate drying out in summer, 8 in. (20 cm). Zone 4.

P. veris. Cowslip. The hardiest and most reliable of the *Primula*. Bright-yellow flowers in spring. An orange seed strain has recently become available, but does not seem to be as vigorous (in limited trials) and the flowers never quite open fully so don't live up to their promise. 8 in. (20 cm). Zone 3.

P. vialii. Pagoda primrose. Striking lavender and magenta-red flower spikes to 12 in. (30 cm). Zone 4.

P. vulgaris. Oxslip. The wild form is yellow. Cultivars and hybrids

Primula saxitilis. Photo Darwin Paton

are available in a wide range of colours; also available are many double and "hose-in-hose" types (that look like one flower tucked inside of another). To 8 in. (20 cm). Zone 4.

Perennial Maintenance

A healthy and diverse perennial garden should not need a lot of maintenance. The woody perennials such as thyme and lavender can benefit from an annual haircut in May or the first half of June, before they really get going but after growth has started, to remove last year's twiggy growth. The rest of the perennial garden should get only as much cleanup as you really feel impelled to give it. My garden gets one general cleanup in the spring, and that is mostly just a redistribution of dead plant material to even it out. In warmer coastal

gardens it is necessary to remove dead plant material in the fall, due to all the pests and diseases that grow along with the plants, but northern gardens are harder on pests as well as plants. With fewer problems comes less work. Not to mention longer winters in front of the fire reading gardening books.

Marvellous things happen when you let plants grow where and how they want to. *Echinacea purpurea* 'Ruby Star' and *Verbascum bombyciferum*.

In my garden, all the leaves, stems and debris on the plant or ground remain as they are over the winter, providing a layer of protection in the event the snow is light or late. This ground litter, which approximates the duff layer in the forest, also harbours a great many beneficial insects in hibernation over the winter, including everyone's favourite, the ladybug beetle.

The routine for my spring cleanup is becoming simpler and simpler every year, as my garden builds up populations of those specific micro-organisms and creepy-crawly things that break down the myriad specific cellulose materials. I lift handfuls of old leaves off the more sensitive plants, pull away brittle stems and any dead foliage that volunteers to let go, and prune the roses (hardy shrub roses that only need a tidying, not a formal pruning). I remove prickly debris from the garden for the benefit of the dogs, and throw away (in the garbage, not the compost) any remaining seed heads of plants that tend to self-seed in excess.

Once the initial cleanup is done, I start a month-long war with dandelions that have snuck into the empty places (fewer every year) between plants. I usually run out of energy by the time the dandelions finish blooming, and spend the rest of the summer wandering the garden contemplating things I should move or divide or do something about but never do. Part of the reason for the lack of follow-up is that I get distracted by the beauty of the forms and shapes and textures and movement around me, all the more attractive for knowing it isn't under my control, only in my care for this little while.

This sounds like sacrilege to any old-school gardener, and I still have trouble with it sometimes, but nonetheless it is working. By that I mean that more of the garden debris is breaking down in place faster every year, as the garden develops the ability to compost its own waste in place, just like the forest does. I use a soft garden rake to sweep the debris around and break it up a bit, and snap off dead stems and twigs, but that's about it. With many plants, such as irises, the old leaves fall off to the sides, forming a circle around themselves through which the new foliage grows. This suppresses weeds and acts as a natural mulch. Other plants, such as hostas, have leaves that simply turn to mush, basically disintegrating by spring. Some leave a handful of hard flower stalks that can just be pulled off by hand and thrown on the ground to rot. Those too become part of someone's habitat.

Deadheading, as you may have realized by now, isn't on my agenda except for a very few plants, and these are the thugs that I introduced in the first place: Maltese cross (*Lychnis chalcedonica*), perennial cornflower (*Centaurea montana*) and mullein (*Verbascum nigrum*). I never seem to have time to control and/or eliminate these plants properly by digging them out, so in the meantime am doing my best to keep them deadheaded in the hopes that this will at least slow their spread. It would work better if I had time to get every single one, but this is my reality and as good as it gets.

Above photo Darwin Paton

Above and top right: *Pulmonaria* x 'Highdown.'

Pulmonaria – Lungwort

Woodland or Meadow | *Boraginaceae*

Despite being cultivated for many years, *Pulmonaria* have never achieved fame or trendiness. There are a number of good old varieties still available, as well as many new ones. While some claim mildew resistance, most of mine are largely covered by deciduous shrubs by the time the foliage is mature, so if they get powdery mildew I don't know it.

This is, quite accidentally, also my solution to the problem of what to do with all those messy flower stems after they are finished and the new year's leaves start to grow. Many references suggest cutting off flower stems after the blooms are finished, so that the foliage can be appreciated for the rest of the season. This kind of pruning and deadheading just isn't on the agenda here, but it turns out that the shrubs that leaf out and grow over the lungworts cover up most of that mess, and the plants don't seem to mind—I suspect that this is much like their native habitat.

The species form of *Pulmonaria* themselves are seldom seen, although they can easily be grown from seed. Most cultivars on the market are of mixed parentage, taking to one linage or the other in size and colouring. Flowers are some shade of pink, blue or purple, usually starting out one colour and turning darker as they age. The foliage is spotted or overlaid with silver, and prone to powdery mildew. The plants are all mounding in habit, usually about twice as wide as they are tall.

Varieties

Pulmonaria **hybrids.** Most of the named cultivars available are of mixed parentage, and are hardy in the north, to zone 3, as far as they have been tested. (The cultivars all start looking the same after a while. No complete northern trials have been attempted.) The old favourite 'Roy Davidson' has light-blue flowers and long strappy foliage spotted with silver. 'Majeste' starts off with light-pink buds that open to dark blue; the leaves are almost solid silver. 'Highdown' has bright-blue flowers and lightly spotted foliage. 'Opal' has pale whitish-blue (opal-coloured, in fact) flowers.

P. angustifolia. Numerous cultivars and hybrids are available. 12 in. (30 cm). 'Blue Ensign' has large showy blue flowers. Zone 3.

P. longifolia. Numerous cultivars and hybrids, 24 in. (60 cm). 'Bertram Anderson' has been around for a while, for good reason. Bright-blue flowers and long dark-green leaves generously spotted in silver. Zone 4.

P. mollis (P. montana). Numerous cultivars and hybrids, 16 in. (40 cm). 'David Ward' is the most common in this group, with green leaves edged in cream, and salmon-pink flowers. Zone 3.

P. officinalis. Numerous cultivars and hybrids, 12 in. (30 cm). 'Sissinghurst' has white flowers and lightly spotted foliage. Zone 3.

P. saccharata. Many of the commonest named cultivars and hybrids are lumped together under this "species" heading. 12 in. (30 cm). 'Mrs. Moon' is reliable, pink buds opening to bright-blue flowers, and round silver spotted leaves. The leaves of 'Argentea' are almost solid silver, with red flowers fading to blue. Zone 3.

Pulsatilla – Pasque Flower

Meadow or Prairie | *Ranunculaceae*

Pulsatilla bloom in early spring, and do best in full sun and moist well-drained soil. They have characteristic hairy (silver-grey

Pulsatilla vulgaris. Photo Darwin Paton

fuzzy) flowers and buds, and form large clumps over time, but don't spread.

Varieties

Pulsatilla occidentalis (Anemone occidentalis). Pasque flower. White or off-white flowers, blooms in late spring. Grows to 20 in. (50 cm). Zone 4.

P. patens (Anemone patens). Prairie crocus. Blue-purple flowers in spring; there is also a yellow subspecies (*Pulsatilla patens* ssp. *trisecta* f. *flavescens*—which is a mouthful, admittedly), a beautiful sunny yellow on the inside and pinkish-red on the outside, which I am going to try now that I know about it. *P. patens* is native to the Canadian prairies, and prefers slightly more alkaline soils than the commonly available *P. vulgaris*. This is usually the species that prairie gardeners are referring to, rather than plants in the *Crocus* genus, when they talk about crocus. To 8 in. (20 cm). Zone 4.

P. vulgaris (Anemone pulsatilla). Pasque flower. A number of different named cultivars and seed strains exist. The wild form is usually some shade of blue-purple; seed strains in different shades and mixes of red, pink, lilac and white also exist. I can never make up my mind which I like the best—the deep red is glorious, until I see the pale lilac, but then there's the soft fuzzy palest pink. These are somewhat clay tolerant, but grow larger, healthier and happier in well-drained soil; to 12 in. (30 cm) tall. Zone 3.

Rabbit-resistant Plants

Many rabbit-resistant plants are also resistant to deer, for the same reason of taste or texture that the animals find unappealing. How rabbit or deer resistant a plant is depends, unfortunately, on how hungry the creature is. A hungry rabbit will gobble things he or she wouldn't in times of plenty, and varying populations have different acquired habits and tastes. It is possible to keep the local bunnies busy elsewhere with a lush planting of clover and grasses at the far side of the property, if you have enough room, but there is no guarantee they won't wander to the lettuce patch. A well-fenced yard with a dog works, most of the time. It is, however, surprising how many plants a dog will eat or dig up.

Astilbe – *Astilbe*
Bee balm, bergamot – *Monarda*
Catnip – *Nepeta*
Christmas rose – *Helleborus*
Daylily – *Hemerocallis*
Elephant's ear – *Bergenia*

False indigo – *Baptisia*
Foxglove – *Digitalis*
Garden sage – *Salvia*
Iris – *Iris*
Lamb's ear – *Stachys*
Lavender – *Lavandula*

Ornamental onion – *Allium*
Peony – *Paeonia*
Sage, silvermound – *Artemisia*
Speedwell – *Veronica*
Yarrow – *Achillea*

Clockwise from top left: Allium, daylilies and
Astilbe – rabbit-resistant plants.

Bottom left photo Jon Sullivan

Ratibida columnifera f. *pulcherimma*.
Photo Georg Ubelhart, Jelitto Perennial Seeds

Ratibida – Prairie Coneflower, Mexican Hat Flower

Prairie | *Compositae*

These coneflowers are valuable additions to any dry sunny border, with an unusual prominent central cone standing above the richly coloured rays, creating an effect reminiscent of a Mexican sombrero. *Ratibida* isn't as well known as some of the other genera in the coneflower family (*Echinacea*, *Rudbeckia*) and adds an extra element of interest to the garden because of its relative rarity. With unique structure and long-lasting beauty, they also make an excellent cut flower. Both species listed here are prairie natives that do best in deep soils and sunny locations, and are hardy to zone 3.

VARIETIES

Ratibida columnifera. The more compact of the two, reaching 28 in. (70 cm). Several subspecies and cultivars are available in rich tones of rusty red and golden yellow, including bi-colours. There is also a dwarf cultivar ('Red Midget'), with red-brown flowers tipped with yellow, and reaching only 18 in. (45 cm).

R. pinnata. Bright gold, and a good height for the back of the border or along a fence, sometimes reaching 48 in. (120 cm).

Rheum – Rhubarb

Meadow or Bog Garden | *Polygonaceae*

We are all so familiar with the common garden rhubarb that we seldom appreciate its ornamental qualities. The large deeply textured leaves, bright-red stems and towering flower stalks topped by creamy-white plumes are all quite striking. Unfortunately there are two problems with garden rhubarb as an ornamental plant. First, it falls apart, literally, in the heat of the summer, collapsing outwards as it goes dormant. Secondly, it self-seeds and makes every effort to take over the country. I have seen an old lane-side farmyard by Vanderhoof where the entire landscape seemed to consist of hundreds of rhubarb plants, all thriving but not leaving much room for anything else.

Fortunately there are several species of purely ornamental rhubarb selected for their looks alone. *Rheum tanguticum* is fairly common, *Rheum wittrockii* spectacular but less seldom seen. Preferring the same conditions as ordinary rhubarb—rich moist soil, with regular watering during the growing season and occasional fertilizer, they will look at home at the top edge of a bog garden or near a stream-side or pond. Mine are situated in a low spot in my Rain Garden, and are one reason for the occasional supplemental watering over the summer. Zone 3.

Rheum wittrockii.

Rodents in the Garden

When the cat who owns me was young and a mighty hunter I didn't have a lot of trouble with the assorted northern small rodents, including field mice, house mice and voles. (Thankfully, we don't have rats in northern BC.) I would lose a few plants here and there, especially when I had covered them with protective straw or blankets too early so as to unwittingly provide winter homes for the mice, or grouped the containerized plants together to make it easier for the voles to carve runways. Eventually I learned to wrap the trunks of young fruit trees and others that were favoured by the rodents, and to leave the perennials uncovered until the ground was frozen solid.

The voles, rather than the mice, do the most damage, to lawns as well as shrub and perennial borders. Voles have shorter tails, only half the length of their bodies, and stubby ears. They lack the Walt Disney characteristics of field mice, with their large ears and eyes, and long tails. Voles create runways in lawns under the snow (the perfect protective cover for them) and girdle young trees, also under cover of snow. Cats are not the only predators—in years with no snow cover, or late snow, rodent populations plummet as owls, foxes, coyotes and wild cats take their toll. Conversely, that heavy blanket of snow that is so good for plant survival also ensures an explosion of rodents the next year. Boom and bust is normal in the natural world.

Miss Josephine Lightfoot.

Apart from damaging lawns, voles harvest perennials at ground level or below, and in the case of grasses, or plants such as irises with grassy foliage, make little straw igloos (mouse houses) in the middle of clumps. I suppose this could be seen as a reason to clean up in fall rather than spring, but the voles have to live somewhere (and foxes and owls have to eat too; I am especially fond of the owls) and I don't really mind the rodents chomping at dead plant material I was planning to cut off in the spring anyway. I am striving for a low-maintenance balance of nature, not total control and order.

My worst rodent damage came the year I invested in expensive nursery blankets (insulated layers of breathable fabric almost an inch thick). The voles couldn't have been happier. Each bed was a smorgasbord protected from predators, and they thrived. The blankets now rot up in the attic of my shop, too expensive to throw away but with no use that I can think of. (A rose-growing friend back east had a comparable negative experience with a similar type of product meant for overwintering roses. These things sound good in theory, but you really have to wonder if they have ever been field-tested.)

I do mind when the voles get too enthusiastic about digging up bulbs, including—surprisingly—the ornamental onions, apparently a delicacy for rodents. I've solved this partly by scattering the plantings of onions throughout the garden instead of concentrating them in one area. I've also been planting them deeper, and between the two strategies the predation problem has pretty much come to an end. I find this particular battle ironic because interplanting onions with deer favourites can deter the deer, who don't like onions or their smell.

While I could spray against the rodents (see below), I can't be bothered. In peak rodent years I lose some plants, but nothing lives forever— and I always want to plant more things than I have room for anyway.

Trees and shrubs are quite another matter: they are expensive and I have more time and energy invested in them than perennials. Voles can girdle everything from roses to maples, and I am not prepared to be philosophical about this. The trees, fortunately, are relatively easy to protect with physical barriers bought or constructed. Most of the commercial barriers are plastic, either coil wraps or adjustable sleeves; it is important to remember to take them off before they strangle the tree.

Sometimes it is impossible to wrap the tree high enough—in heavy snow years and in snow belts, the cover can be so deep the voles can safely girdle major branches right up in the tree. These are the same branches that deer nibble and moose munch, so sprays would do double duty. Homemade wraps can be as simple as a fine-mesh chicken-wire or thin sheet metal—anything that surrounds the trunk(s) and keeps those sharp little teeth away from the bark, without itself doing damage to the trunk (which has to breathe).

The loose-fitting hard-plastic tree shields can be left on during the summer to protect against the worst of all urban predators, the lawn trimmer. The nylon line so efficient at cutting off grass and weeds will also slice into young tree trunks, quite effectively killing by cutting off circulation, even though the wound is narrow and barely visible. (This is one more reason to have a shrub or perennial bed around the base of a tree, rather than lawn right up to it.)

Low-growing trees and shrubs, especially the multi-stemmed ones, are best protected by one of the deterrent sprays on the market. These taste bad but do not poison anything, including the plants they are supposed to protect. Beware of homemade concoctions that can do more damage to the plants than the rodents they protect against. There are certified organic as well as non-organic sprays available, for those who prefer that choice. I have used whatever was locally available in any given year, and they all seem to work well if applied according to the directions. (They do not work at all while still in the bottle—it seems to be unfortunately common to buy the spray, think about applying it, and then never get around to it.)

Keeping long grass mowed (especially in orchards), encouraging snakes by building habitat for them in the form of rockeries or wood-piles, and an alert cat (belled to protect the birds) all help to keep the rodent population under control. As with much else in the garden, there is no one big solution—just a number of small ones which, if used in conjunction with some common sense (and a degree of fatalism), can deal well enough with any problem. Sometimes you just aren't meant to grow a certain crop, although that is a harsh reality for any gardener, seeing as by definition we are people who want to grow things that don't grow there in the first place.

Rodgersia – **Rodgersia**

Woodland | *Saxifragaceae*

Rodgersia aesculifolia is a striking plant grown for its foliage, which looks very much like that of a horse-chestnut tree, as is suggested by its epithet (the epithet is the second of the two Latin names). In this case, *Aesculus* is the genus name of the horse chestnut, and *aesculifolia* means, literally, "leaves like those of the horse chestnut."

Rodgersia aesculifolia.

With a mounding habit, *Rodgersia* does well in moist, rich soils, where the foliage can spread to 12 in. (30 cm) and the whole plant can reach 36 in. (90 cm) across and high if you include the spikes of whitish flowers it produces in summer. It has a great coarse texture to add contrast to a planting of fern, meadowsweet (*Filipendula*), or astilbe (*Astilbe*). Dark-red astilbe would bring out the red tones in the *Rodgersia* foliage. Hardy to zone 3, more vigorous in zone 4.

Rudbeckia – **Black-eyed Susan, Gloriosa Daisy, Outhouse Plant, Perennial Sunflower, Yellow Coneflower**

Meadow or Prairie | *Compositae*

Rudbeckia are North American prairie natives, sometimes found in their species form, sometimes as improved cultivars, with the newer introductions seemingly almost always bred in Germany. Mostly golden-yellow daisy-type flowers with dark centres, they are useful late-summer bloomers in dry sunny gardens, blending well with ornamental grasses and native asters. Most are tall, some are huge; and they all grow higher and do better in deep soils, although they will survive in clay.

VARIETIES

Rudbeckia fulgida. Coneflower. 'Goldsturm' (1999 Perennial Plant of the Year) is the best known of the cultivars, but there are also several other good selections from this species. To 32 in. (80 cm). Zone 3. A new dwarf version, 'Little Goldstar,' reaches 16 in. (40 cm). Zone 3 or 4.

R. hirta. Black-eyed Susan. Short-lived, usually grown as annuals, with overwintering a bonus in short-season cold-climate gardens. They will be longer lived on the prairies, which have longer, hotter summers. Most of the named cultivars have rich colours and large flowers with dark centres. 'Irish Eyes' has

Left to right: *Rudbeckia hirta* 'Irish Eyes,' *Rudbeckia hirta* 'Cherokee Sunset' and *Rudbeckia laciniata*.

a bright-green "eye." The dwarf varieties can be nice in large containers with ornamental grasses. To 32 in. (80 cm). Zone 4 or 5.

R. laciniata. Perennial sunflower, outhouse plant. Light-yellow to gold flowers, some forms are fully double; the tallest and heaviest blooms may need staking. Versions of this have been popular in northern gardens for a century or more. It became traditional to plant this towering specimen beside the outhouse as a discreet signpost for visitors. To 8 ft. (240 cm). Zone 3.

R. maxima. Perennial sunflower. Large yellow flowers, tall dark cone-shaped centres, blue-green foliage to 6 ft. (180 cm). Zone 4.

R. nitida. Perennial sunflower. Golden-yellow flowers with green centres. 'Herbstonne' is the most popular variety of this species—a gloriously over-sized plant at 6 ft. (180 cm). Zone 3.

R. occidentalis 'Green Wizard.' Perennial sunflower. Large brown centre cone, with barely any petals at all—this is an unusual flower, and interesting in fresh or dried flower arrangements, but not nearly as hardy as some of the other species. To 36 in. (90 cm). Zone 5 or 6.

R. subtomentosa. Sweet coneflower. Large showy flowers with dark centres; a pretty but short-lived perennial, to 24 in. (60 cm). Zone 4.

R. triloba. Brown-eyed Susan. Tall open plant with yellow-gold flowers with dark centres. A new densely branched cultivar called 'Prairie Glow' has flowers in shades fading from rust to orange, all blooming on one plant simultaneously, with yellow tips on the petals. This one has made my "must grow" list for next year. To 36 in. (90 cm). Zone 3.

Sagina – Irish Moss, Scotch Moss

Woodland | *Caryophyllaceae*

Sagina subulata are not mosses, and they are native from Iceland down to Spain, which leaves the common names a bit of a mystery. Pretty little ground-hugging plants, in bright green (Scotch) or the chartreuse green ('aurea,' of Irish), they sport tiny starry white flowers in summer. Hardy to zone 3.

Sagina does look like moss when draped over and around rocks and old stumps, if the plants can be persuaded to grow according to plan. They need a cool moist habitat to prevent the foliage from burning in full sun. Ideally suited to small landscapes, including troughs and shady rockeries, they grow only 1 in. (2.5 cm) tall. They can be propagated easily by dividing the clumps. I had plans to build a checkerboard of the two colours once upon a time—one more good idea that never happened. (It would have had small ceramic mushrooms for checker pieces.)

Sagina subulata.

Salt-tolerant Perennials

Most hardy salt-tolerant plants evolved near the ocean and are useful in landscapes near sidewalks and roads where salt is used in the winter. Others evolved in desert conditions, such as the great salt flats of Utah, but those plants are seldom hardy enough to make them useful in climates where snow and ice prevail half the year.

Salt applied in the vicinity of a plant impacts the plant's health in one of two ways, either through the salt spray on the foliage or by build-up in the soil. In areas that have cold winters but high rainfall in the spring and summer, salts leach out of the soil more rapidly; in times of drought or areas of low rainfall the build-up can be enough to render the soil sterile. A thorough and deep spring watering of flower beds and lawns that have been affected by winter salting of nearby sidewalks and driveways will help prevent salt from building up to toxic levels.

Along highways and freeways, the salt spray becomes a fine mist thrown out from under the wheels of high-speed traffic. The faster the traffic, the wider the salt-tolerant buffer zone must be.

Hemerocallis.

Salt tolerant (not necessarily salt proof!)

Alyssum – *Alyssum*	Delphinium, larkspur – *Delphinium*	Rock cress – *Arabis*
Aster – *Aster*	Foxglove – *Digitalis*	Sage – *Salvia*
Baby's breath – *Gypsophila*	Peony – *Paeonia*	Sea holly – *Eryngium*
Bellflower – *Campanula*	Phlox – *Phlox*	Sea thrift – *Armeria maritima*
Blue oat grass – *Helictotrichon*	Pinks, carnation – *Dianthus*	Snow-in-summer – *Cerastium*
Candytuft – *Iberis*	Reed grass (incl. 'Karl Foerster') –	Stonecrop – *Sedum*
Coral bells – *Heuchera*	*Calamagrostis*	Wormwood – *Artemisia*
Daylily – *Hemerocallis*	Ribbon grass – *Phalaris*	Yarrow – *Achillea*

Salvia – Garden Sage

Prairie or Herb Garden | *Lamiaceae*

The perennial *Salvia* species (there are many popular annuals as well) thrive in well-drained, slightly alkaline soil and full sun. The sages all bloom in the summer, attracting hummingbirds.

The nomenclature for the hardy perennial varieties is a bit confused due to both reclassifying and hybridizing—some cultivars can be found listed under several different species names in different references or catalogues. A lot of these varieties are also sold under either their German names (having been developed and released in that country) or the English translations. Regardless of any confusion over the names, they are all beautiful in bloom and—more importantly—beloved by hummingbirds.

Many of the *Salvia* varieties are borderline hardy in zone 3; they would rather be on the real prairies.

Varieties

Salvia nemorosa. Sage. Flowers usually violet purple, sometimes with contrasting reddish bracts. A number of cultivars are available, including some in rose and pink as well as shades of purple and violet. The sturdy subspecies *S. nemerosa* ssp. *tesquicola*, with brilliant large violet flowers, is in this group and worth looking for. Dwarf varieties reach 12 in. (30 cm), the taller ones 24 in. (60 cm). They are all hardy to zone 3.

S. officinalis. Common garden sage. A popular culinary herb that would be happier growing in a more Mediterranean climate, but will sometimes overwinter if planted in very well-drained soil in a hot dry location. Usually lavender-purple flowers, sometimes white. To 30 in. (75 cm). Zone 4 or 5.

S. officinalis ssp. *lavandulifolia* (*S. lavandulifolia*). Spanish sage. Blue-violet flowers over narrow and aromatic grey-green foliage to 16 in. (40 cm). Zone 5.

159

Salvia nemerosa 'East Friesland.'

Alaska. The small cylindrical summer blooms have a typical bottle-brush shape, either upright or arching. The foliage is fairly fine-textured, and the species vary in size and flower colour more than habit. The varieties listed are all hardy to zone 3.

VARIETIES

Sanguisorba canadensis (S. stipulata). Canada burnet. Creamy-white flowers. 6 ft. (180 cm).

S. menziesii. Alaska burnet. Long maroon-red flowers, dark blue-green leaves. Makes a good cut flower. Clay tolerant. 32 in. (80 cm).

S. officinalis. English burnet. Upright red flowers. 24 in. (60 cm).

S. tenuifolia. Burnet. Usually dark red, sometimes white; arched nodding flower heads. Good cut flower. 48 in. (120 cm).

Sanguisorba menziesii.

S. pratensis. Meadow sage. Flowers usually purple blue, sometimes white, pink or lavender. This is the hardiest of the genus, and a parent/ancestor of most hardy hybrids, 36 in. (90 cm). Zone 3.

S. sclarea. Clary sage. Showy rose-red bracts are prominent; broad foliage, 36 in. (90 cm). Biennial. Zone 4.

S. × superba. Garden sage. This hybrid is *S. nemerosa × S. × sylvestris* or *S. × sylvestris × S. villicaulis* depending on who you listen to. Several cultivars are available, with violet, purple or purple-blue flowers. To 36 in. (90 cm). Zone 4.

S. × sylvestris (S. nemerosa × S. pratensis). Garden sage. The widest range of colours appears in this group, including white, pink, almost true blue, violet and deep purple. 'May Night' was the 1997 Perennial Plant of the Year. Grows to 26 in. (65 cm). Zone 3.

Sanguisorba – Burnet

Meadow | *Rosaceae*

Sanguisorba are plants of moist meadow and woodland edge. They do best in damp soils, and some (as noted) are quite clay tolerant. Several of these are native to Western Canada and

Saponaria – Soapwort, Bouncing Bet

Meadow or Rockery | *Caryophyllaceae*

There are two distinct kinds of hardy *Saponaria*—the tall-growing *S. officinalis* and low-lying *S. ocymoides*. Both flower in summer in shades of pink and need well-drained moist soil to do well.

Saponaria officinalis is tougher than it looks, and naturalizes quite happily without being too aggressive. It grows to an airy and open 24 in. (60 cm), and is available in white and shades of pink, including a light-pink double-flowered form that comes about 50 percent true from seed (a mix of single and double flowers, all pretty). Hardy to zone 3.

A named cultivar of *Saponaria ocymoides* out of the English plant breeders, Blooms of Bressingham, is one of the best and

Left to right: *Saponaria officinalis* and *Saponaria ocymoides* 'Bressingham.'

most distinctly improved selections of anything I have ever seen. Most of the time "new and improved" is a bit of an advertising gimmick, but *Saponaria ocymoides* 'Bressingham' is in a class by itself. The species form of *S. ocymoides* is a loose mound, with a nice show of pretty flowers for a short period in early summer before the whole plant falls apart. 'Bressingham' is a tight mound absolutely covered with masses of flowers that last for half the summer; the plant maintains the tight shape even after the bloom is finished. It's quite an achievement, and well worth the higher price. To 8 in. (20 cm). Zone 3.

Saxifraga – Saxifrage

Woodland or Rockery | *Saxifragaceae*

Most *Saxifraga* do best in semi-shaded or filtered light conditions, although the succulent varieties are more sun tolerant. The several native species, being alpine, are happiest in rocky calcareous soils. Most hybrids of garden origin do well in moist but well-drained soil in filtered light or part shade.

There are many species beyond those listed here that could very well grow in northern gardens, given a match to appropriate soil types. Saxifrages are one of those genera that drive gardeners to addiction. There are whole books written about them, and they can provide endless amusement for those collecting and growing them in rockeries and troughs. It should be no surprise that there is a Saxifrage Society that proudly bills itself as "the only international organization dedicated to the best plants in the world; the genus Saxifraga and its relatives."

VARIETIES

Saxifraga aizoides. Yellow saxifrage. Yellow flowers rise above overlapping rosettes of fleshy leaves. Tolerant of full sun but best in light shade, 6 in. (15 cm). Zone 3.

S. × *arendsii.* Mossy saxifrage. White, pink or red flowers over low mounds of green mossy foliage. Prefers moist humus-rich soil; partial shade or filtered light. Grows to 8 in. (20 cm). Zone 3.

S. oppositifolia. Purple saxifrage. Dark-pink to purple flowers. Native across the north. Prefers moist humus-rich soil, light shade or filtered sun. To 4 in. (10 cm). Zone 2.

S. paniculata (S. aizoon). Encrusted saxifrage. White flowers over tight rosettes of "encrusted" grey-green foliage. Needs sharply drained alkaline soil in a trough or rockery. 8 in. (20 cm). Zone 2.

S. stolonifera. Saxifrage. White flowers, flecked with yellow or orange. Best in moist humus-rich soil in partial or full shade. 12 in. (30 cm). Zone 3.

Saxifraga paniculata.

161

Saxifraga x arendsii.

S. tricuspidata. Three-toothed saxifrage. Off-white flowers marked with dark-orange or maroon dots. Mat-forming native species, probably the most common of our dozen or so native saxifrages. 8 in. (20 cm). Zone 2.

S. × urbium. London pride. Delicate pale-pink flowers over leathery succulent-like foliage. Some cultivars have gold- or white-spotted foliage. Tolerant of poor dry soils, best in light or partial shade. 12 in. (30 cm). Zone 4.

Scabiosa – Pin Cushion Flower, Scabious

Meadow or Prairie | *Caprifoliaceae*

Scabiosa are supposed to be the perfect plant in sunny borders, doing best in well-drained soils but surviving in clay. They have a long flowering period from midsummer on, and make good cut flowers. Beneficial insects are attracted to them, and they seldom self-seed and do not spread by runner. 'Butterfly Blue' was Perennial Plant of the Year in 2000. I'm not sure why I find them boring; maybe it's the insipid lavender blues and wishy-washy lavender pinks. They're not vigorous enough to be fillers, and don't have the drama to take centre stage. They just sit there being fuzzy around the edges. I plan to try some new cultivars next year, in a flower bed that needs renovating, to see if I can get excited about them.

VARIETIES

Scabiosa caucasica. Pin cushion flower. Large flowers in shades of pink and lavender, occasionally white. The 'Fama' and 'Perfecta' series reach to about 20 in. (50 cm), others including 'Kompliment' are slightly larger. 24 in. (60 cm). Zone 3.

S. columbaria. Small scabious. Very similar to *S. caucasica*, with slightly smaller plants and flowers in the same shades

Scabiosa columbaria 'Pincushion Pink.' Photo Georg Ubelhart, Jelitto Perennial Seeds

of lavender blue or pink. 'Misty Butterflies' is the seed-grown version of the vegetatively propagated award-winning 'Butterfly Blue.' Grey-green foliage, 16 in. (40 cm). Zone 3.

S. lachnophylla (S. comosa var. lachnophylla). Pin cushion flower. This one is showing promise, although it is still new to my garden—violet-blue flowers over a long bloom period, upright habit and leathery fine-textured foliage to 24 in. (60 cm). Zone 4.

Scutellaria – Skullcap

Meadow or Woodland | *Lamiaceae*

Scutellaria are little-known summer-flowering plants with small snapdragon-like flowers, suitable for the sunny or lightly shaded border. They seem to be clay tolerant, but are more vigorous in well-drained soils. Apart from the two species described below, there are also half a dozen species rated zone 5 that are new in trials here but might do well in the right place: *S. alpina, S. altissima, S. incana, S. integrifolia, S. orientalis* and *S. pontica.*

VARIETIES

Scutellaria alpina. Alpine skullcap. Blue and white flowers. Named seed strains have a colour range from pale yellow

Scutellaria alpina.

('Moonbeam') to the full spectrum of white, yellow, rose, violet and dark blue ('Arcobaleno'). Grows to 8 in. (20 cm). Zone 3.

S. baicalensis. Baikal skullcap. From the shores of Lake Baikal in Siberia comes this densely branched little plant, with purple-blue flowers accented with a white throat. Very nice, growing to 12 in. (30 cm). Zone 3.

Sedum – Stonecrop

Rockery , also Prairie, Meadow, Woodland or Forest Floor
Crassulaceae

Sedum is a large and diverse group of useful plants, well suited to hot dry locations but also surprisingly adaptable to moist (but not water-logged) soil. They are relatively clay tolerant, and many of the low-growing varieties are shade tolerant.

Most are usually found in commerce only as the named cultivars listed. A few (noted as such) can be invasive. The zone-5 varieties listed here would probably do just fine in sheltered sunny locations with well-drained soil. Note: some species of *Sedum* have been reclassified into *Hylotelephium*.

VARIETIES

Sedum acre. Stonecrop. Yellow flowers, bright-green fine-textured foliage. This is one of the invasive ones—it pops up everywhere and is very hard to eradicate. Grows to 2 in. (5 cm) tall, infinite spread. Zone 3.

***S. album* 'Murale.'** Stonecrop. White flowers. To 4 in. (10 cm). Zone 3.

***S. brevifolium* 'Blue Spruce.'** Stonecrop. Yellow flowers. To 4 in. (10 cm). Zone 4.

S. kamschaticum. Russian stonecrop. Dark-green foliage, yellow flowers turning to dark-red seed heads. Excellent groundcover that grows to 6 in. (15 cm). Zone 2.

***S. k.* 'Variegatum.'** Variegated stonecrop. One of the few variegated stonecrops without a tendency to revert to solid green. Yellow flowers turning to dark-red seed heads. To 6 in. (15 cm). Zone 3.

***S. lanceolatum* (*Amerosedum lanceolatum*).** Stonecrop. Yellow flowers. Foliage sometimes powdery in appearance, grows to 4 in. (10 cm). Zone 4.

***S. oreganum* (*Breitungia oregano*).** Stonecrop. Yellow flowers. Grows to 2 in. (5 cm). Zone 4.

***S. reflexum* (*S. rupestre*).** Stonecrop. Yellow flowers. To 10 in. (25 cm). Zone 3.

Sedum sp. Photo Darwin Paton

Sedum album 'Murale.'

S. sexangulare. Six-sided stonecrop. Pink or red flowers. To 4 in. (10 cm). Zone 3.

S. spathulifolium. Stonecrop. Yellow flowers, blue-green powdery foliage. To 2 in. (5 cm). Zone 4.

S. spurium. Two-row stonecrop. Flowers are usually dark or purple red. Most of the low-growing dark-leaf forms ('Purple Carpet', 'Dragon's Blood', etc.) are of this parentage. Can spread—some gardeners consider this a problem, others don't. "The right plant in the right place" makes all the difference. To 6 in. (15 cm). Zone 3.

Sempervivum – Hen and Chicks

Rockery or Prairie | *Crassulaceae*

Excellent in troughs, living wreaths, rockeries and alpine beds, *Sempervivum* thrive in dry poor soils and hot sunny locations. There are hundreds of named cultivars for the aficionado. Foliage can be any tone of green, and shaded or tipped with red, purple, coral or amber; it can be tiny or broad, sharply pointed or widely triangular, tightly wedged into the rosette or loosely formed, as a single rosette or a cluster.

If you want to grow a variety of these intriguing plants, try starting your own from seed—you can have a hundred different plants for the cost of a seed packet. Flowers appear in mid to late summer on long phallic stalks, in pink or red.

Sempervivum flower stalk. Photo Darwin Paton

....

Self-seeding Perennials and Biennials

Iberis sempervirens.

All plants, unless sterile, live and flower for the single-minded purpose of setting seed. This isn't a problem. The trouble comes when they try to take over the whole garden. It is a rule of thumb, and as usual one with exceptions, that the biennials and short-lived perennials tend to self-seed more than longer-lived species. Live fast, die young. Those perennials that cause problems in the garden by self-seeding a bit too enthusiastically are the guppies of the plant world.

Many of these are wonderful candidates for the garden apart from this tendency, sometimes because of it (free plants!) and any of them could cause gardeners to argue whether or not that variety really does self-seed enough to be called a weed (or worse). The ones marked with an asterisk have hit noxious-weed status somewhere.

Baby's breath – *Gypsophila* – tall species *	Grasses, ornamental – almost all	Pansy – *Viola* – many
Bellflower – *Campanula* – some	Jacob's ladder – *Polemonium caeruleum*	Star thistle, knapweed, perennial
Catchfly – *Silene* – most	Maltese cross – *Lychnis chalcedonica*	cornflower, mountain bluet – *Centaurea*
Crane's bill – *Geranium* – some	Mullein – *Verbascum*	– most
Dame's rocket – *Hesperis matronalis*	Ornamental onion – *Allium* – some	

Slugs in the Garden

Slugs, like almost everything else, flourish if they have the right type of habitat and do less well if they don't. Like most pests, they can be kept under control but never entirely eliminated. To control them, take a three-pronged attack: eliminate habitat, use varieties of plants less attractive to slugs, and kill or discourage them by use of various physical means.

Habitat

As slugs prefer moist shady places to hide during the day, the first line of defence is in eliminating as many of these as possible. The traditional practice of laying boards over the soil in the vegetable garden to create a path also creates a slug haven on the underside. The wooden sides of raised beds likewise give the slugs a perfect place to live, tucked between the wood and soil. This would be a good argument for raised beds that were only raked-up soil, if the wood wasn't so convenient for keeping the gardens tidy and providing an edge to kneel or sit on.

Plant Choices

Slugs are, it turns out, sensitive creatures that do not like coarse surfaces. This includes rough or fuzzy plants such as mullein (*Verbascum*) and lamb's ear (*Stachys*). They also tend to avoid tough or leathery choices such as elephant's ear (*Bergenia*), aromatic plants (most herbs), and very fine-textured foliage such as meadowsweet (*Filipendula*). What they love are large and soft succulent leaves—think young delphinium (*Delphinium*) and most hostas (*Hosta*). When choosing hostas, select varieties with the thicker, heavier leaves sometimes advertised as "slug-proof," not quite the truth but close enough. And, to break up the buffet, interplant your hostas with other species less attractive.

Deterrence

Slug barriers and deterrents can be effective on various scales. Some people claim great success with strands of copper (from uncurled copper kitchen scrubbies) laid out on the ground around plants. In a small garden with a few vulnerable plants this might be all that is needed. Crushed eggshells and coarse wood ash are also effective, in that the slugs do not like the rough texture. Both of these also add nutrients to the soil.

In my perennial garden, I have used a lot of aged wood chip as mulch and this seems to have much the same effect. Granular rather than flaky, it remains loose on the surface, a texture slugs dislike. The surface is also dry most of the time, because the loose wood chips do not wick water up from below and I do not irrigate; this again makes it less attractive to slugs.

In shadier areas where there may be a lot of slug favourites growing and the moisture levels are higher, I resort to an annual application of diatomaceous earth. This is an organic material harvested from old sea beds, the graveyards of billions of microscopic silica-based prehistoric creatures. The silica is sharp, on a

Hosta 'Zager's Blue.'

microscopic level, and it slices at the soft tissue of the slugs. Diatomaceous earth is safe for people and pets (and it is used for worming livestock, being fatal to worms in cows' guts the same way it is to slugs in the garden). The use of a dust mask when spreading it is recommended.

I sprinkle it lightly throughout the susceptible areas like a fine dusting of snow, a bit heavier around the hostas, and also in the cabbage beds and other problem areas. I don't use any poison slug baits because of the animals, and I don't have the time or patience to mess around with beer traps.

Snow Load

Perennials are much better than woody plants at dealing with heavy winter snow load. Herbaceous perennials by definition are dormant during the winter, with only their roots alive beneath the ground. In fact, having more snow rather than less is a good thing, as snow is a nearly perfect insulator.

Deep snow protects perennials— and mice.

Heavy accumulations of snow in shady locations take longer to melt in the spring, but this doesn't appear to hurt the plants. Each winter the snow piles up to the windowsill or higher under my eaves from snow sliding off the metal roof. The soil underneath is screened rock (backfill against the foundation), providing good drainage. Every year, just one day after the snow has crept back, sickly yellow leaves of early daffodils, already emerged from the frozen soil, turn green and stand upright. The tulips bloom soon after and by the time the bulbs are done the dozen species of hardy geraniums (*Geranium*) are a good size, as are the old-fashioned bleeding hearts (*Lamprocapnos* that used to be *Dicentra*). By late fall the colours are muted gold and rust shades as the geraniums go dormant just before they are covered with snow again. It's a predictable cycle and reassuring.

If you are new to the north, it is important to note that snow load doesn't just fall from the sky—it comes from different sources and can have different effects. Snow off a metal roof flows off in an avalanche and is dense and deep. The plume from a snow blower is spread out lightly over a large area. Shovelled snow ends up in a bank close to the path, heavy and mounded. Snow pushed by a plow blade is the most destructive, as it collects rocks and gravel (rather like a glacier scraping along), and can do a lot of damage to lawns and flower beds. It's hard to remove the gravel from some types of flower beds; the easiest thing would be to create an alpine plant collection that would welcome the addition.

Soil Amendments

Soil amendments change the texture and structure of the soil as much or more than they affect the nutrient levels. In many ways they are more important to the health of the soil and hence the plants than just straight fertilizers are.

Soil amendments can be a wide variety of things. When we talk about soils we mean both the organic component derived from previously living organisms, and the mineral component originating from some form of rock broken down into gravel, sand, silt or clay. An organic soil is one with a relatively high percentage (usually greater than 5 percent) of peat or other previously living material in it. A sandy or gravel soil is a mineral soil.

The purpose of soil amendments such as manures (animal or green), compost, peat, coir, sand, gypsum, seaweed, guano, or anything else, is to modify the texture of the soil. The nutrient content cannot be overlooked, but is really secondary. Northern post-glacial soils tend to be very young (relatively speaking) and lacking organic matter. The organic component is what holds the moisture and nutrients in the soil, and—along with all the living things—creates that lovely spongy tilth that is rich healthy soil. The humic acids and micro-organisms that are in the organic component of the soil are what work to break the nutrients down into forms plants can absorb through their roots. (With apologies to the soil scientists—this is very much the short form of what really happens, and I can feel you wincing. This is close enough for our purposes, though. There are some excellent gardener-level soil books available for anyone who wants more—and more accurate—information.)

Our existing native soil (primarily sand, loam, silt and/or gravel) may be rich in all kinds of nutrients (those bits of the Periodic Table that go by N, P, K, Mg, B, etc.) but it is the organic component (of which our soils have very little) that bring it to life. This is why we work so hard at adding leaves and peat and compost and grass clippings and such to our flower and vegetable beds.

I can live with baled peat as a soil amendment because I know that the peat industry is working hard to make that business sustainable. I have more trouble with bagged compost and manure at the local garden centres, because these tend to have a high moisture content (they are bagged and sold by weight), the contents are not regulated, and they create an awful lot of plastic waste from the packaging. Next time you are by a big-box store in the spring, look at all those pallets of soil-improvement products out front. Think about the truckloads and truckloads of that stuff coming up the highway, and then all that stretch wrap and plastic going into the garbage. Is there not a local source of organic material?

In the long run, the old-fashioned methods of soil improvement are probably the best and safest. Green manure or plow-down crops have fallen out of favour in today's smaller gardens, but are still safe and effective. Plant a suitable crop (vetch, field peas, annual clover, buckwheat, annual rye, etc.) in any empty bed or between rows, and dig or till it under while it is still young and soft. Do not let it get old and stringy or go to seed. (See the West Coast Seeds catalogue or website for some great information on cover crops, including quantities to sow.)

Locally obtained manures (preferably well-aged) are good, although they will be full of weed seeds. Mushroom manure is great, but the Prince George mushroom grower has shut down, so there might not be a local source in this area anymore. Compost is good, from a local source if not your own backyard, but again may be full of weed seeds. Partly decayed leaves, wood chips, chopped straw—use anything you can get locally. Add it in moderate quantities to your soil or compost pile. It requires time and takes a variety of different materials to build up the life in your soil to the point that your garden can be truly sustainable.

Or—simply grow what is happy in your soil. Remember that fireweed started blooming on the hardened lava slopes of Mount St. Helens a couple of years after that volcano erupted. For every soil type there is a plant community that will thrive in it.

Everything I know about the soil/mulch/organic-matter cycle has been learned while sitting under a tree in an undisturbed area behind my shop, contemplating how well that little piece of the earth runs without any help or interference from me.

Soil-texture Types

Gardeners, both novice and experienced, are often frustrated by the phrase "moist well-drained soil." How, they ask, can it be both? It turns out it is not really a contradiction in terms. If you think of the soil as being a sponge it is easier to visualize.

A fine-textured sponge can hold a lot of moisture; even after being wrung out, it is still moist to the touch. This is similar to a soil that contains a lot of organic matter such as peat or compost. It holds a lot of moisture when saturated and the pores are full of water, and also can stay moist for a long time as it loses the water very slowly. This sponge is what plants that need "moist well-drained soil" are wishing for—lots of space to get their roots down into the soil, with plenty of moisture as well.

By contrast, a kitchen strainer or colander provides excellent drainage, but by design does not hold water—these match the definition of well-drained, even "perfectly drained," sandy or gravelly soils. Water can cling to the surface of the large particles for a little while, but is soon gone. There are, of course, plants well adapted to this type of soil, and these are the ones that rot when we plunk them into ordinary garden soil—they can't tolerate moisture around their roots or their crown.

In northern gardens, soils tend to be at one extreme or another, and even the well-drained fine-textured sandy loams—the best soils we have—contain very little organic matter (although they grow the greatest carrots in the world). They hold moisture better than the gravel, sand and other almost purely mineral soils leftover from river beds and moraines, but not as well as peat (bog) soils, which are pure sponge.

Well-drained soil. Photo Darwin Paton

At the other end of the extreme are the clay soils, consisting of microscopic platelets in layers that become glued together by moisture. This is what makes clay so hard to work (or easy to work, if you are a potter and not a gardener) and sticky. When that moisture is extracted by very persistent plants or evaporation, the flat particles stick together in the same way two wet pieces of glass will stick together—there is very little water between them but what is there refuses to let go. As the excess moisture is removed, the soil becomes one hard mass similar in texture to concrete. Although there is a great deal of water in the soil when it is wet, it is not easy for the plants to unglue it, and there are also no spaces for roots to easily gravitate down and through the soil. Gypsum works to make clay soil more open and porous by re-arranging the flat particles into small aggregated round lumps with pores between them that roots can penetrate (again, my apologies to the soil scientists out there, several of whom have made attempts to educate me on this topic).

Silene dioica.

Silene uniflora 'Compacta.'

Silene – Catchfly, Moss Campion

Meadow or Rockery | *Caryophyllaceae*

Silene tend to be short-lived and self-seeding, and are very pretty additions to the meadow garden or natural rockery. They do best in loose sandy or gravel soils of poor fertility; they can get leggy in well-fertilized ground. The alpine varieties are excellent in rockeries, blooming in summer, usually in shades of light pink.

VARIETIES

Silene acaulis. Moss campion. Pink or white flowers, low mat-forming mossy foliage. Native in alpine regions of northern BC. To 4 in. (10 cm). Zone 2.

S. hookeri. Pale-pink starry flowers, grey-green foliage, 4 in. (10 cm). Zone 4.

S. schafta. Catchfly. Bright-pink flowers, mat-forming foliage, 10 in. (25 cm). Zone 3.

***S. uniflora* 'Compacta.'** Cupped pale-pink flowers, flushed with rose. There is also a white-flowered form known as 'Icecups.' Grey-green foliage, 8 in. (20 cm). Zone 3.

Solidago – Goldenrod

Prairie or Meadow | *Compositae*

The native species of goldenrod, as well as the introduced garden cultivars, are useful summer bloomers tolerant of many types of soil, all preferring full sun. The tall ones make good cut flowers. They coordinate well with wild asters, and the fine-textured

Solidago canadensis 'Baby Gold.'

168

spikes play off the bright gold daisy shapes of many other late-summer bloomers.

Solidago canadensis. Goldenrod. The species is one of several native goldenrods in northern BC. Tall pyramidal panicles of golden-yellow flowers appear in mid to late summer. The whole plant tends to fall apart after blooming, especially in good garden soil; it has a tidier habit when growing in poor soil. To 4 ft. (120 cm). Zone 2.

S. canadensis **'Golden Baby,' 'Baby Gold,' or 'Goldkind.'** This was bred in Germany from North American seed, and then sent back to us better behaved—like a plant going off to finishing school. It is more compact and holds its shape well; a vast improvement in habit without losing the spirit of the parent plant. To 28 in. (70 cm). Zone 3.

S. nemoralis. Goldenrod. Tall and slightly pendulous spikes of gold. To 28 in. (70 cm). Zone 3.

Stachys – Lamb's Ears, Betony

Meadow or Rockery | *Lamiaceae*

The *Stachys* are best known for the silver-leaf species *S. byzantina*, usually grown for the soft fuzzy foliage beloved of children and young of heart. Although the tall fat spikes of pink flowers are attractive, they tend to fall over and smother nearby plants unless staked or propped up. Some old-fashioned gardeners (i.e., the kind who fondly remember the days of hired help) recommend keeping these tidy by cutting the flower spikes off early in summer. Supposedly it is only the ornamental foliage, not the "coarse" flower stalks, that we should admire. These are probably the same people who recommend cutting the flowering stems off the hostas for the same reason—they are "unsightly." I quite like

the tall stalks of white or lavender lily flowers that hostas produce, and try not to do any work I don't have to. I also like the whole plant of lamb's ear, not just the foliage—those fat fuzzy stalks have character. The flopping flower stems and large leaves of the lamb's ear have also taken care of any overly delicate small plants (including weeds) in the immediate neighbourhood, which is not counted as a bad thing in my garden.

Stachys byzantina **(S. lanata).** Lamb's ear. Lilac-pink flower spikes over exceptionally soft fuzzy silver-grey foliage. Grow to 36 in. (90 cm) when stalks don't fall over, 12 in. (30 cm) when they do. The cultivar 'Helen von Stein' is supposed to be flowerless, solving the problem, but mine had flowers—which would suggest an error in labelling or propagation, if not some failure in testing it after putting it into mass production (all of which happen, unfortunately). The cultivar 'Silky Fleece' is a dwarf with low mat-forming foliage and short spikes of purple-pink flowers. 'Silky Fleece' is only hardy to zone 4.

S. macrantha **(S. grandiflora).** Betony. Purple-red flowers, rugose (wrinkled) dark-green foliage similar to that of *Salvia*, 18 in. (45 cm). Zone 4.

S. officinalis **(S. monieri).** Alpine betony. Purple–red flowers, smooth-textured dark-green foliage, 18 in. (45 cm). Zone 3.

Foliage of *Stachys byzantina*.

Stachys macrantha 'Rosea.'

Tanacetum coccineum 'Robinson's Rose' (a mutant flower).

Tanacetum – Feverfew, Painted Daisy, Tansy

Meadow or Prairie | *Compositae*

Tanacetum includes some of the species previously lumped together under *Chrysanthemum*. They all prefer moist soil and full sun but are fairly adaptable; some are so much so that they can become nuisances with self-seeding. One is a noxious weed.

VARIETIES

Tanacetum coccineum. Painted daisy. Long-stemmed yellow-centred daisies in bright shades of pink, red and magenta, occasionally white. The 'Robinson' strain is available in individual colours or a mix. 'Duro' is a long-stemmed bright-magenta colour bred for the cut-flower trade. They are all good vase flowers; and cutting them at their prime solves the problem of the plants falling apart in the garden after blooming. They grow to 36 in. (90 cm). Zone 3.

T. parthenium. Feverfew. Masses of small white flowers over vigorous mounding foliage. Cultivars with gold foliage are attractive in filtered light or part-day shade, but the foliage burns in hot sunny locations. Good cut flower. To 36 in. (90 cm). Zone 4.

T. vulgare. Tansy. Warning!—this is officially a noxious weed; please kill it on sight, or at least report your sighting to *www. nwipc.org*. It's hard to miss with clusters of small mustard-yellow flowers and ferny green foliage with a distinct aroma, especially when crushed. (It has been used as a medicinal, but some people have an allergic reaction to skin contact with the foliage.) Grows to 36 in. (90 cm) or more. If you want this for herbal purposes, there are many badly infested areas that you could harvest from, especially along transportation corridors and waterways in and around Prince George.

Thalictrum – Meadowrue

Meadow | *Ranunculaceae*

The *Thalictrum* are well suited to cold-climate gardens, species of them originating in moist meadows throughout the northern hemisphere. They thrive in sun and light shade, and in well-drained soils or heavy clay. Meadowrue blooms from spring to midsummer, and some species develop persistent ornamental seed heads that remain attractive in the garden right into winter. The flowers can be cut for fresh arrangements, and the seed heads are splendid as dried flowers. They do self-seed, but not annoyingly so. Most of the species are quite tall, but it is a light airy height, and perfect for mixing into meadow gardens or adding to the edge of woodlands along with ferns and hostas.

Thalictrum aquilegiifolium.

Thalictrum flavum var. *glaucum.*

VARIETIES

Thalictrum aquilegiifolium. Meadowrue. Mauve or white flowers, turning into the most attractive and lasting seed heads of all the species, maturing to gold and purple-russet tones. These self-seed a bit, more often in the white form than the mauve, which is a bonus. The foliage is very similar to that of the columbines (*Aquilegia*) hence the name. Easy and beautiful. 48 in. (120 cm). Zone 3.

T. delavayi. Meadowrue. Small bright-lilac or white flowers, with very dark purple-black stems. 36 in. (90 cm). Zone 4.

T. flavum* var. *glaucum. Meadowrue. Sulphur-yellow flowers, glaucous grey-green foliage to 5 ft. (150 cm). Zone 3.

T. rochebrunnianum. Meadowrue. Clusters of bright-lilac flowers with contrasting yellow stamens, on tall dark arching stems. Tall but airy, so can be at the front of the border where the flowers can be appreciated. The showiest of the hardy species' to 5 ft. (150 cm). Zone 3.

Thermopsis – False Lupine

Meadow | *Leguminosae*

The *Thermopsis* are related to true lupines, as well as the rest of the pea family, which means the plants fix nitrogen in the soil on their roots. This adaptation allows them to do well in poor soils, and although they prefer deep well-drained ground they are also somewhat clay tolerant. Blooming in mid spring or early summer, they self-seed but not aggressively.

VARIETIES

Thermopsis chinensis. Loose spikes of bright-yellow flowers take up one-third of the height of the plant, creating a mass of colour in spring. Does not spread. Grows to 24 in. (60 cm). Zone 3.

T. montana (T. rhombifolia). Bright-yellow flowers in spring, silky-haired foliage. It has a tendency to spread by runner, although is more of a weaver than a weed. Grows to 16 in. (40 cm). Zone 3.

Thymus – Thyme

Rockery or Herb Garden | *Lamiaceae*

Thyme thrives in hot dry locations, especially in sandy soils and rockeries in neutral to alkaline soil. The low-growing varieties of this popular herb and ornamental are perfect fillers between pavers and stepping stones, as the plants are very low-growing and will tolerate some foot traffic. The taller varieties have woody bases; they could be trimmed into a miniature hedge for a knot garden or simply left to grow into their natural mounding shape. The aromatic foliage is popular in the kitchen and for potpourri.

Years of hybridizing and selecting for specific sizes and flavours have created a nomenclature tangle, the unravelling of which is beyond the scope of this book. Suffice to say there are a lot of varieties, and (another Rayment's Rule of Thumb) the fancier they are in terms of variegation or alleged flavour or any

Thermopsis montana. Photo Darwin Paton

Above: *Thymus praecox* 'Nutmeg.'

other characteristic, the less hardy they are likely to be. On the other hand, none of them would be a huge investment to experiment with, and most are quite happy overwintering in a clay pot on a windowsill.

VARIETIES

Thymus × citriodorus. Lemon thyme. Lavender-pink flowers, solid-green foliage. Solid-gold leaf and both gold/green and white/green variegated leaf forms exist, but don't seem to be quite as hardy as the solid green. To 10 in. (25 cm). Zone 4.

***T. doerfleri* 'Bressingham.'** Creeping thyme. Dark pink-lavender flowers, grey-green foliage. This may be a hybrid, as it is considerably hardier than the species form. It is one of my favourites here, growing to 4 in. (10 cm). Zone 3.

***T. praecox* (*T. polytrichus*).** Creeping thyme. Flowers in various shades of lavender to purple. Some marketed under this name are *T. serpyllum* var. *coccineus* cultivars or hybrids. I'm not quite sure where the cultivar 'Nutmeg' fits into the family tree, but it is a favourite, hardy and always looking good. Grows to 4 in. (10 cm). Zone 3.

***T. praecox* ssp. *ligusticus* (*T. pseudolanuginosus*).** Woolly thyme. Mat-forming fuzzy grey-green foliage, covered with tiny mauve flowers in late spring. This seems to be rather fussy about drainage; excellent between paving stones set in sand, or as a filler in a hot dry rockery. To 2 in. (5 cm). Zone 4.

T. serpyllum. Mother-of-thyme. Variable species and/or group, with flowers from pale pink to dark purple, and foliage from glossy to fuzzy, dark green, variegated or gold. To 10 in. (25 cm). Zone 3.

T. vulgaris. Common thyme. Commonly grown as a culinary herb. To 12 in. (30 cm). Zone 4.

Tiarella cordifolia 'Rosalie.'

Tiarella – Foamflower

Woodland | *Saxifragaceae*

Tiarella are North American native wildflowers, adapted to woodland conditions of moist shade and humus-rich soil. Quite a bit of breeding work has been done with them lately, leading to many named introductions of mixed or unknown parentage and hardiness. They are all beautiful, and slightly more graceful in appearance than the closely related *Heuchera* (with which they can be crossed, creating *Heucherella*).

VARIETIES

Tiarella cordifolia. Foamflower. Native to eastern North America. Sprays of tiny white flowers. The cultivar 'Rosalie' has pale-pink blossoms and dark markings on the leaves. This is one of the oldest named cultivars and still the best and hardiest. To 12 in. (30 cm). Zone 3.

Thymus praecox. Photo Darwin Paton

T. trifoliata. Three-leaved foamflower. Western native. A delicate beauty that doesn't really need to be improved upon. White flowers to 16 in. (40 cm). Zone 3.

T. wherryi. Foamflower. Eastern native with the showiest flowers of all, and for this reason used as a parent of many of the new named introductions. To 16 in. (40 cm). Zone 5.

Tradescantia virginiana 'Osprey.'

Tradescantia – Spiderwort

Meadow or Woodland | *Commelinaceae*

Tradescantia is named after a British plant explorer (or actually two of them: John Tradescant the elder and John Tradescant the younger, a father-and-son act) who botanized four centuries ago in the New World. One of their plant discoveries in Virginia was named after them—*Tradescantia virginiana.*

Spiderwort plants are grassy clumps topped by exquisitely engineered flowers in a range of cool shades from pure white to pale blues and lilacs, to deep violet purples and carmine reds. Growing a mixed batch from seed can be exhilarating, as all the colours are clear and beautiful. The only trouble for me is that mine all decided to up and die one winter for no particular reason, after going along beautifully for several years. (I lost more than 20 different cultivars and seed-grown specimens one winter—and this left a hole in my heart as well as in my garden.) I wondered if it was something to do with the heavy wet soil combined with a nasty wet and cold fall and then spring: but even gardeners with better-drained soil lost their spiderworts that year.

Tradescantia virginiana (also known as *Tradescantia × andersonia*) form a large clump over a few years, growing to 24 in. (60 cm) and blooming from early summer on. Hardy to zone 4 (until they die.

Trollius – Globeflower

Meadow | *Ranunculaceae*

Trollius are related to buttercups, but with larger and far showier flowers. Growing best in moist soils, full sun or filtered light, they will re-bloom some years if cut back hard and fertilized after their initial spring bloom. The species are much hybridized, resulting in some confusion over nomenclature: the classification tends to groups rather than species, and some cultivars show up in different "species" in references or catalogues. It may not really matter in the long run, as they aren't all that different from each other in hardiness.

Some have cup-shaped flowers with five petals and a prominent cluster of stamens, others double with ten petals and stamens barely showing, still others globe-shaped with stamens hidden from view. I don't have a preference as to flower shape, but admit to being fonder of the dark-orange varieties than the bright-yellow ones—there are many flowers that bloom in bright yellow in the spring and early-summer garden (many of them dandelions) and very few in bright orange. I am also enamoured with the pale buttery yellow of 'Cheddar' and the light-yellow 'Cressida.' 'Alabaster,' even paler, is on my wish list.

Trollius 'Orange Queen.'

Trollius 'Cressida.'

VARIETIES

Trollius altaicus. Siberian globeflower. Bright-orange cupped double blooms with dark stamens showing in the centre. Very nice. To 32 in. (80 cm). Zone 3.

T. chinensis. Chinese globeflower. Cup-shaped golden-yellow flowers with exposed stamens. 'Golden Queen' is the most common in this group, 36 in. (90 cm). Zone 3.

T. × cultorum. Hybrid globeflower. From palest yellow to dark orange, this group of hybrids includes both cup- and globe-shaped forms, to 36 in. (90 cm). A relatively new cultivar, 'New Moon,' pale yellow and semi-double with dark-gold stamens—almost like a peony flower—is on my wish list. The very nice 'Cheddar' and slightly creamier 'Cressida' both do well here. Zone 3.

T. europaeus. European globeflower. Globe-shaped lemon-yellow flowers to 20 in. (50 cm). Zone 3.

T. pumilus. Dwarf globeflower. A compact plant with cup-shaped golden-yellow flowers, to 8 in. (20 cm). Zone 3.

Typha – Cattail, Rush

Pond or Water Garden | *Typhaceae*

The cattail is a familiar resident of lakes, ponds, lagoons and even ditches across the northern hemisphere, and many water-gardeners add this seemingly essential vertical element to their backyard ponds. It will introduce itself, sooner or later, if the pond is big enough, as it is not shy. An essential part of the ecology of any wetland, cattail provides food and habitat to a myriad of creatures from mammals and birds to microscopic life forms. This is

There are many ways of creating vertical accents in small ponds.

a good reason not to transplant it from the wild, as there may well be hitchhikers.

The native species, *Typha latifolia*, reaching 8 ft. (240 cm), is sometimes found for sale as nursery-grown plants at pond-supply outlets and mail-order dealers, and although buying such a common plant may seem silly, it is a small price to pay for keeping your pond clean and fish healthy. The fluffy seed heads can also be collected and scattered at pond edge with a reasonable degree of success, although with no control over exactly where it grows.

For a smaller pond, there are several non-native choices, but the compact (24 in./60 cm) *T. minima* is probably only hardy to zone 4 or 5. Hardy to zone 3 and growing to around 5 ft. (150 cm), *T. laxmannii* looks like a reasonable alternative but is extremely invasive and can quickly take over a small pond. It may even have designs on the rest of the neighbourhood. If you want a mid-sized vertical accent in your pond, try one of the non-invasive water irises, or one of the sweetflag (*Acorus*) or rush (*Scirpus*) species. Or maybe a metal sculpture of a heron.

Uvularia – **Merry Bells**

Woodland | *Asparagaceae*

Uvularia grandiflora is an eastern North American native looking somewhat like a smaller version of the western fairy bells (*Disporum*) but with yellow flowers in summer. Thriving in moist humus-rich soils, and spreading slowly by rhizome, it makes a pleasant addition to the beauty and diversity of the woodland garden. While it can grow to 30 in. (75 cm) in its native habitat, it is usually half that here. Hardy to zone 3.

Valeriana – **Valerian**

Meadow | *Caprifoliaceae*

The hardy species of *Valeriana* will grow well in most soils, preferring moist, well-drained soil in full sun, but also being somewhat clay tolerant and even a little bit shade tolerant.

Varieties

Valeriana montana. Mountain valerian. Rounded clusters of mid-pink blooms in early summer, over compact clumps of dark-green foliage. To 12 in. (30 cm). Zone 3.

V. officinalis. Valerian. Sprays of small white flowers in summer. The plant is an aphid magnet in my garden, although some other northern gardeners report no problems. I keep a few plants in the back corner; the aphids have to be somewhere and this gives them a place where they don't annoy me. (No aphids = no ladybugs. If I want a permanent population of predator insects—and I do—I have to make sure they have a buffet available.) To 6 ft. (180 cm), although my aphid-stressed specimens growing in clay top out at 4 ft. (120 cm). Zone 3.

Verbascum – **Mullein**

Meadow | *Scrophulariaceae*

Officially *Verbascum* includes some biennial species as well as tender and hardy perennials. In my garden the categories are non-hardy perennials and self-seeding nuisances. Fortunately they make good cut flowers and snipping enough of them prevents the tendency to self-seed from being too much of a problem. Clay and drought tolerant, *Verbascum* will grow almost anywhere but is happiest in deep, moist well-drained soils.

Varieties

Verbascum × '**Jackie**,' '**Pink Petticoats**,' '**Caribbean Crush**.' Mullein. There are a number of "new" cultivars available in luscious colours that seem to be complex hybrids (no parentage is given). None of these tested to date have proven to be hardy in zone 3, or even tried to overwinter in my garden—a pity. Probably zone 5.

V. bombyciferum. Silver mullein. With woolly silver-grey leaves

Uvularia grandiflora. Photo Darwin Paton

Valeriana montana.

Verbascum chaixii. Photo Darwin Paton

175

and long stems studded with yellow flowers, this biennial, if you are lucky, will self-seed so that a small population maintains itself. While its huge leaves may smother everything around it, they are also eminently soft and touchable, and the flower stalks are conversation pieces. Zone 3.

V. chaixii. Mullein. Yellow or white flowers with contrasting violet-purple stamens. Stocky compact plants with dark-green foliage. 'Sixteen Candles' is a very nice full-flowered yellow form; 'Wedding Candles' is white. To 36 in. (90 cm). Zone 4.

V. nigrum. Mullein. Yellow flowers (occasionally white) with violet-purple stamens. Mid-green felted leaves. This one self-seeds quite badly, and although it is a striking plant in late summer, I now have about a thousand striking plants. To 5 ft. (150 cm). Zone 3.

V. phoeniceum. Roman candles. Flowers in shades of dusty pink to dark rose, and lilac to dark purple, with the occasional white. There are several named varieties available in one colour or another. This blooms the first year from seed, very fortunate as it isn't always reliably hardy in zone 3. To 36 in. (90 cm). Zone 4.

from seed, and self-seed non-aggressively to maintain a presence in suitable conditions.

VARIETIES

Verbena hastata. This is the taller of the two, growing to 48 in. (120 cm) and available in a number of cultivars with dark-blue, pink or white flower spikes. The wild type has purple-blue flowers. Zone 3.

V. stricta. Lavender-purple flowers and grey-green foliage; grows to just 24 in. (60 cm). Zone 3.

Vernonia fasiculata.

Verbena hastata.

Verbena – **Vervain, Hoary Vervain, Verbena**

Prairie | *Verbenaceae*

Verbena are best known as those popular annuals used in containers and hanging baskets, but there are at least two hardy perennials in the genus. They are both native to prairie regions, and are tough drought-tolerant plants for the sunny garden. Good cutting flowers, *Verbena* are also useful for attracting pollinating insects. Not long-lived, they nevertheless bloom in the first year

Vernonia – **Ironweed**

Meadow | *Compositae*

William Kennedy's great book (*Ironweed*) inspired me to grow this plant, which turns out to be very tough and hardy. An interesting if not spectacular addition to the late-summer garden, its dark flower heads are a nice contrast to the lavender blues and golden yellows prevalent at that time.

Vernonia are at home in wet meadows, and do their best in full sun and heavy—even clay—soils, achieving the best height and largest flower spikes in moist soils, yet tolerating drier conditions. They are excellent for attracting and feeding pollinating insects, and also make good cut flowers.

VARIETIES

***Vernonia arkansana* (*V. crinita*).** Ironweed. With purple-violet flowers, this late bloomer (possibly too late for north-central BC) does better with more heat and a longer growing season as found around Williams Lake, Quesnel and even Vanderhoof. To 6 ft. (180 cm). Zone 3.

V. fasciculata. Ironweed. Flat reddish-purple umbels. To 36 in. (90 cm). Zone 3.

V. noveboracensis. Ironweed. Purple umbels. To 6 ft. (180 cm). Zone 4.

Veronica peduncularis 'Georgia Blue.' Photo Darwin Paton

Veronica – Speedwell

Meadow | *Plantaginaceae*

The genus of *Veronica* includes a wide variety of useful plants, ranging from groundcovers to tall border specimens. Speedwells thrive in moist soils and full to part sun, generally blooming from midsummer on, and include an abundance of low-growing species with slightly varying textures and flower colours. Most if not all would do well in a rockery, a fine place for a collection.

Beware of a number of confusions: *Veronicastrum* is sometimes lumped into this genus but is actually distinct. Quite a few species of *Veronica* have been reclassified into the *Pseudolysimachion* genus, a change not likely to be reflected in literature or plant catalogues in our time (but noted below). The genus *Veronica* also used to contain the New Zealand sub-shrubs *Hebe*, but they were calved off some years ago. None of the *Hebe* are hardy (most are zone 8 or 9), including one alleged variety circulating in the Prince George area under the name of *Hebe* 'Karl Teschner' (a.k.a. *Hebe* × *youngii*), having been grown from seed and traded around the garden-club circuit for years now. In the end, it turns out to not be the miracle it would have been if it really was a zone-3 *Hebe*. While indeed beautiful, it is a *Veronica* and not a *Hebe*. This was verified courtesy of a nice gentleman who is the Secretary of the Hebe Society in Britain (and who knew there was even such a society?!). The leaf structure and the way the foliage attaches to the stems is distinctly different. (We still don't know which *Veronica*, of course, and probably never will. Which is fine.)

VARIETIES

***Veronica* × 'Crystal River' ('Reavis').** Lavender-blue flowers, mat-forming foliage to 4 in. (10 cm). Zone 3.

***V.* × 'Sunny Border Blue.'** Speedwell. Bright blue-purple flowers, vigorous plant with dark-green foliage. The 1993 Perennial Plant of the Year. To 32 in. (80 cm). Zone 3.

Veronica spicata 'Giles von Hees.'

177

V. allionii. Alpine speedwell. Purple-blue flowers, evergreen foliage, 6 in. (15 cm). Zone 2.

V. filiformis. Bird's-eye speedwell. Bright-blue flowers, feathery foliage, grows well in dry conditions, 6 in. (15 cm). Zone 4.

V. fruticulosa. Pink speedwell. Pink flowers, mat-forming foliage, 8 in. (20 cm). Zone 3.

V. gentianoides. Speedwell. Spikes of light sky-blue flowers in spring, 24 in. (60 cm). Zone 3.

V. incana (*V. spicata incana, Pseudolysimachion incanum*). Speedwell. Compact spikes of dark-violet flowers, silver-grey foliage. Needs good drainage, prefers slightly alkaline soil, 8 in. (20 cm). Zone 4.

V. liwanensis. Turkish veronica. Mid-blue flowers, dark-green leaves, mat-forming, 2 in. (5 cm). Zone 3.

V. montana 'Corinne Tremaine.' Variegated speedwell. Unusual specimen with white-trimmed foliage, 4 in. (10 cm). Zone 3.

V. officinalis. Creeping speedwell. Light blue, mat-forming, 6 in. (15 cm). Zone 3.

V. peduncularis 'Georgia Blue.' Speedwell. Blue flowers with white eye, 6 in. (15 cm). Zone 4.

V. pinnata (*Pseudolysimachion pinnatum*). Speedwell. Mound-forming, light-blue flowers, feathery-green foliage, 12 in. (30 cm). Zone 3.

V. prostrata. Creeping speedwell. Small bright-blue flowers, mat-forming dark-green foliage.

V. repens. Speedwell. Blue-white flowers, low mat-forming foliage, thin rounded leaves. Needs moist soil, does best in partial shade, 2 in. (5 cm). Zone 3.

V. spicata (*Pseudolysimachion spicatum*). Spike speedwell. Spikes of blue, pink or white flowers. Cultivars vary in height as well as colour; 'Sightseeing Mix' is common and very reliable, 24 in. (60 cm). Zone 3.

V. teucrium (*V. austriaca*). Speedwell. The old variety 'Crater Lake' is still my favourite, probably because the colour reminds me of that very blue lake, 20 in. (50 cm). Zone 3.

V. whitleyi. Speedwell. Sapphire-blue flowers with white eye, olive-green foliage, 4 in. (10 cm). Zone 3.

Veronicastrum – Culver's Root, Bowman's Root

Meadow or Bog Garden or Rain Garden | *Plantaginaceae*

*V*eronicastrum have palmate leaves emerging in a radial pattern from the stems, offering an interesting structural look even when they aren't in bloom. The late-summer favourites of bees and other pollinators, they do best in moist heavy soil and are happy at stream-side or the edge of any wet area, forming large clumps in time but not spreading beyond that.

Veronicastrum are sometimes lumped in with *Veronica*,

Veronicastrum virginicum 'Rosea.'

similar in appearance but smaller in scale, but they are sufficiently different genetically to warrant their own genus. The following two (of 15 or so species currently recognized) are known to be hardy.

VARIETIES

Veronicastrum sibiricum. Siberian culver's root. Tall spikes of pinkish-white flowers are produced in late summer. To 5 ft. (150 cm). Zone 3, maybe 2.

V. virginicum. Culver's root. White, pink or purple flower spikes to 6 ft. (180 cm). The selections in white ('Alba') and pink ('Rosea') are attractive and worth a place in the garden, but the newer cultivars are truly outstanding and can be used as specimen plants, holding their colourful blooms for a longer period of time. 'Fascination' is violet purple, 'Lilac Karina' is lavender purple and 'Apollo' a light lilac blue. Zone 3.

Vinca – Periwinkle, Myrtle, Creeping Myrtle

Woodland | *Apocynaceae*

Vinca minor is a semi-evergreen trailing vine with woody stems; as an evergreen, it does best in a sheltered location, developing brown desiccated foliage where exposed to drying winter winds.

Vinca minor. Photo Darwin Paton

Viola canadensis.

While it does well under deciduous trees, the relatively fine foliage and long vining stems get in the way of leaf raking in the fall. (This might actually be a good reason to use that urban blight, the leaf blower.) The more finely textured foliage of mountain ash (*Sorbus*) or flowering crabapple (*Malus*) tends to filter down through the *Vinca*, and has less need to be raked than the larger leaves of maple (*Acer*) or linden (*Tilia*). Conveniently, *Vinca* needs the same well-drained soils as the mountain ash and crabapple.

Although we tend to take this common low-growing (4–6 in./10–15 cm) groundcover for granted, it is a bit of an oddball taxonomically, with its closest North American relative being the dogbane (*Apocynum*), a widely spread native shrub. *Vinca* is hardy to zone 4, but sometimes survives (if not thrives) in a sheltered location and well-drained soil in zone 3. As a bonus, it is also deer resistant.

There are a number of cultivars, varying in vigour as well as flower or foliage colour; they all seem to be more firmly zone 4 than their parent, with less room for tolerance of poor soil conditions and winter cold.

Viola – Violet, Pansy

Woodland or Meadow | *Violaceae*

Viola is a large and prolific genus. In fact, some varieties can be far too prolific. Despite this, they are widely planted in many northern gardens, including mine, because of their beauty and cold tolerance. They are annuals or short-lived perennials, with

the exception of the native species that are longer lived. Despite a reputation for fragrance, only the little sweet violet (*V. odorata*) is strongly so—this is the flower so popular in ladies' posies in the days before deodorant. Only hardy to zone 5, but less necessary in these days of improved hygiene.

Many of the generic pansies sold as bedding plants in the spring (also in the fall in warmer climates) are marginally hardy, and either they or their offspring pop up again the following year. Seedlings may or may not be the same colour as the original plants; after a generation or two they tend to revert back to purple blue with a yellow eye, although not all do this. I have a very pretty ivory-white pansy that pops up here and there around my yard every year, the descendent of a flat of plants that went in more than 10 years ago. (I have collected seed from it and sown that where I want the plants to grow, to no avail. It has a mind of its own—and a preference for growing in pure gravel.)

I don't know of anyone who has had to purchase the tiny Johnny-jump-up violas, but they seem to appear in lawns and gardens everywhere. They wouldn't be such a nuisance if they would restrain themselves, but they can actually choke out other plants by the volume of seedlings, and have a talent for sprouting up right in the middle of other plants where they are hard to get at.

A friend who shall remain nameless (because I owe her much gratitude for many other plants and favours over many years of friendship) once gave me a small seed-grown pansy labelled (probably incorrectly, as it turns out) 'Orchid Penny Frost.' It was a delightful plant, with cream, violet and purple shading, and a tidy mounding habit. I was overjoyed. The next year there were hundreds of seedlings for 20 ft. (6 m) around the original plant. I was less overjoyed, but let some of them live. The year after that the azalea bed was smothered with delicate little purple-flowering pansies. The nursery staff at the time pleaded for clemency because the flowers looked so pretty carpeting the ground. Which they did. I let the little purple darlings live until I realized they were actually sucking all the moisture and nutrients out of the soil; the azaleas (the University of Minnesota 'Northern Lights' series, spectacular in bloom) were dying. That was better than five years ago, and I am still ripping out purple pansies wherever I see them. The azaleas never did recover.

That said I planted a variety of pretty hybrid cultivars this past spring, in shades of rose and burgundy, and surely they won't be as bad. . .

VARIETIES

Viola adunca. Early blue violet. This is early, mid and late in my garden, happily (but not aggressively) spreading around one semi-shaded corner of my garden. It is a pretty little thing, to barely 4 in. (10 cm), and I encourage this native species wherever it wants to grow.

V. canadensis. Wood violet. One of several native species (of at least half a dozen), with white flowers and a tendency to spread in moist shade. Mine is planted under an aggressive white Rugosa rose (*Rosa rugosa* 'Alba'), and they are a good match for each other. The rose is more than holding its own, a good thing because it is too prickly to even try to weed under.

V. cornuta. Violet. Delicate and variable small-flowered species, with flowers in white or shades of light to dark violet and purple black usually with a yellow eye. ('Bowles Black' claims to be black but isn't quite.) Grows from 2–8 in. (10–20 cm). Zone 4.

V. labradorica. Labrador violet. The usual variety of this is 'Purpurea,' which has dark-purple leaves and comes true from seed, producing a moderate number of offspring , all of which also have purple leaves. It displays tiny violet-coloured flowers in the spring, then produces seed pods through parthenogenesis (i.e., without further flowering) for the rest of the summer. While it self-seeds enough to cover an area under shrubs, it doesn't try to take over. Pretty, it nevertheless can be a bit too dark a colour in the shade. I am thinking of trying it partnered with a fairly sturdy gold-leaved shrub or taller perennial for a (hopefully) stunning contrast—perhaps a spirea (*Spireae*) or a meadowsweet (*Filipendula vulgaris* 'Aurea'). We shall see.

V. pedata. Bird's foot violet. Compact and polite little wood violets, to 4 in. (10 cm), with long-lasting blooms in violet with a bit of white at the throat. Fairly reliable perennial but not long-lived. Zone 3.

V. pedatifida. Similar to above, but even hardier. There is a white ('Alba') form of this that is outstanding under shrubs. Again, not long-lived, but at least it doesn't try to take over the world. Zone 2.

V. sororia. The most popular of this species seems to be the small treasure 'Freckles,' which is white and variably freckled with violet or purple blue. This and its sister cultivars need to be planted where they can be seen and appreciated up close— they haven't been vigorous enough (at least not in zone 3) to be useful as a groundcover. Still, they would be sweet in a hypertufa trough with other small-scale plants. Protect these delicate beauties from slugs.

Zizia aptera.

Zizia – Golden Alexanders

Prairie or Meadow | *Apiaceae*

Zizia aptera and *Zizia aurea* seem to be virtually unknown in northern gardens, which is a pity because they are totally hardy (to at least zone 3), drought resistant, clay tolerant and free of any pest or disease issues as far as I can tell. Lovely as cut flowers, they produce deep yellow-gold umbels of flowers in midsummer, at a time when a shot of fresh colour and food for the pollinators is very welcome. Clump-forming, with no tendency to take over, they are surviving quite happily with little or no care at the back of my garden.

Zizia aptera is the smaller of the two, forming a clump 16 in. (40 cm) tall and a bit wider, with shiny dark-green foliage. *Zizia aurea* is similar but taller, up to 24 in. (60 cm) with darker stems as an added attraction. Both of these prairie natives are easy to grow from seed.

Zone Ratings

"What zone are we in?" "What zone is this plant?"

Zone ratings are the subject of much discussion in gardening circles. The Canadian zone system was originally devised based on a handful of benchmark shrubs for each designated zone, combined with minimum average winter temperatures. These zones (slightly different in range from the American zone system, so check the publishing location of any reference material) are reasonably useful for woody plants, but little more than a guideline for perennials and bulbs, both dormant for the winter and not affected by the same factors.

Northern gardeners in zone 2 and 3 regularly grow perennials supposedly hardy only to zone 5 or more. A number of variables other than minimum winter temperature come into play. The volume of snow cover, which insulates the ground and plants in it, is perhaps the most important. I am convinced (rightly or wrongly) that I could overwinter anything under 48 in. (120 cm) of snow. Two more variables out of the gardener's control are the length of the growing season and the amount of heat and hours of sunshine that occur within it. Miserable wet years, when the last frost occurs in very late May and the first by the end of August with only half a dozen sunny days in between, don't give plants much time to grow, ripen, and go into dormancy with adequate energy stored in their roots to tough it out for the winter. This is the reason zone 3 on the prairies is quite different from zone 3 in the northern interior of BC.

Soil type plays a bigger part than we generally think when it comes to the ability of plants to overwinter, yet it is not taken into consideration with regard to zone ratings at all. Heavy clay can be extremely destructive to plant roots and crowns, especially in a cold and wet spring or fall. Much "winter-kill" is in fact caused by the season before or after.

Humidity, the amount of moisture in the air, is also important. Coastal plants that evolved in a maritime climate do not do well—even in the same temperature ranges—when asked to cope with the harsh dry air of the interior continental climate. This is especially relevant to evergreen plants, which suffer badly in dry air.

Next, there is the human-error factor, with some plants being rated quite differently in varying resources and seed catalogues. I have noticed that some retail catalogues tend to be overly optimistic, while reference books err on the side of caution.

And, of course, plants don't read books, and can survive and even thrive in an incredible range of conditions we wouldn't have thought possible. I have learned to never say "That won't grow here," because inevitably if I do someone will turn around and tell me they are growing it.

Clearly, zone ratings, especially when it comes to perennials, should be looked at as probability ratings rather than absolute law. Most zone-5 bulbs and herbaceous perennials seem to do quite well here in zone 3 as long as they have good drainage. Despite being rated zone 4 or 5, though, the large ornamental grasses seldom get the long days of light and heat they need to flourish in our short-season climate; they never really do well, although they usually overwinter.

Within any genus, there is almost always a large number of species that have adapted to varying growing conditions and are found at different latitudes and altitudes in their native lands. As a rule of thumb, when experimenting with a new genus, I try the hardiest species first, then work my way up. I usually run out of enthusiasm (how many different *Allium* or *Primula* can one person grow, after all?) and garden space before I run out of potentially hardy species.

So many plants, so little time.

Bibliography

These are foremost amongst the books that have shaped my thinking and my garden. Most are still in print and available from your local bookstore; these days many out-of-print books can be found at reasonable prices (plus shipping charges) through Internet book-sellers' consortiums such as *abebooks.com* and *alibris.com*.

Armitage, Allan M. *Armitage's Garden Perennials: A Colour Encyclopedia*. Portland, OR: Timber Press, 2000.

Bartholomew, Mel. *All New Square Foot Gardening: Grow More in Less Space!* Brentwood, TN: Cool Springs Press, 2006.

Biles, Roy. *The Complete Book of Garden Magic*. Chicago: Ferguson, 1951.

Brickell, Christopher, Trevor Cole and Judith D. Zuk, eds. *Reader's Digest A-Z Encyclopedia of Garden Plants*. Westmount, QC: Reader's Digest Assoc. (Canada), 1997.

Callaway, Dorothy J. and M. Brett Callaway, eds. *Breeding Ornamental Plants*. Portland, OR: Timber Press, 2000.

Cannings, Sydney, JoAnne Nelson and Richard Cannings. *Geology of British Columbia: A Journey Through Time*, rev. ed. Vancouver: Greystone Books, 2011.

Chatto, Beth. *Beth Chatto's Woodland Garden*. London: Cassell Publishing, 2002.

Davitt, Keith. *Water Features for Small Gardens*. Portland, OR: Timber Press, 2003.

DiSabato-Aust, Tracy. *The Well-Tended Perennial Garden: Planting & Pruning Techniques*, rev. ed. Portland, OR: Timber Press, 2006.

Eck, Joe. *Elements of Garden Design*. New York: Henry Holt and Co., 1995. Reprint, New York: North Point Press, 2005.

Fukuoka, Masanobu. *The One-Straw Revolution: An Introduction to Natural Farming*. Translated by Larry Korn, Chris Pearce and Tsune Kurosawa. Emmaus, PA: Rodale Press, 1978. Reprint, New York: New York Review of Books, 2009.

Gerber, H.S., D.J. Ormrod and M.A. Waring. *A Gardener's Guide to Pest Prevention and Control in the Home and Garden*. Victoria, BC: Crown Publications, 1995.

Gershuny, Grace. *Start With the Soil*. Emmaus, PA: Rodale Press, 1997.

Gershuny, Grace and Joe Smillie. *The Soul of the Soil: A Soil-Building Guide for Master Gardeners and Farmers*, 4th ed. White River Junction, VT: Chelsea Green Publishing, 1999.

Griffiths, Mark, ed. *Index of Garden Plants*. Portland, OR: Timber Press, 1994.

Harvard, David. *Gardening Between Frosts*. Smithers, BC: D.G. Havard, 1986.

Hayward, Gordon. *Garden Paths: Inspiring Designs and Practical Projects*, 3rd ed. Buffalo, NY: Firefly Books, 1999.

Hemenway, Toby. *Gaia's Garden: A Guide to Home-Scale Permaculture*, 2nd ed. White River Junction, VT: Chelsea Green Publishing, 2009.

Johnson, Hugh. *Principles of Gardening: The Practice of the Gardener's Art*, 2nd ed. New York: Simon & Schuster, 1996.

Kingsbury, Noël. *Natural Gardening in Small Spaces*. Portland, OR: Timber Press, 2003.

Knowles, Hugh. *Woody Ornamentals for the Prairies*, rev. ed. Edmonton: University of Alberta Press, 1995.

Leapman, Michael. *The Ingenious Mr. Fairchild: The Forgotten Father of the Flower Garden*. London: Headline Book Publishing, 2000.

Ministry of Agriculture and Land. *Home and Garden Pest Management Guide*, rev. ed. Victoria, BC: Crown Publications, 2009.

Mollison, Bill. *Introduction to Permaculture*, rev. ed. Sisters Creek, Tasmania: Tagari Publications, 1997.

Oudolf, Piet. *Designing with Plants*. Portland, OR: Timber Press, 1999.

Oudolf, Piet and Noël Kingsbury. *Planting Design: Gardens in Time and Space*. Portland, OR: Timber Press, 2005.

Ouellet, Kerstin P. *Contain Yourself: 101 Fresh Ideas for Fantastic Container Gardens*. Batavia, IL: Ball Publishing, 2003.

Pollan, Michael. *Second Nature: A Gardener's Education*. New York: Atlantic Monthly Press, 1991. Reprint, New York: Grove Press, 2003.

Reich, Lee. *The Pruning Book*, 2nd ed. Newtown, CT: Taunton Press, 2010.

Rose, Robin, Caryn E.C. Chachulski and Diane L. Haase. *Propagation of Pacific Northwest Native Plants*. Corvallis, WA: Oregon State University Press, 1998.

Royer, France and Richard Dickinson. *Weeds of Canada and the Northern United States.* Edmonton: University of Alberta Press / Renton, WA: Lone Pine Publishing, 1999.

Springer, Lauren. *The Undaunted Garden: Planting for Weather-Resilient Beauty.* Golden, CO: Fulcrum Publishing, 1994.

Stein, Sara. *Noah's Garden: Restoring the Ecology of Our Own Back Yards.* New York: Houghton Mifflin, 1993.

van der Gulik, Ted W. and Rick J. Williams. *BC Frost Protection Guide.* Vernon, BC: Irrigation Industry Assoc. of BC, 1988.

White, Lee Anne. *Landscaping Your Home: Creative Ideas from America's Best Gardeners.* Newtown, CT: Taunton Press, 2001.

Yepsen, Roger B., Jr. *The Encyclopedia of Natural Insect & Disease Control.* Emmaus, PA: Rodale Press, 1984.

McDuff and Lucy on the trail home.

Barbara Rayment's 2008 self-published book, *From the Ground Up: A Horticultural Guide for Northern Gardeners*, is available through Books & Co. in Prince George, BC, or Barbara's website, northerngardeners.com. This reference volume consists of 400 pages of first-hand information on hardy plants of all types that are known to grow in north-central BC.

Index

More Great Canadian Gardening Books from Harbour Publishing...

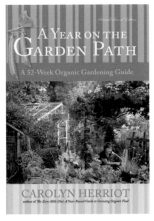

A YEAR ON THE GARDEN PATH

A 52-Week Organic Gardening Guide,

Revised Second Edition

by Carolyn Herriot

Full of seasonally relevant, practical information, this bestselling weekly gardening guide can be picked up any day of the year for timely advice on how to create a beautiful, healthy ornamental landscape and food garden.

Full of helpful tips and recipes, this highly illustrated book covers everything from soil building, non-toxic solutions to common garden problems, plants for impossible places and perennials with personality to pruning and four-season food growing and seed saving, all interspersed with recipes, poetry and humour.

978-1-55017-515-8, paperback, 200+ B&W photographs and illustrations, 6 x 9, 176 pages

THE ZERO-MILE DIET

A Year-Round Guide to Growing Organic Food

by Carolyn Herriot

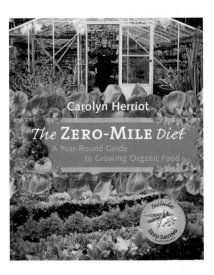

Take a journey through a year of sustainable backyard food production with Carolyn Herriot, one of BC's top organic gardening gurus.

This definitive month-by-month guide brings gardeners into the delicious world of edible landscaping and helps take a load off the planet as we achieve greater food security. Full of illustrative colour photos and step-by-step instructions, *The Zero-Mile Diet* shares wisdom gleaned from 30 years of food growing and seed saving with comprehensive advice on growing organic food year-round, small fruit orchard and backyard berries, preserving your harvest, backyard poultry and an A–Z guide to growing the best vegetables and herbs.

Put organic home-grown fruits and vegetables on your table throughout the year, using the time-saving, economical and sustainable methods of gardening outlined in *The Zero-Mile Diet.*

978-1-55017-481-6, paperback, 100+ colour photographs and illustrations, 8 x 10, 256 pages

THE BOOK OF KALE

The Easy-to-Grow Superfood

by Sharon Hanna

Despite the fact that kale is lauded as a miracle food, and most people know that they should be eating it, many don't know how to make it taste good. This garden-to-kitchen guide gives readers all they need to know to grow this super-sustainable crop organically—as edible landscaping, on balconies and boulevards and even indoors. And, aspiring locavores take note—purple, silvery-green, frilly, stately Tuscan and rainbow-hued kale can all be grown year-round throughout North America, helping families save hundreds of dollars a year on grocery bills.

978-1-55017-576-9, paperback, 50 colour photographs, 8 x 10, 192 pages

HOW TO GET YOUR LAWN AND GARDEN OFF DRUGS

A Basic Guide to Pesticide-Free Gardening in North America

by Carole Rubin

A completely revised, updated and timely edition of Canada's first organic lawn-care book, and a must for all gardeners and homeowners who want to tread lightly on the earth.

This inspiring guide covers all regions of North America, and demonstrates how lawns and gardens can flourish by replacing synthetic chemicals with balanced organic alternatives. It contains clear instructions on how to properly choose, feed, water, aerate and cut your lawn and garden plants, plus a glossary and an updated list of organic suppliers.

978-1-55017-320-8, paperback, b&w line drawings, 5.5 x 8.5, 144 pages

ABCs OF WEST COAST GARDENING

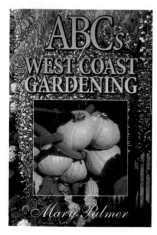

by Mary Palmer

Here is a gardening book encompassing the broad spectrum of plants available to West Coast gardeners, with handy tips on adapting a garden to the extremes of the region.

After six decades of gardening—running a nursery in Seattle, working as the gardening columnist for the *Seattle Times* and homesteading on a British Columbia gulf island—Mary Palmer has gained the experience to turn even the most infertile ground into a thriving garden of vegetables, flowers, trees, shrubs—whatever your preference may be. There are sections covering every aspect of creating a garden from initial soil improvements to final landscaping and beautification techniques. Moss, deer and blackberries will become obstacles of the past. The only problem left to tackle may be finding enough friends to share the bountiful harvest.

978-1-55017-253-9, paperback, 100+ colour photos, 6 x 9, 240 pages

Sow Simple

100+ Green and Easy Projects to Make Your Garden Awesome

by John Gillespie & Christina Symons

Gillespie and Symons inspire and delight with a gorgeous collection of tips, tricks and projects that are sure to increase enjoyment of outdoor spaces, save money and sustain the environment.

Plants thrive thanks to back-sparing and thrifty techniques for propagation, fertilization and transplanting, plus tips on beneficial fungi and bugs, magical mulches, edible weeds, water-wise wildflowers and native plants. Design-wise, make a spectacular entrance with a living gate, or see how easy it is to create a vertical or rooftop garden, a whimsical water garden or a stone courtyard. Home-crafted concrete troughs stuffed with succulents stand strong alongside dry-stack stone walls, and simple ideas for playhouses, gazebos and backyard benches will keep readers busy through all seasons. *Sow Simple* invites all gardeners, whether they have a large acreage or a tiny urban oasis, to have fun, experiment and see how wonderful it can be to spend time in the garden.

978-1-55017-574-5, paperback, 200+ colour photographs, 8 x 10, 208 pages

Everyday Eden

100+ Fun, Green Garden Projects for the Whole Family to Enjoy

by John Gillespie & Christina Symons

Using inexpensive, often recycled, materials and easy techniques, this lively collection of garden projects and practices will delight beginner and experienced green thumbs alike. Whether you have just five minutes or an entire weekend, this full-colour book is designed to delight and inspire. Here are step-by-step instructions and gorgeous photography for lovely gifts from the garden, delightful recipes and cocktails and inspiring weekend garden projects, plus fun things especially for children to make and grow like flowerpot cupcakes and personalized pumpkins. With ideas on everything from gorgeous succulent sculptures and living willow fences to fresh ways to arrange flowers and plan stylish garden soirées, *Everyday Eden* maximizes enjoyment of outdoor spaces—from balcony-sized urban green spaces to rural acreages.

978-1-55017-538-7, paperback, 200+ colour photographs, 8.25 x 10.5, 208 pages

To purchase these gardening titles please visit your favourite bookseller or contact

Harbour Publishing

Toll-free order line: 1-800-667-2988 • E-mail: info@harbourpublishing.com • Online: www.harbourpublishing.com

ABOUT THE AUTHOR

BARBARA RAYMENT has lived and gardened from one coast to the other and now lives in Prince George, BC, where she runs Birch Creek Nursery. A passion for experimentation, along with long winters devoted to reading and research, has placed Barbara at the forefront of contemporary northern gardening experts.

Rayment's blog is northerngardeners.com

Author photo by Susan Hallum

ABOUT THE PHOTOGRAPHER

Originally from the Shuswap, photographer DARWIN PATON moved to Prince George, BC, in 1981. As a photographer he seeks to capture the essence of fragility in the environment without impacting his subject matter. He is also an avid conservationist, outdoorsman and alpine hiker. He has participated in numerous group exhibits and solo exhibitions.

Paton's website is wfphoto.ca